RIGHT TURN

American Life in the
Reagan-Bush Era, 1980–1992

Michael Schaller

University of Arizona

New York   Oxford
OXFORD UNIVERSITY PRESS
2007

Oxford University Press, Inc., publishes works that further Oxford University's
objective of excellence in research, scholarship, and education.

Oxford   New   York
Auckland   Cape Town   Dar es Salaam   Hong Kong   Karachi
Kuala Lumpur   Madrid   Melbourne   Mexico City   Nairobi
New Delhi   Shanghai   Taipei   Toronto

With offices in
Argentina   Austria   Brazil   Chile   Czech Republic   France   Greece
Guatemala   Hungary   Italy   Japan   Poland   Portugal   Singapore
South Korea   Switzerland   Thailand   Turkey   Ukraine   Vietnam

Copyright © 2007 by Oxford University Press, Inc.

Published by Oxford University Press, Inc.
198 Madison Avenue, New York, New York 10016
http://www.oup.com

Library of Congress Cataloging-in-Publication Data

Schaller, Michael, 1947–
   Right turn: American life in the Reagan-Bush era, 1980–1992/by Michael Schaller.
      p. cm.
   ISBN-13: 978-0-19-517257-7 (pbk.)
   ISBN-10: 0-19-517257-4 (pbk.)
   ISBN-13: 978-0-19-517256-0 (cloth)
   ISBN-10: 0-19-517256-6 (cloth)
      1. United States—Politics and government—1981–1989. 2. United States—Politics and
   government—1989–1993. 3. Conservatism—United States—History—20th century.
   4. Reagan, Ronald. 5. Bush, George, 1924–I. Title

E876.S295 2006
320.97309'048—dc22   2005054749

9 8 7 6 5 4 3 2 1

Printed in the United States of America
on acid-free paper

For Nick, Gabe, and Daniel—
children of the '80s

CONTENTS

INTRODUCTION

For most Americans, 1980 began badly and got worse. The United States, like the hapless comedian Rodney Dangerfield, "got no respect." A decade earlier President Richard Nixon had warned that if the United States faltered in Vietnam, it would become a "pitiful, helpless giant." His premonition, some thought, had come true. In 1979, a pollster told President Jimmy Carter that a "malaise" like a choking haze had descended upon Americans. In the wake of the Watergate scandal and retreat in Vietnam, people craved leadership but had lost faith in government and most politicians. Since the mid-1970s, a litany of growing federal deficits, accelerating inflation, slow economic growth, factory closings, gasoline shortages and price hikes, and rising rates of crime, divorce, welfare, single parenting, and drug use had put tremendous pressure on ordinary families. For the first time since World War II, a majority of Americans reported that rather than a better life, they expected to pass on to their children mounting debts and a declining living standard.

Society seemed divided against itself along racial lines as well. For a quarter of a century, federal courts and Congress had chipped away at the laws and customs that promoted segregation in American life. Yet, many schools, neighborhoods, jobs, and professions remained nearly as monochromatic as before. In neighborhoods such as South Boston, Irish- and Italian-Americans bitterly resisted efforts by federal courts to integrate schools through busing and other remedies. So-called white flight to suburbs left cities such as Detroit and Baltimore predominantly black and poor. Growing numbers of wealthy Americans retreated within "gated communities" patrolled by private security firms. "Judicial activists," as critics labeled them, had deeply offended many Americans through decisions such as those that banned organized prayer in public schools, expanded the legal rights of accused criminals, placed restraints on the police, and upheld a woman's right to choose an abortion.

Things weren't much better abroad. Competition from countries such as Germany and Japan took a growing toll on manufacturing jobs in bedrock industries such as steel, electronics, textiles, and automobiles. Americans also felt physically less secure. Since 1969, Presidents Nixon, Gerald Ford, and Jimmy Carter had engaged the Soviet Union and China through détente—a policy of substituting trade, arms control, and negotiation for confrontation. But conservative critics ridiculed détente as a "one-way street" that allowed the Soviets and their proxies to increase their nuclear arsenal and support radical groups in Latin America, Africa, and the Middle East. Who could feel secure when since November 1979—ultimately for 444 days—nightly TV broadcasts described America as "held hostage" by Iranian militants who had seized fifty-three U.S. embassy personnel? The hostage-takers demanded that President Carter return the exiled shah or his money to gain the hostages' release. On April, 24, 1980, after months of fruitless negotiations, Carter authorized a military rescue that ended in disaster when two of the American aircraft collided during a desert refueling stop, killing eight of the would-be rescuers. Had it not been so tragic, the incompetence might seem comic.

Events mocked even America's self-image as a beacon of hope for refugees, such as the several hundred thousand Vietnamese and other Southeast Asians who had arrived since the fall of Saigon in 1975. In April 1980, Cuba's Fidel Castro responded to Carter's offer to accept a small number of asylum-seekers by permitting an almost seven-month exodus in small boats from the port of Mariel. Among the 125,000 refugees who fled the island were a few thousand ordinary criminals and mental patients whom the cigar-smoking strongman happily offloaded onto the United States. As journalists highlighted these hard cases, many Americans concluded that their well-meaning but naïve president had been hoodwinked by the wily Castro.

Late-night TV entertainers captured the mood of national despair when they rhetorically asked audiences if they recognized the ten most frightening words in the English language: "I'm from the government, and I'm here to help you." When Republican presidential aspirant Ronald Reagan referred to a rising "misery index" to describe the combined high inflation and unemployment rates of 1980, the public had a visceral sense of what he meant.

Over the next twelve years—the "long" 1980s both politically and culturally began in the late 1970s and blended into the first two years of the 1990s—Americans lived on a roller coaster. During the 1980s, bold policy innovations reduced taxes and business regulations in an effort to reinvigorate entrepreneurship. At both the local and national levels, government promoted a more conservative vision of justice, personal responsibility, and business power. Technological innovations, including the use of computers to manage information, as well as regulatory reform encouraged new forms of corporate management and financing. Through campaign contributions that provided access to officials, large businesses exercised growing influence over public policy. Meanwhile, the loss or "outsourcing" of many well-paying manufacturing jobs diminished the size and clout of organized labor and undermined a key pillar of the Democratic Party.

In the realm of ideas—sometimes called the "culture war"—conservatives in control of the Republican Party marshaled evangelical Christianity, new legal concepts, and a reverence for the market to challenge the primacy of secular liberalism and big government that had dominated American life since the 1930s. These conservatives portrayed government regulation as a dead hand restraining progress and sapping initiative in everything from public education to banking. Markets, not bureaucrats, were seen as the best mechanism to create and distribute wealth efficiently. The term *tax payer* (and its pejorative inverse, *tax taker*) displaced the more egalitarian notion of "citizen."

Although a growing number of women worked outside the home and earned college and professional degrees, feminism came under attack for hurting the "traditional family." Even as popular culture depicted sexuality, both "straight" and "gay," more openly than ever before, religious conservatives and their political allies mounted spirited campaigns against abortion, sex education, and gay rights. In a further reaction against the legacy of 1960s "permissiveness," federal and state governments launched a new "war on drugs" and an anticrime campaign that more than doubled the nation's prison population and took an especially heavy toll among blacks and Latinos.

Determined to enhance national strength and to challenge foreign foes, President Ronald Reagan confronted the Soviet Union and its proxies by doubling military spending and intervening—both openly and in secret—in conflicts that stretched from Latin America to Africa to Southeast Asia and the Middle East. These interventions produced controversial and often unanticipated results. Yet, Reagan, the most anti-communist of American presidents, ultimately embraced a reformed Soviet Union and facilitated an end to the Cold War.

As the Soviet Union withered away in the early 1990s, the United States organized an international coalition that forced Iraqi troops out of Kuwait. President George H. W. Bush proclaimed a "new world order" to replace the half-century-long Cold War. Yet, popular misgivings about the results of the short but inconclusive Gulf War, fear of foreign competition, and a sharp economic recession in 1992 tarnished conservatism's claims of success and breathed new life into the Democratic Party. After twelve years of national conservative leadership, American voters elected as president former Arkansas governor and Democratic moderate Bill Clinton. But the contest to dominate the nation's values and determine its policies continued and in some ways grew even more intense. Jim Johnson, a longtime Clinton foe from Arkansas, described the newly elected president as a "queer-mongering, whore-hopping adulterer; a baby-killing, draft-dodging, dope-tolerating, lying, two-faced, treasonous activist." Clearly, under the surface calm of the 1980s and early 1990s, Americans remained deeply uncertain about the recent past, the current state of affairs, and future direction of their society.

This account of American life during the Reagan-Bush era begins with two chapters that examine how conservative ideas and organizations reemerged from the shadows cast over them by the Great Depression and New Deal. The economic, political, social, and diplomatic crises of the 1970s tarnished the claims of "big government" liberals that they alone could steer a course of domestic prosperity and international security. The middle chapters describe national politics and public policies implemented by conservative Republicans as well as the dramatic heating up and cooling down of the Cold War. The final chapters describe how economic, legal, social, and cultural developments affected ordinary Americans in all their diversity. I conclude each chapter with a description of books upon which I have relied and annotated recommendations for further reading on specific topics.

In addition to the readers selected by Oxford University Press, several friends and colleagues critiqued earlier versions of the manuscript. Robert Schulzinger, Brint Milward, Daniel Ball, Gail Schwartz, Gabriel Schaller, and Daniel Schaller read the manuscript in whole or part and offered especially valuable suggestions for its improvement. I thank all of them for making this, I hope, a better book.

Right Turn is dedicated to Nick, Gabe, and Daniel Schaller, all children of the '80s.

Conservatism

From Margin to Mainstream,
1945–1980

Fellow citizens, fellow conservatives, our time is now, our moment has arrived.

Ronald Reagan, 1981

Ronald Reagan and the conservative movement he spoke for drew strength from issues, causes, and personalities that long preceded the economic, social, political, and diplomatic crises that afflicted the United States in 1980. Relying heavily on support from white voters in the Sunbelt states of the South and Southwest, as well as from disillusioned "ethnic" Democrats (largely Catholics of Irish, Italian, and east European descent) in northern cities, conservatives gradually took control of the Republican Party during the 1960s and 1970s. By 1980, they stood poised to dominate national politics. This movement, sometimes called "Sunbelt conservatism," promoted free markets and limited government over regulation and planning by state and federal agencies. It championed so-called traditional values (often shorthand for public expression of Christian faith and opposition to abortion, sex education in schools, and equal rights for homosexuals) as the cure for many of the nation's problems. Sunbelt conservatives reveled in patriotism and promoted a more militant anti-communism as the best way to meet foreign challenges.

Since at least the 1950s, critics of liberalism and big government had voiced the sentiments later expressed by Reagan and his successor, George H. W. Bush. They denounced the prevailing foreign policy of containment as a morally suspect compromise with communism, embraced market-based solutions to most economic and social problems, criticized "activist" judges for "legislating" from the bench and coddling criminals, and often spoke fervently of their Christian faith. After 1965, even while liberal Great Society programs such as Medicare and Food Stamps expanded, a backlash against big government gained traction. By the late 1970s, economic stagnation, inflation, racial polarization, rising rates of crime, and growing fear of Soviet nuclear power and advances in the third world tipped the scales in favor of a conservative movement that found its voice in Reagan.

The Great Depression of the 1930s had buried traditional conservatives in a hole so deep that it took them nearly fifty years to climb out of it. In response to the economic crisis, President Franklin D. Roosevelt cobbled together a diverse coalition that included poor southern whites and northern blacks, the Catholic and Jewish descendants of Irish, east European, and Italian immigrants, trade unionists and small farmers, intellectuals and urban politicians. In spite of their sometimes-clashing interests, the failure of the old order to stop economic hemorrhaging or alleviate human suffering prompted all these groups to abandon their traditional reliance on private enterprise and local government to manage public affairs. They turned toward and supported an activist federal government. Roosevelt's New Deal included programs that provided public jobs to the unemployed, propped up agricultural prices, regulated commerce, banks, and capital markets, and encouraged union organizing efforts. The federal government made modest efforts to redistribute income more equally by using a progressive tax system and by funding old age and disability insurance programs such as Social Security. Although the programs sometimes fell short of the mark, Roosevelt's optimism and energy nurtured faith in democracy and in the ability of the federal government to actively regulate the economy for the public good.

Federal spending and power accelerated during World War II when hundreds of billions of dollars poured into factories to modernize technology and boost military production. After 1945, the federal government remained committed to Keynesian (referring to the British economist John Maynard Keynes) economic policies of regulating and stimulating the private economy to maximize employment and growth. These policies, most Americans believed, produced a higher standard of living more or less steadily until the early 1970s. Democratic and Republican politicians, from the era of Roosevelt through that of Richard Nixon, launched program after program. Frustrated conservatives could do little more than deride these initiatives as "tax and tax, spend and spend, elect and elect."

Most Democrats and many Republicans agreed that the federal government had the obligation and ability to promote full employment and economic growth in order to raise living standards for all Americans, including those at the bottom of the economic pyramid. In contrast to the pre–World War II era when big business opposed efforts by governments to regulate the economy, after 1945 most large corporations made their peace with big government. Corporate leaders concluded that the profits they earned from defense and other public expenditures outweighed the burdens of regulation and taxes as well as the power of labor unions to demand a bigger share of the pie for workers.

Conservatives felt shut out even during the administrations of Republican presidents such as Dwight Eisenhower (1953–1961) and Richard Nixon (1969–1974). Democratic domination of Congress from 1932 until 1981 meant that conservative ideas and criticism of big government received short shrift.

Critics of liberalism gained little traction in large part because during the three decades after World War II the real income of working- and middle-class Americans more than doubled. Unionized blue-collar workers—around one-third of the workforce until the 1960s—did especially well. A typical male automobile worker in Detroit or steelworker in Pittsburgh could rely on steady employment for most of his working career. On a single income, he could support a family in a small home, buy a car, send his children to a state college, enjoy two weeks of annual paid vacation, and probably keep his same job with health insurance, other benefits, and a supplementary pension until retirement. Typically, such a worker looked to his union leadership for political guidance and usually voted Democratic.

This equilibrium began eroding in the 1960s and collapsed during the 1970s. Seeking election in his own right following the assassination of President John F. Kennedy, Lyndon Johnson called for creating a "Great Society" through a "war on poverty." Excited by the prospect of something like a renewed New Deal and put off by Republican candidate Barry Goldwater's grumpy conservatism, voters swept Johnson into the White House along with huge congressional majorities. Prompted by the president, Congress enacted an array of laws and programs to redress racial discrimination, promote health care, improve nutrition and childhood education, rebuild cities, and support the arts. Within a short time, however, these initially popular initiatives fractured the Democratic Party along regional, racial, and class lines.

Americans by and large appreciated broad-based social welfare programs such as the New Deal's Social Security and Johnson's Medicare health assistance for the elderly. These so-called entitlements helped nearly everyone over age sixty-five. But programs that primarily benefited the poor and non-whites, such as Medicaid, Food Stamps, and Model Cities, enjoyed considerably less support and often provoked bitter resentments. For example, in the late 1960s, a Polish-American steelworker in Pittsburgh might be appalled by Ku Klux Klan violence against African-Americans trying to vote in Mississippi, but he also worried about rising levels of street crime, court-ordered school busing, and growing welfare rolls that he associated with blacks. As economic growth slowed and then virtually stopped in the 1970s, many steel mills closed and skilled jobs migrated overseas. The loss of well-paying jobs undermined union clout, both in the marketplace and in politics. Federal and state taxes—once accepted as a price to be paid for valuable government services—now seemed like one more burden on hard-pressed workers who were expected to fund programs helping those who did not work, had children they could not support, and broke the law.

Social strains, including more open drug use and sexuality among his children, changing expectations in marriage, frequent divorce, and new career roles for women, also alarmed the steelworker, who feared for his continued employment. While liberal politicians stressed the difficulty of quickly solving entrenched problems such as the legacies of racism and poverty, conservatives placed the blame for high taxes and unsafe streets on elitist judges from the Supreme Court on down who banned organized school prayer, offered constitutional protection for contraception and abortion, and stressed the need to defend the rights of accused criminals, homosexuals, and others who lived on society's margins. Why, the steelworker wondered, did so many Democratic liberals show so little appreciation for his family's well-being, his job, and his values? By 1968, he joined millions of southern white Protestants, suburban white-collar workers, and northern urban Catholics who were drifting away from the Democratic Party, first in presidential elections, then in state and local elections. Gradually, these "disaffiliated" Democrats became Republican voters and embraced a variety of distinctly conservative causes and beliefs under the GOP banner.

CONSERVATISM ON THE MARGINS

Edmund Burke, the British political theorist of the late eighteenth century, characterized his conservative creed as distrusting state power, placing a greater value on individual liberty than equality, celebrating patriotism, relying on religion as a core source of values, distrusting notions of human progress, and respecting a natural human hierarchy. For much of American history, the ideals that linked equality to liberty and celebrated the goal of human progress over natural limits made Burke's ideology a hard sell.

Well into the 1950s, Republican conservatives dissipated much of their energy by attacking popular New Deal social reforms and foreign policy. For example, conservatism's most respected political voice, Senator Robert Taft of Ohio, defended isolationism and a hands-off economic policy long after most Americans concluded that national security justified foreign alliances and prosperity required measures such as a federal minimum wage and agricultural price supports. The most notorious critic of liberalism and the New Deal legacy, Wisconsin Senator Joseph McCarthy, reduced most complexities to a charge that Democrats or anyone else who opposed his crusade against domestic subversion must be a "communist or a cocksucker."

By the end of 1954, however, Taft had died, and McCarthy's increasingly reckless charges—some leveled at fellow Republicans—led to his censure by the Senate. In 1952 and 1956, large majorities of Americans had elected as president a moderate Republican and retired general, Dwight D. "Ike" Eisenhower. Espousing what he called "modern Republicanism," Ike agreed that a "gradually expanding federal government" was an acceptable price to pay for "rapidly expanding national growth." With considerable insight, he told his brother Milton, president of Johns Hopkins University, "Should any political party attempt to abolish Social Security and eliminate labor laws and farm programs, you would not hear of that party again in our political history." Instead of repealing the New Deal, Eisenhower helped enshrine it. Among other acts, he created the Department of Health, Education and Welfare (HEW) to oversee the network of social programs he inherited from Roosevelt and Truman and then expanded.

By the mid-1950s, with Taft gone and McCarthy an outcast, the "Old Right" scarcely had enough leaders or followers to be called a movement. Conservative intellectual Ayn Rand, a Russian émigré writer whose novels *The Fountainhead* (1943) and *Atlas Shrugged* (1957) were especially popular among adolescent males, considered herself a movement icon. But her extreme libertarian philosophy (she despised, for example, Christianity as a faith for weaklings, claimed that people had a duty to have as many orgasms as possible, and urged everyone to smoke cigarettes as a symbol of man's triumph over fire) put off many potential converts.

Another fringe figure of the period, the Reverend Billy James Hargis, roamed the heartland in a customized bus as spokesman for his "Christian Anti-Communist Crusade." At political rallies that doubled as religious revivals, Hargis denounced most elected officials as communist traitors in league with Satan. He eventually fell afoul of the law when his youthful acolytes complained that he sexually abused them while warning about the Red Menace.

More serious conservative thinkers included Austrian émigré economist Friedrich von Hayek, author of *Road to Serfdom* (1944), a weighty book popularized by *Reader's Digest* in abridged form. However well intentioned, Hayek argued, government economic regulation inevitably stifled freedom and led to totalitarianism. He and his disciples, such as economist Milton Friedman at the University of Chicago, where Hayek moved in 1950, believed that aside from national defense and a few limited functions, government should pretty much leave everything else to the free market.

Other conservative thinkers, however, questioned the morality of the Rand and Hayek doctrines of unfettered capitalism. Richard Weaver, author of *Ideas Have Consequences* (1948), Russell Kirk, who published *The Conservative Mind* (1953), and Whittaker Chambers, who chronicled his own disillusionment with communism in *Witness* (1952), criticized both democracy and raw economic competition as degrading to the human spirit. Literary critics praised some of their ideas about the failures of modern society, but few people implemented their nostrums.

Conservatives were also divided along party lines. In the North, for example, conservatives were typically Republicans concerned mostly with economic issues. By tradition, most southern conservatives voted Democratic and cared far more about race than markets. To retain its vital southern base, the national Democratic Party from the 1930s to the 1960s usually tried to appease southern Democratic politicians by soft pedaling challenges to segregation. As late as 1950, Republicans held only two congressional seats out of the entire House and Senate delegation from the South. Trent Lott, who became Senate Republican majority leader a half-century later, recalled that while growing up in Mississippi in the 1940s and 1950s, he "never met a live Republican."

Conservatism had other problems in attracting a national audience. Besides their discomfort with racial equality, some well-known conservatives from the pre–World War II era continued to embrace a crude anti-Semitism that had, since 1945, gone out of public favor. Among the several currents of conservative thought, libertarians favored low taxes, small government, free markets, and few restrictions on personal behavior. In contrast, religious conservatives believed government was obliged to censor what people read and to control what they smoked or drank and with whom they slept. And among conservatives who professed a strong religious faith, Protestants often distrusted Catholics and vice versa. By nature all conservatives despised communism, but many considered foreign aid a waste and military alliances such as the North Atlantic Treaty Organization (NATO) risky entanglements.

More than anything else, however, the conservative movement's gloom-and-doom caricature of big government planning and social welfare programs leading the nation to the brink of collapse fell flat because for nearly thirty years after World War II the American economy thrived, personal freedom remained intact, and Republican and Democratic presidents kept communism contained behind the Iron Curtain. Among the few scholars who studied conservatism in the 1950s, most dismissed it as an evolutionary throwback, a last gasp among downwardly mobile individuals terrified by rapid social and economic change.

New Trends in Conservatism

Even as critics wrote this obituary, conservative thought evolved along paths that found a wide audience. By the later 1950s, people such as the writer James Burnham and the young founder of the *National Review* magazine, William F. Buckley, along with conservative policy think tanks such as the American Enterprise Association (later renamed the "American Enterprise Institute" or AEI) in Washington, DC, and the Hoover Institution in Palo Alto, California, "Fused," as they put it, the seemingly contradictory tenets of conservatism into a forward-looking movement.

In articles published in his *National Review,* Buckley proposed to bridge the gap dividing "libertarians" who believed in market-determined outcomes and "traditionalists" who insisted that government should impose on society a religiously based moral order. According to Buckley, both big government and the welfare state undermined human autonomy, morality, *and* economic freedom. A smaller federal government (defense aside) with less power would naturally result in both religious and local authorities playing an increased role in everyday life. Buckley also urged conservatives to abandon what he characterized as the quaint notion of a well-armed but isolated America. But rather than merely contain communism—at best an accommodation with evil—he proposed using military and other pressure to dismantle the empires controlled by the Soviet Union and China.

Conservatives also attracted new blood from the racial tensions that beset the Democratic Party. During World War II, many rural African-Americans entered military service or flocked to newly opened factory jobs in cities in both the North and the South. By the early 1950s, the increased mechanization of cotton agriculture pushed millions more black and poor white

William F. Buckley used his magazine, *The National Review*, to rally conservatives beginning in the 1950s. © Bettman/CORBIS.

sharecroppers off the land. This flood of rural migrants flowed both north and west. Freed from the stifling effects of sharecropping and rural peonage, these black veterans and urban migrants played key roles in challenging segregation. Rural white southerners who moved north and west often carried their harsh traditionally racial views to their new homes.

In 1948, some northern Democratic politicians moved to support the struggle for racial justice. For example, that year Minneapolis Mayor Hubert Humphrey pushed through the Democratic national convention a modest statement in support of racial equality. In response, southern Democrats such as Mississippi Senator James Eastland accused liberals of trying to "mongrelize" America. Some outraged southern delegates bolted the party convention and organized their own States' Rights or Dixiecrat Party. Their presidential candidate, South Carolina Governor Strom Thurmond, appealed to the economic interest and racial bias of many poor southern whites.

Thurmond blamed the region's poverty on an improbable alliance of Wall Street millionaires and communists. He condemned African-American and Jewish advocates of civil rights as Red stooges. Dixiecrats, Thurmond explained, stood for the "deepest emotion of the human fabric—racial pride, respect for white womanhood, and the superiority of Caucasian blood." (Although not widely known until his death a half-century later, Thurmond in 1925 had fathered a child with a young African-American woman who worked for his family.)

Although Thurmond (who formally became a Republican in 1964) failed to attract a national following, he carried four states in the presidential election of 1948—South Carolina, Louisiana, Alabama, and Mississippi—breaking the traditional Democratic lock on the South. In 1944, three-fourths of white southerners had voted for Roosevelt. In 1948, only one-half voted for Truman. The trend continued during the 1950s and accelerated after 1964 as Republicans attracted a growing share of this white, conservative voting bloc.

Conservatives found a real national spokesman in 1958, when Arizona Senator Barry Goldwater assumed that role. Elected to the Senate in 1952, he broke with Eisenhower six years later, accusing the president of "aping the New Deal." Frustrated by the Republican national convention of 1960, which selected the centrist Richard Nixon for president, Goldwater urged conservative activists to "grow up" and "take this party back." Nixon lost the election, and in 1964 Goldwater delegates dominated the convention and nominated him for president.

Racial politics played an important role in that year's contest between incumbent Lyndon B. Johnson and Goldwater, the Sunbelt (a term not actually coined until 1969) conservative. Determined to solidify his standing among liberal Democrats while promoting a cause he deeply believed in, Johnson pressured Congress to pass the landmark 1964 Civil Rights Act, outlawing racial (as well as gender) discrimination in public accommodations, housing, and employment. Despite opposition from many southern Democratic senators, most Republicans supported the bill. Goldwater led a group of eight GOP senators who opposed it even while insisting that race had nothing to do with their stand. Couching his dissent in the traditional language of states' rights, Goldwater said he could not vote to impose federal power on "the people of Mississippi and South Carolina." Yet, Goldwater appeared to ignore the fact that few African-American citizens in these states could vote. Thus, the "people" whose autonomy Goldwater defended were virtually all white.

Other Sunbelt Republicans echoed Goldwater's theme. Strom Thurmond switched parties and campaigned for the Arizonan. In Texas, the thirty-eight-year-old transplanted Connecticut Yankee, George H. W. Bush, running for the Senate on the GOP line, denounced the Civil Rights Act as an abuse of power that "trampled upon the Constitution." He warned white Texans that their jobs were threatened by the antidiscrimination provisions of the law, which "was passed to protect 14 percent of the people." If elected, Bush promised to protect "the other 86 percent."

In his autobiography, *Conscience of a Conservative* (1960) and during the 1964 race, Goldwater dismissed liberal gibes that conservatism was outdated. "The laws of God and of nature have no dateline," he thundered. Anticipating Ronald Reagan's 1981 assertion that government was not the solution but rather the problem, Goldwater explained that unlike his chief rival for the GOP nomination, New York Governor Nelson Rockefeller, he had no interest in "streamlining government or making it more efficient, for I mean to reduce its size." "My aim," he added, "is not to pass laws, but to repeal them." If elected he would slash domestic spending 10 percent annually and institute a flat income tax. He also promised to confront and defeat "the communist empire."

Goldwater's gruff demeanor and sometimes offensive remarks frequently undercut his ideological appeal. His candidacy also suffered because so many Americans were enthusiastic about Johnson's proposed Great Society programs. In addition, the still-small Vietnam War had not yet become a major problem for the Democrats or the nation.

Moreover, no matter how stridently Goldwater criticized the alleged failure of big government, liberalism, and containment, the United States had not only held the line against communism but also continued to enjoy stable economic growth and a rising standard of living. Whereas Goldwater grumbled about the abuses of big government, Johnson told boisterous supporters "I just want to tell you this . . . we're in favor of a lot of things and we're against mighty few." In 1964, a substantial majority of Americans continued to support big government activism and an agenda that promoted growth, addressed problems of poverty and racial discrimination, expanded health care coverage, assisted the elderly, and increased educational spending.

Nationally, Johnson trounced Goldwater, while in Texas Bush lost his Senate bid. LBJ received 61 percent of the popular vote, and Democrats racked up large congressional majorities. But the apparently grim outcome for conservatives contained a silver lining. Goldwater attracted 55 percent of the white (mainly Democratic) vote in the South and carried five of eleven southern states. This marked the emergence of what Nixon later called the Republican "southern strategy," the effort by the GOP to recruit large numbers of southern and southwestern white Democrats disillusioned by their party's racial, tax, and social policies. An allied strategy sought to attract ethnic and blue-collar northern Democrats troubled by rising rates of crime and welfare, by job losses, and by court rulings that promoted school integration by mandatory busing of students.

Even as the newly elected Johnson claimed the high moral ground in getting Congress to pass the Voting Rights Act of 1965, he privately worried that his victory in opening politics to millions of African-Americans had inadvertently "delivered the South to the Republican Party for a long time to come." As Johnson hoped, African-Americans took advantage of the new law by boosting their voter registration numbers in Mississippi from 7 percent to 60 percent. But an even larger number of southern whites bolted the Democratic

Party in favor of the GOP, more than offsetting any political gain. Gradually, as historian Dan Carter has pointed out, the politics of racial conservatism in the South "broadened into a general program of resistance to the changes sweeping American society" nationally.

HOME ON THE RANGE: NEW SUNBELT CONSERVATISM

Although Goldwater won majorities only in the Deep South, he appealed to many Sunbelt conservatives in the bustling suburban enclaves stretching from Virginia, around the Gulf Coast, and into Arizona and southern California. Engineers, defense workers, doctors, and white-collar professionals in these communities admired Goldwater's outspoken support for religious values, rugged individualism, property rights, small government, and low taxes. They also liked his strident denunciation of communism.

Yet, Goldwater remained a marginal candidate who conveyed mixed messages. Although he often posed in cowboy outfits and invoked Christian morality, he came from a wealthy urban family of recent converts from Judaism. Never comfortable with the social agenda of religious conservatives, he supported his wife's prominent role as an officer of Planned Parenthood and soft pedaled calls for mandated school prayer. For all his talk about individualism and private enterprise, the Goldwater family made its first fortune securing Government contracts to supply goods to army units in the Arizona Territory. Goldwater's hometown, Phoenix, thrived on government aid. Federally subsidized irrigation and electric power made the arid Southwest bloom and generated cheap energy for the air-conditioners that made desert life comfortable. Interstate highways linked the Southwest to national markets. The state's many Air Force bases and defense contractors also spurred growth.

In spite of the many ways in which his rugged individualism actually relied upon government largesse, Goldwater appealed to many Sunbelt residents in rapidly growing suburban communities around Atlanta, Miami, Dallas, Houston, Phoenix, San Diego, and Orange County, California. The predominantly white population of these communities shared Goldwater's disdain for wasteful federal spending and big government programs. They expressed a strong preference for state and local government over federal authority and saw little merit in promoting additional civil rights.

California's Orange County typified this demography, growing rapidly and prospering with the advent of defense and aerospace production in the 1940s. Culturally conservative engineers and other professionals flocked from the South and Midwest to this former farm community, where they found well-paying jobs with companies that comprised what some called the "buckle on the Gunbelt." The region's many World War II veterans took advantage of their GI Bill benefits to continue their education, start small businesses, and, with the assistance of low-interest Veterans Administration loans, buy homes in the new suburban subdivisions. Abundant state spending on freeways and education made life still better for this group.

Nevertheless, many Orange County residents resented what they saw as government-sponsored "collectivism," the erosion of traditional values, and a growing communist threat. They embraced a belief in free enterprise and looked disdainfully at labor unions. By the early 1960s, tens of thousands of area residents attended rallies organized by ultraconservative groups such as the John Birch Society, the Christian Anti-Communist Crusade, and the School of Anti-Communism. People at these events heard speakers such as Ronald Reagan warn of a communist master plan to dominate America by using government, the media, schools, and even churches to undermine "tradition." Race played a secondary role among these early Sunbelt conservatives in the Southwest because relatively few African-Americans lived in the region. Hispanics, although more numerous, were not yet politically active.

Although (or because) many Sunbelt conservatives were financially well off, they resented taxes and income redistribution schemes. In their view, personal failings and interference in the operation of the free market by government and labor unions caused poverty. Welfare programs actually *hurt* the poor by distorting capitalism, rewarding failure, and providing disincentives to work. These "handouts" also encouraged crime, divorce, and out-of-wedlock births.

A strong identification with evangelical Christianity motivated many conservatives. They condemned the United Nations, communism, liberal educators, federal regulators, and government bureaucrats for threatening the nation's moral core. As federal rules and programs displaced the authority formerly exercised by local officials, family, and churches, the nation strayed farther from its Christian roots.

Orange County's rapidly growing evangelical Protestant congregations embraced these beliefs with special fervor. Their churches, many of which reflected a set of beliefs most common among southern Christians, promoted social conservatism and an apocalyptic vision of an imminent battle between good and evil. The biblically prophesized "end of times" would follow this battle, marked by the return of Jesus, who would transport true Christians to heaven and consign those not "born again" to oblivion.

These beliefs reflected and were reinforced by an "underground" bestselling book by Hal Lindsey in which he superimposed the Cold War between the U.S. and the Soviet Union, the creation of Israel, and the nuclear arms race onto biblical scripture. Lindsey published his vision of an imminent day of judgment in 1970 under the title *The Late Great Planet Earth*. By 1980, it had sold over fifteen million copies, more than any other nonfiction book of the era. Lindsey's writing inspired Tim LaHaye, another politically active Christian conservative, to begin organizing evangelicals on behalf of the Republican Party. In the late 1970s, LaHaye joined the Reverend Jerry Falwell in founding the Moral Majority, a religiously based lobbying group. During the 1990s, LaHaye followed Lindsey's literary example by publishing a hugely successful series of "Left Behind" novels that foretold the battle between evangelical Christians and the anti-Christ, symbolized by godless liberals and the United Nations.

Lindsey and later LaHaye condemned communism as both antifree market and anti-God. In many ways Ronald Reagan anticipated their message in talks he gave on behalf of General Electric and to audiences at anti-communist rallies in southern California. As the final conflict approached, Reagan declared at a rally in 1961, "one of the foremost authorities on communism in the world today has said we have ten years. Not ten years to make up our minds, but ten years to win or lose—by 1970 the world will be all slave or all free."

Like other Sunbelt conservatives, Reagan and Goldwater advocated a hard line to deal with the Red Menace. Merely containing the Soviets and negotiating with them appeased rather than defeated evil. Instead, the United States should create overwhelming military superiority and bring relentless pressure to bear on what Reagan later called "the evil empire." Meanwhile, Cold War defense spending greatly enriched places such as Orange County.

Sunbelt enclaves from Cobb County, surrounding Atlanta, to the suburbs of Dallas and Orange County exemplified a major change in American demographic patterns. The post–World War II rise of the suburbs accelerated from 1960 on. The percentage of Americans living in rural areas and small towns declined from around 44 percent to 20 percent between 1950 and the early 1990s. Cities barely held their own, shrinking from 33 percent to around 30 percent. Suburbs, however, nearly doubled in size, ballooning from about 25 percent of the population to nearly 50 percent. From the 1950s through the 1980s, cities became economically poorer and racially darker, whereas suburbs became richer and whiter. So-called white flight transformed cities such as Detroit from 16 percent to 75 percent black between 1950 and 1990. Baltimore followed the same trajectory, going from 25 percent to over 60 percent black. As cities became more Democratic, suburbs trended strongly Republican. With their dependence on the automobile rather than public transportation and their reliance on the shopping mall rather than downtown commercial centers, suburbs embodied a "privatized" ethic that corresponded closely with conservative ideas.

By the early 1960s, conservative challengers to state power spoke a language familiar to those who came of age in the 1980s. They complained that liberal school curriculum and sex education mandated by bureaucrats undermined religious and family values. They condemned the civil rights movement as a "big government" assault on personal freedom. Sunbelt conservatives denounced fair housing and employment laws, such as the 1964 Civil Rights Act, without using openly racist language. Instead, they depicted these laws as unconstitutional assaults on private property and local control.

By 1966, as the Vietnam War escalated and as the backlash against several Great Society programs intensified, conservatives in California expressed mounting frustration. Local developments, such as the Berkeley Free Speech Movement, anti–Vietnam War rallies, and the Watts (Los Angeles) ghetto riots, sharpened their anger. In response, Ronald Reagan emerged as the redeemer first of California conservatism and then national conservatism.

A former actor, president of the Screen Actors Guild, and since the early 1950s a motivational speaker for the General Electric company, Reagan seized the limelight by making a televised fundraising speech entitled "A Time for Choosing" for Goldwater late in the senator's faltering 1964 presidential campaign.[1] Drawing material from after-dinner speeches he had delivered on GE's behalf over the previous decade, Reagan was by turn humorous and indignant as he spoke of bloated bureaucracies and the government threat to personal freedom. Brazenly lifting phrases made famous by Franklin Roosevelt, Abraham Lincoln, and Winston Churchill, Reagan declared:

> You and I have a rendezvous with destiny. We can preserve for our children this, the last best hope of man on earth, or we can sentence them to take the first step into a thousand years of darkness. If we fail, at least let our children and our children's children, say of us we justified our brief moment here. We did all that could be done.

He criticized high taxes and the national debt, adding that the "founding fathers" knew that "government does nothing as well or as economically as the private sector."

Goldwater lost, but in a real sense Reagan won. Where the senator grimaced and scowled, Reagan smiled and cajoled. Although Reagan's beliefs were as conservative as Goldwater's, he radiated a self-deprecating and inspirational quality, honed by decades of acting and public speaking.

Reagan's effectiveness as a political speaker soon led to his being hired by the American Medical Association (AMA) as their public voice in opposition to Lyndon Johnson's proposed Medicare program to help pay medical bills for the elderly. In a series of radio commercials, Reagan portrayed Medicare as the first wave of socialism or even totalitarianism that would erode "every area of freedom" in America. If Medicare became law, he predicted, the current generation of Americans would spend their "sunset years telling our children and our children's children what it was like in America when men were free."

Despite AMA opposition and Reagan's appeal, Congress passed the bill. The setback barely registered, however. During 1965 a group of wealthy Californian businessmen, including automobile dealer Holmes Tuttle, organized

---

1. Born into a modest Illinois family in 1911, Reagan admired the New Deal programs that provided a job for his father during the Depression. As late as 1948, Reagan campaigned for liberal Democrats. He began espousing conservative ideas in the early 1950s and formally became a Republican in 1962, shortly before endorsing Goldwater. Even after rejecting the New Deal legacy, Reagan continued to admire FDR's inspirational leadership and borrowed many of his best phrases for his own speeches. As Reagan moved right, the threat to freedom he spoke of changed from "big business" to "big government."

Ronald Reagan campaigns on behalf of Senator Barry Goldwater, 1964. Courtesy Ronald Reagan Library.

a "Friends of Ronald Reagan" committee to promote his candidacy for governor of California.

In the ensuing campaign, Democrats disparaged Reagan as both an amateur and an extremist. Neither label fit. As in his later race for the White House, Reagan promised voters a few simple things: to reduce the size and scope of governments and to throw the rascals out. "I am not a politician . . . I am an ordinary citizen" opposed to high taxes, government regulations, big spending, waste and fraud, he declared in 1966. For six years as governor and for eight more as president, Reagan stayed on message. He used dramatic, if sometimes fanciful, anecdotes—many sent to him by admirers—to point out the excesses or absurdities of government regulation. When speaking of liberalism, his voice oozed with contempt. If the topic was communism, he sounded resilient and impervious. Describing the plight of hard-pressed taxpayers or small business owners, he radiated empathy and recalled his own humble origins.

Reagan worked closely with consultants who recognized his "mastery of the electronic media." As much as possible, they waged the campaign on television, where Reagan's ability to deliver a prepared script in an off-the-cuff manner excelled. After coasting to an easy primary victory, Reagan went on to challenge two-term incumbent Governor Pat Brown in the general election.

A moderate Democrat, Brown had presided over one of California's fastest growth spurts. During his administration the state university system expanded along with a network of roads, water projects, and social services. These projects cost billions of dollars and were paid for by raising taxes. Not surprisingly, the improved public services were popular, and the taxes that funded them were not. At the same time, many middle-class Californians also felt threatened by the virtual black uprising in Watts, the raucous Free Speech Movement at the flagship Berkeley campus, and the growing antiwar movement that questioned the Cold War, challenged authority, and mocked traditional patriotism.

As a candidate, Reagan spoke largely about symbolic issues such as freedom, personal autonomy, and traditional values. He blamed Brown for condoning riots, ignoring welfare cheats, raising taxes, and appointing judges who "coddled" criminals. Although as a moderately conservative Democrat Brown actually supported the Vietnam War and voiced little sympathy for student protesters, Reagan tied the incumbent to spoiled "bums" at Berkeley who indulged in "sexual orgies so vile I cannot describe them to you." Hippies, he quipped, "act like Tarzan, look like Jane, and smell like Cheetah." But, relying mostly on inspiration, Reagan told audiences, "We can start a prairie fire that will sweep the nation and prove we are number one in more than crime and taxes . . . this is a dream, as big and golden as California itself." His sincerity and ability to tell jokes on himself (asked what kind of governor he might be, he quipped, "I don't know, I've never played a governor") undercut Brown's effort to portray him as a wild extremist. Most voters viewed Reagan as a pleasant man aroused by grievances they shared. In November 1966, they swept him into office with a million-vote margin.

Reagan assumed the governorship in January 1967 at a midnight inauguration, the time recommended by an astrologer consulted by wife Nancy Reagan. Over the next two decades Mrs. Reagan consulted with several astrologers, most famously Joan Quigley. Although sophisticates later ridiculed the Reagans' reliance on this advice, the Reagans' interest in astrology resembled that of millions of Americans who read with devotion astral predictions by Jeanne Dixon and other practitioners in their daily newspapers. The Reagans, like most of their peers, relied on horoscopes to bolster their existing beliefs.

"For many years now," the new governor told Californians, "you and I have been hushed like children and told there are no simple answers to the complex problems which are beyond our comprehension." In truth, he countered, "There are simple answers—they're just not easy ones." But Reagan seemed unsure of what they were. Shortly after taking office, he appeared stumped when asked by a journalist about his priorities. Turning to an aide, Reagan remarked, "I could take some coaching from the sidelines, if anyone can recall my legislative program." Initially, he did little more than impose an across-the-board budget cut on state agencies, impose a hiring freeze, and request that state employees work without pay on holidays.

Eventually Reagan settled into a comfortable governing style that blended conservative rhetoric with flexible policies. He denounced student protesters, forced out liberal administrators from several campuses, and sent state police to quell disturbances at Berkeley. But he abandoned plans to slash education spending and to probe "communism and blatant sexual misbehavior" in the state universities. Reagan blamed Brown for saddling him with a large budget deficit, then approved the largest tax increase in state history. He praised budget cutting, but during his two terms state spending doubled from $5 billion to $10 billion. Although he criticized a casual attitude toward sex, in 1967 Reagan signed into law (after what he privately called an agonizing study of the issue) the nation's most liberal abortion statute. After 1973, when abortion became a sensitive litmus test among conservatives, Reagan claimed he had never read the law and blamed doctors for performing more procedures than intended. Yet, his pragmatic view of social relations also showed in his approval of arguably the nation's most liberal "no fault" divorce law, the 1969 California Family Law Act. Some outraged conservatives charged that Reagan's signature had "wiped out the moral basis for marriage in America."

Reagan's bold rhetoric and cautious governance style are sometimes characterized as "populist conservatism." His favorite targets were "liberal elitists" whose social agenda might be well intentioned but whose policies actually hurt working people, encouraged dependence, and stifled initiative. Reagan's easygoing style disarmed Democratic critics who dominated the state legislature and inspired conservative supporters. He easily won reelection in 1970. During his second term, the governor promoted a modest reform designed to help the taxpayer and punish the "tax taker." He condemned "welfare cheats" but struck a deal with the legislature that only modestly tightened eligibility standards while substantially increasing benefits. Reagan continued to criticize public programs as inferior to private business and insisted that independent ranchers and private entrepreneurs had carved an empire from a wilderness. He either did not know or obscured the fact that public water, power, roads, and defense contracts had helped California and the West to thrive.

THE POLITICS OF RACIAL ANGER

Although the conservative movement of the 1980s avoided overtly racial language, it shared its origins with segregationist appeals of earlier politicians such as Strom Thurmond and especially George Wallace. The Democratic governor of Alabama became a celebrity in 1963 when he proclaimed,

George Wallace was a presidential candidate in 1968. AP/Wide World Photos.

"Segregation now, segregation, tomorrow, segregation forever" and then "stood in the schoolhouse door" to block the enrollment of two African-American students at the University of Alabama. Even Wallace, who used brutal epithets in private conversation, publicly avoided racial name-calling. Instead, he portrayed himself as a champion of states' rights against a bullying federal government controlled by communists, masquerading as liberals, who oppressed hard-working white Alabamans.

Wallace, who began his career as a moderate and then, after losing an election, vowed never to be "out-niggered," gained national attention after his dramatic—if futile—resistance to court-ordered integration. In 1963, less than one-third of Americans agreed with his criticism that the federal government was pushing integration "too fast." By 1968, however, the number topped one-half. Although Wallace's angry tirades contained no coherent critique of the causes of economic or social inequality suffered by poor whites, like Thurmond a generation earlier he blamed millionaires, communists, civil rights activists, and liberals—as if they were one group—for America's troubles. Federal bureaucrats who "can't park their bicycles straight," he raged, presumed to tell ordinary Americans how to live their lives. Wallace, who secretly raised campaign funds through kickbacks from state contractors, connected especially well with working-class males between ages eighteen and thirty-seven who bore the brunt of the economic and social impact caused when manufacturing jobs left cities and blacks moved in.

As the 1968 presidential election neared, Wallace played on the fear of what Nixon later called the "silent majority," working- and middle-class Americans who worried about racial change, urban riots, anti-Vietnam demonstrations, and the "counterculture" of drugs and sex. Wallace lamented the loss of the "traditional moral compass" of God, country, and family. He thundered against an epidemic of crime, obscenity, and abortion that proliferated as "uppity" minorities threw off old constraints and threatened "our schools, our jobs, our streets, and our neighborhoods."

Running for president as the nominee of the American Independent Party in 1968, Wallace ridiculed Nixon as part of the Republican administration in 1953 that had appointed Earl Warren to the Supreme Court. He also targeted the antiwar movement, recognizing that although working-class whites did not especially like the Vietnam War, they resented protests led by well-off college students who seemed to mock traditional religious, cultural, and patriotic values. Wallace attacked liberal politicians who, he claimed, taxed workers to pay for wasteful programs and federal judges who promoted school busing, barred official school prayer, and turned over "lawless streets to punks and demonstrators." He took great delight in skewering "intellectual snobs" who could not distinguish between "smut and great literature." These "limousine liberals" demanded that poor white children be bused to integrated schools but sent their own kids to posh suburban schools or to private academies.

On paper, Wallace's words sounded shrill and whining. But he had an entertainer's instinct and came alive when he spoke before crowds or on television. Radical journalist Hunter Thompson compared the energy at a Wallace rally with what he felt at a Janis Joplin concert. Wallace radiated an aura. As Thompson put it, "The bastard somehow levitated himself and was hovering over us." Crowds roared their approval when he dared protesters to lie down in front of his limousine. "It will be the last one they ever lay down in front," he yelled. "Their day is over." Ultimately, Wallace's crude rage and southern provincialism limited his national appeal. Four years later, in 1972, he ran in primaries as a Democrat until a would-be assassin's bullet left him gravely wounded and forced his withdrawal from the presidential race. But Wallace's campaigns had legitimized a "coded" political language of race resentment whose themes echoed in future conservative rhetoric.

Reagan's two terms as governor, from 1967 to 1975, roughly coincided with Wallace's campaigns and with the presidency of Richard Nixon. Although both Nixon and Reagan proclaimed themselves conservatives, they had little mutual affection or respect. Nixon's skill in appealing to voters' resentments, racial and otherwise, attracted many of the same Democrats who later voted for Reagan. But Nixon remained at heart a "big government" politician. His support for expanded regulation, expressed in new programs such as the Environmental Protection Agency (EPA), the Consumer Products Safety Commission (CPSC), and the Occupational Safety and Health Administration (OSHA), his embrace of wage and price controls, along with his effort to engage the Soviet Union through détente (involving arms control and trade agreements) and to open a dialogue with the People's Republic of China, horrified many conservatives. When, in 1971, Nixon declared, "I am now a Keynesian," a startled conservative economist remarked this was like a "Christian Crusader saying 'all things considered, I think Muhammad was right.'"

One moderate Republican senator remarked that under Nixon, "the conservatives got the rhetoric, we got the action." Nixon privately described himself as a "pragmatist." The only person as bad as a "far-left liberal," he asserted, was a "damn right-wing conservative." When Reagan as governor defended the Vietnam War in the late 1960s, he called for expanded bombing to "turn it into a parking lot." Nixon bombed more heavily than had Johnson but in 1973 signed an agreement with Hanoi that left communist forces in control of much of South Vietnam in return for a truce that allowed Americans a face-saving exit.

Although nowhere near as telegenic as the California governor, Nixon also appreciated the growing importance of television in shaping public opinion. The president and his aides described most voters' decision making as a "gut reaction," not an analytic process. Television could provide him with the correct "aura." Nixon instructed his staff not to waste time trying to communicate his views on complex issues. Instead, they should work on polishing his "public appearance presence." His live speeches should be limited to "naïve type audiences," certainly "no Jewish groups." "Speech," he told his top aide, H. R. Haldeman, "is obsolete as a means of communication."

To distinguish himself from Wallace in both 1968 and 1972 and to avoid driving away moderate support, Nixon shunned explicit appeals to race. Yet, many of the issues he raised in the campaign evoked racial symbolism in a bid to win over Wallace voters. The economic distress experienced by working- and middle-class Americans proved the point. For a quarter-century, purchasing power by these groups had increased nearly 2 percent annually. By 1969, real wage growth nearly ceased. Family income remained stable only because a growing number of women and wives entered the workforce.

Although income growth among whites stalled, blacks and Hispanics made some real economic gains during the 1960s and 1970s. Minority gains did not cause the white slowdown, but it was commonly blamed for it. Nixon, who privately described blacks as "genetically inferior" and "just down from the trees," saw value in using issues such as economic stagnation, fear of crime, and resentment against school busing as code for race. Taking

Nixon celebrates his electoral victory in 1968. Hulton Archive/Getty Images.

a position just to the right of mainline Democrats, he attracted support from disgruntled white Democrats in the South and in the urban North in ways that allowed voters to convince themselves they were not responding to racist appeals of a candidate such as Wallace.

In 1968, Wallace's third-party appeal to Democrats who might otherwise vote Republican represented a real threat to Nixon's candidacy in the South. Harry Dent, an aide to the now-Republican South Carolina Senator Strom Thurmond, developed what became known as Nixon's "southern strategy." Dent convinced Nixon to campaign in the South against "activist judges" and "forced busing" and for "law and order." Nixon pushed these issues and also warned white southerners that a vote for Wallace would only assure the election of Democrat Hubert Humphrey. Ultimately, Nixon's strong showing in the South and the West assured his election in November 1968 and pulled these regions more firmly into the Republican embrace.

Over the next four years, Republican strategists refined their appeal. Studies by Kevin Phillips (*The Emerging Republican Majority*, 1969) and Robert Scammon and Ben Wattenberg (*The Real Majority*, 1970) were parsed by Nixon and his advisers as if they contained magic formulas for winning elections, which, to an extent, they did. Republicans, Wattenberg argued, could coast to success by playing to a majority that was "unyoung, unpoor, and unblack." Phillips pointed out that most of Wallace's supporters in the South and in northern cities had been lifelong Democrats, now in motion between a "Democratic past and a Republican future." In a remarkably cynical assessment, Phillips urged Nixon to promote minority voting rights in the South and in other Sunbelt states. As large numbers of blacks became active Democrats, he predicted, even more whites would bolt and join the GOP.

Elsewhere, such as in northern cities, Phillips noted that support for Wallace ran strongest in white working-class neighborhoods close to black enclaves. These residents, often eastern European and Irish Catholics, viewed African-Americans as encroaching on jobs, housing, and schools. As the tense, urban North became "southernized," it was ripe for Republican picking. Nixon's campaign manager and attorney general, John Mitchell, summarized Phillips's data as showing that the key to electoral success lay in achieving what he called the "positive polarization" of politics along a racial divide. Nixon praised Phillips's book to his chief of staff, H. R. Haldeman, and laid out his (and Republican) future campaign strategy: "go for Poles, Italians, Irish; must learn to understand the Silent Majority. Don't go for Jews and blacks."

As part of his appeal to southerners and more generally to conservatives, Nixon pledged to reverse the perceived liberal bias of the Supreme Court. Two of his nominees, Clement F. Haynesworth and G. Harold Carswell, were rejected by the Senate as unqualified. As one Nixon aide privately admitted, most people considered Carswell "a boob, a dummy. And what counter is there to that? He is." Ultimately, Nixon made four appointments to the Supreme Court—Chief Justice Warren Burger in 1969, followed by Associate Justices Harry Blackmun, Lewis Powell, and William Rehnquist. Although Powell and especially Blackmun proved more moderate than Nixon expected, the other two appointments altered significantly the Court's direction.

With Wallace knocked out of the 1972 race by his grave injury at the hands of a would-be assassin, Nixon faced an unusually weak Democratic opponent in the person of South Dakota Senator George McGovern. (Hoping to provoke a pro-Nixon backlash among Wallace loyalists, Nixon aide Charles Colson tried to plant Democratic campaign literature in an apartment rented by Arthur Bremmer, the deranged gunman who shot Wallace!) The deescalation of the Vietnam War as well as Nixon's success in portraying McGovern as weak on crime, soft on defense, and tolerant of perversion swayed the election. McGovern eased Nixon's task by alienating many southern and ethnic Democrats. For example, as part of an effort to increase diversity within the party, McGovern supporters at the nominating convention barred the seating of an Illinois delegation headed by Chicago Mayor Richard Daley in favor of a rival group who included a large number of African-Americans, Hispanics, and women. Mike Royko, a popular columnist for the *Chicago Sun-Times*, criticized efforts by party liberals to "disenfranchise Chicago's white ethnic Democrats" as a "strange reform." Anyone who would try to revitalize the party by alienating millions of white ethnic voters, he observed, "would probably begin a diet by shooting himself in the stomach." Observing the antics at the Democratic nominating convention, Republicans had a field day by labeling Democrats as the party of the "Three A's—Acid, Abortion, and Amnesty."

THE ROAD TO WATERGATE AND RUIN

Nixon won reelection by an astounding eighteen million-vote margin over McGovern, taking 61 percent of the vote. Less than two years later, in August 1974, with the Senate prepared to try him for a variety of political crimes, he resigned the presidency in disgrace. Probes by journalists, a pair of special prosecutors, several grand juries, and House and Senate committees had revealed the scope of Nixon's lawbreaking. He had approved illegal fundraising, spying on opponents, manipulating Democratic primaries to assure McGovern's nomination, bugging and burglarizing Democratic Party offices in the Watergate building, covering up the botched break-in by paying hush money to the Watergate burglars, and using the FBI and CIA to mislead prosecutors. These actions so tarnished the GOP that former party chairman and Kansas Senator Bob Dole quipped in 1974 that the Republican Party was "*not* involved in the nomination, the convention, the campaign, the election, or the inauguration" of Nixon to a second term.

The previous October, in a separate scandal, Vice President Spiro Agnew resigned after admitting that, while governor of Maryland in the late 1960s, he had accepted bribes from state contractors. Implementing for the first time the Twenty-Fifth Amendment to the Constitution, Nixon nominated House Minority Leader Gerald Ford of Michigan to replace Agnew. Congress quickly confirmed the moderately conservative and affable representative. Nixon barely concealed his contempt for his eventual successor. Just two months before his own forced departure, during an Oval Office chat with Nelson Rockefeller (whom Ford later named as *his* vice president), Nixon quipped, "Can you imagine Jerry Ford sitting in this chair?"

By the first week of August, after the Supreme Court ordered the release of secretly recorded tapes of Nixon's Watergate-related conversations, 75 percent of the public believed Nixon had engaged in a criminal coverup. Republicans in Congress deserted him in droves. As blunt-speaking Barry Goldwater, serving again as senator from Arizona, put it, "There are only so many lies you can take, and now there has been one too many. Nixon should get his ass out of the White House—today." Nixon announced his resignation on August 8, effective the next day. Still disputing the evidence against him, he admitted only to making wrong judgments. As Nixon and his family flew home to California, the new president, Gerald Ford, declared: "My fellow Americans, our long national nightmare is over."

Many Republicans—including conservatives who never liked Nixon— feared that Watergate had consigned their party to permanent minority status. Yet, Nixon's political demise and Ford's disappointing two years as president effectively demolished moderate Republicanism and cleared the path for a revitalized and far more conservative GOP.

Demonstrators demand that Nixon be removed because of the Watergate scandal, 1974. MPI/Getty Images.

STAGNATION, MALAISE, AND THE CONSERVATIVE REPUBLICAN REVIVAL

In spite of Ford's sincerity ("He is a very nice man, who isn't up to the presidency," as one journalist put it), America had not awakened from its nightmare. Even Watergate refused to go away. Ford's decision to pardon his disgraced predecessor (made for humane reasons, as rumors swirled that Nixon might kill himself if forced to stand trial) convinced many Americans that the coverup had continued. The new president's initially favorable approval rating collapsed abruptly and never recovered. Shortly after pardoning Nixon, Ford nominated former New York Governor Nelson Rockefeller to fill the vacant vice presidency, an action that infuriated GOP conservatives who recalled Rockefeller's opposition to Goldwater in 1964. After angering both liberals and conservatives, Ford alienated nearly everyone else by actions such as his lame attempt to tame inflation by handing out buttons with the acronym WIN for "Whip Inflation Now." First Lady Betty Ford outraged religious conservatives by endorsing a woman's right to have an abortion and by touting the advantages of her adult children's cohabitation as preparation for marriage.

The fallout from Watergate along with internal Republican disarray helped Democrats score major gains in the 1974 congressional elections. South Vietnam's collapse in April 1975 as well as evidence of Soviet meddling in Africa further eroded Ford's already frail reputation in foreign affairs.

In November 1975, Ronald Reagan declared he would seek the Republican presidential nomination. Criticizing Ford as a member of the Washington "buddy system" and liberal establishment, Reagan stressed his own opposition to bloated federal spending, school busing for integration, student radicalism, sexual promiscuity, abortion, the Equal Rights Amendment, and détente. He pledged to lower taxes, revive school prayers, and strengthen the military. He rallied patriots by promising never to surrender control over the Panama Canal, as Ford had proposed doing. Although Ford narrowly won renomination, Reagan's challenge had forced Ford to accept a conservative party platform that pledged "less government, less spending, less inflation," and constitutional amendments to ban abortion and permit organized school prayer.

Democrats put forward as their presidential candidate a little-known ex-governor of Georgia, Jimmy Carter. He was a deeply religious and more conservative man than any of his party's recent nominees. His pledge never to lie resonated in post-Watergate America. Audiences cheered his assertion, "I'm not a lawyer, I'm not a member of Congress, and I've never served in Washington." He was elected in 1976 by a narrow margin, but his lack of support among congressional Democrats left him overwhelmed by problems that included bureaucratic infighting, high inflation, rising unemployment, energy shortages, environmental crises, and the emerging threats of terrorism and Islamic fundamentalism.

On July 15, 1979, after two and a half years of disappointing leadership, Carter acknowledged the nation's pessimistic mood in what became ridiculed as his "malaise" speech. Problems such as inflation and energy shortages merely reflected the country's "crisis of confidence." Pessimism posed a more "fundamental threat to American democracy," Carter warned in a televised address, because the nation had been founded on a spirit of optimism. As an antidote, he changed a few of his cabinet members and urged people to cultivate a more positive attitude. This advice seemed about as useful as the "happy face" anti-inflation buttons issued by President Ford. Ronald Reagan, the leader of conservative Republicanism, laid the blame for malaise not on the American people, but rather on the failed leadership of Carter, Democrats, and big government liberalism.

Increasingly, Americans complained about the impact of *stagflation*, the persistent phenomenon of slow economic growth, rising inflation, high unemployment, and steep interest rates. The seizure and confinement of fifty-three American diplomats in Iran beginning on November 4, 1979, added national humiliation to malaise. Conservatives charged that Carter's refusal to stand by America's old friends, such as the shah of Iran or Anastasio Somoza in Nicaragua, virtually invited attack by Islamic fundamentalists and Marxist guerrillas. They also attributed the December 1979 Soviet invasion of Afghanistan (designed to shore up a wobbly communist puppet regime) to American weakness.

On April 24, 1980, Carter authorized a raid on Iran to free the hostages. But a sandstorm and bad luck resulted in the collision of two U.S. aircraft and the death of eight servicemen during a refueling stop. Even as Carter spoke ruefully of "mechanical difficulties," Americans saw the debacle as proof of the erosion of national power. Secretary of State Cyrus Vance, who opposed the raid, resigned in protest, and many American's wondered if the Three Stooges had taken control of foreign policy.

Once admired as an "everyman" who would restore good government and common sense in Washington, Carter now seemed a blunderer. Although he was not an especially liberal Democrat, Carter's failure tainted all Democrats and liberals. Senator Edward Kennedy, who unsuccessfully challenged Carter for the Democratic nomination in 1980, ridiculed the incumbent for "lurching from crisis to crisis." But Carter faced a more daunting problem than Kennedy. Ronald Reagan turned this crisis of confidence into a broad and successful challenge to big government liberalism.

Sources and Further Readings

The evolution of American conservative thought and political action through the 1960s is examined in several excellent books, including John Micklethwait and Adrian Wooldridge, *The Right Nation: Conservative Power in America* (2004); William Rusher, *The Rise of the Right* (1984); Jerome Himmelstein, *To the Right: The Transformation of American Conservatism* (1990); George H. Nash, *The Conservative Intellectual Movement in America since 1945* (1998); Leo Ribuffo, *The Old Christian Right* (1983); Jonathan M. Schoenwald, *A Time for Choosing: The Roots of Modern American Conservatism* (2001); William B. Hixson Jr., *Search for the American Right Wing: An Analysis of the Social Science Literature, 1955–1987* (1992); Godfrey Hodgson, *The World Turned Right Side Up: A History of the Conservative Ascendancy in America* (1996); Garry Wills, *A Necessary Evil: A History of the American Distrust of Government* (1999); Sara Diamond, *Roads to Dominion: Right Wing Movements and Political Power in the United States* (1995); James Morone, *Hellfire Nation: The Politics of Sin in American History* (2003).

For detailed treatment of the rise of "sunbelt conservatism" and the early careers of Barry Goldwater and Ronald Reagan, see Earl Black and Merle Black, *The Rise of Southern Republicans* (2002); Michael Lind, *Made in Texas: George Bush and the Southern Takeover of American Politics* (2003); Rick Perlstein, *Before the Storm: Barry Goldwater and the Unmaking of the American Consensus* (2001); Lisa McGirr, *Suburban Warriors: The Origins of the New American Right* (2001); Matthew Dallek, *The Right Moment: Ronald Reagan's First Victory and the Decisive Turning Point in American Politics* (2000); Kurt Schuparra, *Triumph of the Right: The Rise of the California Conservative Movement* (1998); Lou Cannon, *Governor Reagan: His Rise to Power* (2003); John A. Andrew, *The Other Side of the Sixties: Young Americans for Freedom and the Rise of Conservative Politics* (1997); Mary Brennan, *Turning Right in the Sixties: The Conservative Capture of the GOP* (1995).

The best treatment of the impact of George Wallace and racial polarization on American politics in the 1960s and 1970s is contained in two books by Dan T. Carter, *The Politics of Rage: George C. Wallace, the Origins of the New Conservatism, and the Transformation of American Politics* (1995), and *From George Wallace to Newt Gingrich: Race in the Conservative Counterrevolution* (1996).

The impact of the Nixon presidency and Watergate on the rise of conservatism is discussed in Michael Schaller and George Rising, *The Republican Ascendancy: American*

Politics, 1968–2001 (2002); Melvin Small, *The Presidency of Richard Nixon* (1999). Also see Stanley Kutler, *The Wars of Watergate: The Last Crisis of Richard Nixon* (1992). The domestic political struggle over détente is examined in Robert Schulzinger, *Henry Kissinger: Doctor of Diplomacy* (1989); John Ehrman, *The Rise of Neoconservatives: Intellectuals and Foreign Affairs, 1945–1994* (1995); Jussi Hanhimäki, *The Flawed Architect: Henry Kissinger and American Foreign Policy* (2004).

2

RIGHT TIDE RISING

> The time has come . . . to present a program of action based on political principle that can attract those interested in the so-called social issues and those interested in economic issues.
>
> RONALD REAGAN, 1977

The strong conservative current in American public and private life during the late 1970s and the 1980s represented more than a gut reaction against gasoline lines, inept presidential leadership, and the unresolved fate of American hostages in Iran. Many long-established engines of liberalism, such as the Democratic Party, trade unions such as the AFL-CIO, mainline Protestant churches, citizens' lobbies such as Americans for Democratic Action, the American Civil Liberties Union, and the National Organization for Women, and policy-generating think tanks such as the Brookings Institution and Ford Foundation lost influence as their ideas appeared less and less connected to the problems of everyday life. Gradually their conservative counterparts assumed a more dominant role.

Rising voices on the right came from evangelical Protestant Christian churches who often joined forces with conservative Catholics, single-issue political action committees such as those formed by the National Rifle Association and anti-abortion activists, socially conservative lobbying groups such as the Moral Majority, Concerned Women of America, the Eagle Forum, and the Christian Coalition, and think tanks such as the Heritage Foundation and American Enterprise Institute. They promoted initiatives that appealed to many ordinary Americans and helped to sway elections at the local and national levels. Funds for their activities came from wealthy groups and individuals such as Joseph Coors and Richard Mellon Scaife, from the John Olin Foundation, from corporations and trade organizations, and from direct-mail campaigns. By 1980, liberal organizations found themselves outspent and outmaneuvered by a dynamic conservative movement that provided money, foot soldiers, and ideas to a revitalized Republican Party.

THE END OF THE POST–WORLD WAR II BOOM

Along with its foreign policy achievements, liberal big government's strongest claim of success rested on a nearly thirty-year record of sustained economic growth. After all, most people tolerated taxes and approved government spending as long as their real incomes rose and public expenditures went toward programs that either benefited themselves or seemed like worthy ventures. In November 1973, following the October Yom Kippur War between Israel and Syria and Egypt and the imposition of an Arab oil embargo against the United States, three decades of growth screeched to a halt. The energy crisis triggered an eighteen-month recession, the worst since the Great Depression of the 1930s. The anemic recovery that began in 1975 initiated a prolonged period of slow growth that affected all areas of the economy. After decades of expanding at an average rate of 4 percent, the gross national product (GNP) grew at only 1.8 percent annually from 1973 to 1982. Annual productivity gains, a partial measure of how much workers produced with a given amount of machinery and capital, fell to 0.8 percent, one-fourth the level of the 1960s.

Higher energy costs, along with declining growth and productivity, drove down the value of the dollar. Prompted first by the 1973 oil embargo and then by the 1979 overthrow of the shah of Iran, the cost of petroleum increased from about $3 to $30 per barrel. Because petroleum had so many industrial uses, from gasoline to fertilizer to plastics, the price hikes affected the entire economy. By 1981, the value of the dollar had fallen to half its pre-1973 level. The annual inflation rate, about 4 percent in the decade before 1973, spiked to 13.5 percent in 1980. Even as American consumers imported more Japanese cars and Saudi oil, American exporters found it harder to sell manufactured goods abroad. The declining value of the dollar, along with a rapidly rising foreign trade deficit, sparked inflation.

President Jimmy Carter responded to the energy crisis by proposing investments to develop alternative fuel sources, by urging people to keep their homes cooler in the winter and warmer in the summer, and by retaining the unpopular fifty-five-mile-per-hour speed limit on highways imposed in 1973. Although all these proposals had merit, none had much immediate impact on energy supplies or prices. Conservatives blasted Carter's actions as evidence of inept bureaucratic meddling. "Our problem isn't a shortage of oil," proclaimed Ronald Reagan, "it's a surplus of government." Republicans recognized the public's special frustration with speed limits by promising in their 1980 party platform to repeal the fifty-five-mile-per-hour limit.

American workers bore the heaviest burden of economic decline in the 1970s. Unemployment averaged 4.7 percent from 1962 to 1972. Between 1973 and 1986, it averaged 7.4 percent, hitting a post-1945 high of over 9 percent in 1975. High inflation and slow economic growth added to the pain of high unemployment, creating a new condition—stagflation. Since the 1930s, liberals had relied on the Keynesian formula for promoting growth. Put simply, during a recession the government would increase deficit spending and promote mild inflation by expanding the money supply. This injection of purchasing

Frustrated motorists line up for gasoline, 1979. Library of Congress, Prints & Photographs Division, LC-U9-37734-16A.

power would prompt economic growth and higher employment. As business activity increased, government would collect increased taxes to pay down the deficit and scale back spending. But in the late 1970s, the budget was already in deficit, and inflation had roared ahead without restoring growth or jobs. By 1980, 75 percent of the public agreed with the statement, "We are fast coming to a turning point in our history. The land of plenty is becoming a land of want."

Stagflation drove down the value of the wages earned by ordinary Americans. Real median family income had doubled in the quarter-century before 1973 but stagnated through the rest of the decade and beyond. In 1990, *after* the "Reagan-Bush recovery" described later, 80 percent of families had a lower real income than they enjoyed in 1973. Job and income losses were especially severe among manufacturing workers in the northern and midwestern heartland, a region soon dubbed the "Rustbelt."

Still worse, because inflation drove up the nominal value of incomes and pushed many people into higher tax brackets that were not adjusted for inflation, many working Americans actually paid *higher* income taxes in the late 1970s and early 1980s. Middle- and working-class expectations of improving living standards and improving social mobility were crushed by the reality of stagnant incomes, high inflation, and rising taxes. By 1980, two-thirds of Americans described themselves as economically "worse off" than they had been five years before.

These problems surfaced first during the administrations of Richard Nixon and Gerald Ford, giving Democrats a political boost in the elections of 1974 and 1976. Presidential candidate Jimmy Carter ridiculed Ford for presiding over a rise in what he dubbed the "misery index," a combination of inflation and unemployment rates that reached 12.7 by Election Day in 1976. But Carter's victory that year gave Democrats only a brief respite. During the last half of the 1970s, congressional Democrats focused on issues such as reducing the capital gains tax on investment profits, reforming campaign finance, and cleaning up the environment. However worthy, these issues appealed mostly to wealthier and better-educated Democratic voters, not the party's base. Neither Carter nor most congressional Democrats made much of an effort to stem the job losses and stagnant wages that especially hurt blue-collar workers and minorities, the core Democratic constituencies. By 1980, when the "misery index" hit 20, Democrats had squandered the goodwill and support of a substantial portion of their party.

Economic problems also buffeted large and medium-size corporations. Faced with rising costs, shrinking export markets, intense foreign competition, more intrusive government regulations, and demands by labor unions to sustain good wages and benefits, corporate profit rates plummeted. After-tax profits, which averaged 10 percent in the mid-1960s, fell to 6 percent after 1975 and 5 percent by 1980. Manufacturers responded to this decline by shifting plants to low-wage foreign nations or to nonunionized regions in the American South, where it cost less to do business.

Corporate leaders also adopted new political strategies. From the prosperous 1940s through the mid-1970s, most large businesses contributed money to both major parties and did not actively promote deregulation and anti-union efforts. In the face of a tight profit squeeze, however, management lined up strongly behind Republican candidates who endorsed conservative proposals to slash corporate taxes, to reduce regulations, and to curb union power.

CONSERVATISM ON THE MOVE

Economic woes went a long ways toward mobilizing social conservatives, libertarians, anti-communists, neoconservative intellectuals, and religious traditionalists into a dynamic coalition often referred to as the "New Right." The "New Right" updated longstanding conservative ideas and presented them in a more modern and populist format. Utilizing innovative marketing technologies, such as computerized databases and direct-mail fundraising, proved highly effective in bringing together conservatives of different persuasions, along with their money.

Richard Viguerie, an early supporter of presidential candidates Barry Goldwater and George Wallace, took the lead in this direction by using his firm, RAVCO, to compile computerized lists of individuals, businesses, and organizations that were identified with one conservative issue or another and could be tapped for fundraising. By the late 1970s, several other direct-mail fundraising operations worked the conservative circuit. Tim LaHaye, later chairman of the American Coalition for Traditional Values and the author of the "Left Behind" novels, recalled that early on he and other fundraisers recognized that direct mail and telephone messages that relied upon emotional "wedge issues" elicited the best financial returns. In refining their appeals, conservative fundraisers identified "hot button" issues, such as abortion, gay rights, divorce, crime, pornography, and gun ownership. Reference to these issues not only increased donations, but also drove a wedge between Democratic candidates and their traditional supporters in working-class labor, Catholic, and Protestant households. The "shriller you are," remarked Terry Dolan of the National Conservative Political Action Committee (NCPAC), "the easier it is to raise funds."

THE RELIGIOUS RIGHT

The New Right's use of religious and social wedge issues mobilized voters of faith. It also brought together, for practically the first time, Catholics and evangelical Protestants[1], groups who traditionally viewed each other with suspicion. For example, before the 1970s, many Catholics hesitated to support prayer in public schools because official prayers were typically Protestant. The Catholic Church also had a tradition of communitarian concern and supported government services for the poor. For their part, before the late 1970s Protestant evangelicals typically opposed public subsidies for parochial schools because most were run by the Catholic Church. Traditionally, evangelical Protestants, who emphasized the centrality of individually coming to Jesus, resented the claims of the Catholic Church and its pope to be the one true path to salvation.

New Right religious leaders bridged this divide by focusing on concerns that crossed sectarian lines. These concerns included abortion (especially after the Supreme Court's 1973 *Roe v. Wade* ruling upheld a woman's right to choose to terminate her pregnancy), teenage access to birth control and sex education, gay rights, and public financial aid for religious schools. As discussed later, when white Protestants, especially in the South, created a Christian schools movement partly in response to desegregation, they found common ground with Catholics who—although opposed to racial discrimination—favored public support for parochial education.

Social uncertainty and economic stagnation in the 1970s eroded membership in many mainstream Protestant churches—Episcopalian, Presbyterian,

---

1. People who are "evangelical Christians," a term sometimes incorrectly used interchangeably with "fundamentalists," belong to a variety of Protestant sects. Evangelicals believe that only a personal, life-altering experience that culminates with a decision to follow Jesus guarantees salvation. Often this experience is referred to as being "born again." Evangelicals seek to guide nonbelievers toward the path of salvation through Christ. Fundamentalist Christians, who may or may not be evangelicals, accept the Bible as the literal and unerring word of God. These beliefs clashed with various aspects of Catholic dogma.

President Reagan was applauded by televangelist and Moral Majority founder the Rev. Jerry Falwell, 1981. Courtesy Ronald Reagan Library.

Methodist, Congregationalist, and some Baptist groups—and increased the appeal of fundamentalist, evangelical, and Pentecostal churches. Tradition-ally, these Sects were most common among southern Christians. The outmigration of black and white southerners after 1950 had a religious as well as political and cultural impact on the rest of America. Although the term meant different things to different people, by 1980 surveys found that between 20 percent and 40 percent of Christians described themselves as "born again." That year a literalist faction took control of the Southern Bap-tist Convention, the largest Protestant denomination in the country.

Some Bible-oriented Christian ministers committed to overturning liberal-ism and restoring traditional values took to the airwaves through new "elec-tronic churches." Among the most popular religious TV shows were the *700 Club*, the *PTL Club*, and the *Old Time Gospel Hour*. Nationally, two hundred lo-cal television stations and about eleven hundred radio stations had adopted primarily religious formats by 1980. Within a few years, the electronic church attracted weekly audiences of around 100 million. To pay for air time and other activities, TV ministries relied upon high-pressure fundraising that by 1985 brought in at least $1 billion annually, compared with a mere $50 mil-lion donated in 1975. The most successful of the new "televangelists" in-cluded Jerry Falwell, Pat Robertson, Jim and Tammy Bakker, Jimmy Swag-gart, and Oral Roberts.

Televangelists preached dual sermons. One denounced the threats posed by communism, immorality, abortion, and "secular humanism," the belief that morality comes from humans, rather than from God. The other cele-brated a gospel of wealth that focused on enjoying a life filled with consumer products. Jimmy Swaggart, whose sermons threatened sinners with hellfire and damnation, epitomized the first tendency. Jim Bakker, who described heaven as a genteel retirement community with lots of planned activities, epitomized the second. Both promised grace and a place in heaven via generous contributions while still on Earth. Protestant televangelists often reached out to Catholic viewers by stressing their shared abhorrence of such evils as abortion, gay rights, and pornography. Skirting IRS regulations that barred tax-exempt churches from endorsing candidates, many televangelists provided "voter guidance" to their audience, naming, for example, which candidate for a House or Senate seat defended abortion rights or opposed tighter gun control.

As federal courts pressed harder for integration in the South during the 1970s, a large number of white parents opposed to racial mixing enrolled their children in private, segregated, so-called Christian academies. As non-profit schools, these academics enjoyed tax-free status, so contributions to them were tax deductible. In 1978, President Carter's IRS commissioner, Jerome Kurtz, stripped these private schools of their tax exemption on the grounds that racially biased admissions violated federal civil rights law. Outraged parents denounced the move, which Richard Viguerie described as a "spark" that mobilized evangelical Christians. In response to numerous death threats, Kurtz received full-time protection.

Jerry Falwell, a Lynchburg, Virginia, minister who built a large regional television following on his *Old Time Gospel Hour*, took notice of this grassroots discontent. Like most evangelical preachers, Falwell had long insisted that the church should seek to redeem individual sinners, not society. But by the late 1970s he perceived a need to mobilize religious activists against abortion, homosexuality, the Equal Rights Amendment, and other "ungodly" policies. Angered by the IRS action against the Christian school movement, in 1979 Falwell and other ministers such as Tim LaHaye founded the Moral Majority, a lobbying group promoting conservative Christian beliefs. Falwell and his followers described government regulations, high taxes, and the IRS action as part of an assault on "traditional values." The free enterprise system, he proclaimed, "is clearly outlined in the book of Proverbs." Falwell called for "singling out those people in government who are against what we consider to be the Bible, moralist position." The Moral Majority set out to mobilize evangelical Christians, "to get them saved, baptized, and registered" to vote. In 1980, Falwell and other religious activists began to issue "moral report cards" targeting politicians who failed to make the grade.

In 1979, congressional Republicans condemned the IRS revocation of tax-free status for segregated Christian schools. Republican officials recognized the salience of this issue by including in their 1980 party platform a pledge to end the "unconstitutional regulatory vendetta . . . launched by Mr. Carter's IRS commissioner against independent schools." While campaigning for the presidency, Ronald Reagan told a convention of fundamentalist ministers in Dallas that he considered himself "born again." All of the world's "complex and horrendous problems have their answer in that single book—the Bible," he explained. Reagan called for teaching the biblical account of creation (sometimes called "creation science") alongside Darwin's theory of evolution in public school science classes. He told the cheering ministers, "You can't endorse me, but I endorse you."

Christian conservatives responded to these appeals by switching party loyalty in growing numbers. Traditionally white evangelical Christians, especially in the South, voted at a lower rate than their more secular neighbors. Those who did vote favored Democrats over Republicans. In 1976, for example, Jimmy Carter, a self-described born-again Christian, secured 56 percent of the white evangelical vote. By 1980, however, Reagan, in his race against Carter, received 61 percent of this vote. In 1988, George H. W. Bush's share of the evangelical vote soared to 80 percent.

The trend continued right through 2004. The more religiously involved or self-identified a person is, the more likely he or she is to take a conservative stand on issues such as abortion or gay rights and to vote Republican. The most reliable indicator of voting behavior is not which church a person identifies with (e.g., Catholic, Southern Baptist, Pentecostal, Jewish) but rather the *intensity* of religious devotion and *frequency* of attendance at religious services. Fervent church- and synagogue-attending Christians and Jews are most likely to consider themselves conservatives and to vote for Republican candidates.

Corporate Conservatism

If evangelical churches provided the conservative movement with a mass base and new activists, medium and large businesses made critical funding and the access it provided to politicians available to conservatives. By the late 1970s, corporate America strove to improve its deteriorating profit margin by reducing business taxation, eliminating many regulations, and curbing the influence of labor unions. Business leaders pursued these goals by shifting the bulk of their financial support to the Republican Party.

Corporate managers especially resented the web of new regulatory agencies, such as EPA, OSHA, CPSC, and the Equal Employment Opportunity Commission (EEOC), that had been created or enhanced during the 1970s. They ridiculed regulations that, for example, mandated the number of portable toilets that should be made available to migrant farm laborers or the kinds of chemicals that could be used to exterminate termites in homes. These and other regulations, many business leaders argued, raised their costs and demonstrated a prounion, antibusiness bias. Since World War II, most of the corporate community tacitly supported big government liberalism. Increasingly, however, corporate leaders adopted the more conservative maxim that state regulation of the economy must be reduced for business to thrive at home and compete abroad. Individual businesses hired a growing number of lobbyists to make their case in Washington and state capitals. Between 1971 and 1982, the number of these lobbyists ballooned from 175 to almost 2,500.

Creation of the Business Roundtable in the late 1970s provided large corporations with a unified voice in Washington.

Corporations also pumped an increasing amount of money directly into politics. Post-Watergate reforms limited direct corporate contributions to candidates. Instead, most business or individual donations were made through political action committees (PACs), which bundled small contributions from many donors and provided them to selected candidates who took friendly positions on issues ranging from gun control to reproductive rights to tax cuts and deregulation. Before 1974, labor union-funded PACs outnumbered business PACs by 201 to 89. By 1976, business-oriented PACs held a 433-to-224 edge, an edge that increased to 1,700-to-400 in the mid-1980s. Candidates who wanted access to campaign funds thought twice before adopting "antibusiness" or "prolabor" positions.

In addition to funding campaigns of friendly candidates, corporations and wealthy family foundations, such as those connected to Joseph Coors, John Olin, and Richard Mellon Scaife, provided substantial amounts of money to create a conservative "counterestablishment" of nonprofit foundations and policy institutes. Contributions from these donors now flowed into right-wing organizations such as the Heritage Foundation (originally funded by Coors), the American Enterprise Institute, the Federalist Society, and the Hoover Institution. These groups, which had an aura of respectability that rivaled that of "liberal" think tanks such as the Brookings Institution, promoted policies that distinctly favored probusiness, antilabor, low tax, and deregulatory approaches to government.

Among those who played a major role in this new counterestablishment were two groups of economists who rejected the Keynesian theory that government could promote steady growth and full employment through increased spending on projects such as roads, social welfare programs, and health care initiatives. So-called monetarists, led by Milton Friedman and his followers at the University of Chicago, insisted that prosperity and freedom required less, not more, government spending and regulation. Although generally favoring lower taxes, Friedman held that steady, moderate expansion of the money supply, partly by controlling interest rates, would by itself curb inflation and promote growth and employment. Government efforts to promote growth by taxing and spending were bound to be inefficient and counterproductive.

A more flamboyant and maverick group of economists known as "supply siders" offered another alternative to Keynesianism that promised to solve the problem of stagflation: large tax cuts for businesses and wealthy individuals to promote savings, investment, and growth. This approach relied on the premise that economic growth resulted primarily from stimulating the market's supply side (producers) rather than its demand side (consumers). Because supply was more important than demand, government should encourage entrepreneurs and wealthy investors to put their money into the marketplace by slashing their capital gains taxes (taxes paid on profits from investments) as well as their income taxes. Money saved by the rich on taxes would, theoretically, go to work through additional savings and investments by the wealthy.

Most liberal and some conservative economists warned that the vast tax cuts envisioned by supply siders would create enormous budget deficits. Not so, insisted supply siders, because lower tax rates would actually stimulate the economy and thereby increase tax revenues while reducing the deficit. Among the most influential supply siders was a somewhat obscure economist, Arthur Laffer, who plotted a graph (supposedly on a napkin at lunch) that "proved" that at very high or very low tax rates, the government would collect nothing. As the tax rate approached a confiscatory 100 percent, no one had an incentive to work; if the rate dropped to 0 percent, people would work, but the government would collect no revenue. But if, like the porridge in the story of Goldilocks and the Three Bears, the rate was set "just right," people would have an incentive to work harder, the economy would grow, and, happily, the government would collect all the taxes it needed. Laffer and his acolytes boasted they had discovered the proverbial free lunch. Put another way, it solved the problem of everyone wanting to go to heaven but no one wanting to die. Now government could cut taxes, allow people to keep more of their money, and still collect all the revenue it needed.

Many skeptics, including Reagan's opponent for the GOP nomination in 1980, George H. W. Bush, dismissed Laffer's notions as "voodoo economics." Like most liberals and mainstream conservatives, Bush realized that the Laffer Curve proved accurate only at the two theoretical extremes of taxation, 100 percent and 0 percent. But because everyone else lived in the real world, the Laffer Curve begged the question of just where to set the tax rate. Nevertheless, as a candidate in his 1980 campaign and as president, Reagan embraced supply-side logic and used it to justify steep income tax cuts. As critics predicted, enormous federal deficits resulted.

But this lay in the future. Whatever its deficiencies, supply-side theory provided conservatives an easy-to-understand and popular plan to raise productivity, speed growth, lower inflation, cut taxes, decrease the budget deficit, and generate enough money to fund existing popular social programs. For politicians, it avoided the painful choice of having to cut programs if revenues declined. According to Laffer, you could cut taxes first and then sit back while the revenue flow increased enough to fund existing and new programs.

Some conservatives, to be sure, recognized the theory as a Trojan horse. The tax cuts would help business and wealthy individuals up front. If tax receipts declined, that would be fine, too, because reduced revenue would create the justification to slash "big government" or, as some conservatives such as antitax crusader Grover Norquist put it, "to starve the beast."

Among Laffer's acolytes was Jude Wanniski, an editorial writer for the *Wall Street Journal*. The *Journal* vigorously promoted supply-side theory and in 1978 helped persuade two Republican legislators, Congressman Jack Kemp of New York and Senator William Roth of Delaware, to introduce legislation that called for a 30 percent reduction in federal income tax rates. Kemp predicted this reduction would liberate the "creative genius" of Americans that lay "submerged, waiting like a genie in a bottle to be loosed."

In 1980, as he campaigned for president, Reagan conferred with Laffer, Kemp, and Wanniski. In the words of David Stockman, Michigan congressman and later Reagan's head of the Office of Management and Budget, these true believers "thoroughly hosed him down with supply-side doctrine." The prospect of stimulating growth by cutting taxes and shrinking government, Wanniski recalled, "set off a symphony" in Reagan's ears. He knew "instantly that it was true and would never have a doubt thereafter." Tax cuts became a conservative mantra in the 1980s and beyond, a solution to all economic problems from stagflation to recession.

THE NEOCONSERVATIVES

Laffer's nostrums impressed Reagan but found little support in academic circles. But another group of intellectuals, known as "neoconservatives," abandoned the Democratic Party and joined the ranks of the New Right late in the 1970s. Irving Kristol described his fellow "neocons" as "liberals mugged by reality." As younger men and women, many neoconservatives had been committed liberals and in some cases even socialists. They had believed that government should tear down racial and other barriers to equality in American life. By the end of the 1960s, however, many had grown weary and wary of what they saw as misguided and counterproductive efforts by government to assure an equality of *outcome*, as distinct from opportunity. Liberalism and the Democratic Party, they claimed, had been hijacked by a well-educated, self-serving cabal of government bureaucrats, peace activists, social workers, radical professors, teachers' unions, and public-interest lawyers. This elitist "new class" abandoned core principles of anti-communism, merit-based social mobility, and traditionalist values. Instead of removing barriers that blocked progress, they championed, in the words of R. Emmett Tyrrell Jr., "consciousness raising, self-realization, group therapy, human rights, animal rights," gay rights, prisoners' rights, and other causes "light-years removed from the New Deal."

By the start of the 1970s, many liberals criticized the war in Vietnam, excessive defense spending, interventions in the third world, and the failure to fully fund antipoverty programs. Neoconservatives, in contrast, lamented the failure to pursue victory in Vietnam, criticized the pursuit of détente with the Soviet Union, spoke out in defense of many despotic but anti-communist leaders in the third world, and charged that wasteful social spending perpetuated the poverty it sought to cure. Neocons still supported broad-based programs such as Social Security but rejected more narrowly focused programs such as affirmative action. They voiced their ideas through influential policy journals such as *Commentary, The Public Interest, The New Republic,* and *Encounter.* Unlike the religious right, neocons criticized liberalism while speaking the language and relying on the techniques of social science to expose what they saw as the failure of government programs. Many developed close ties with think tanks such as American Enterprise Institute and Heritage Foundation.

Several leading neocons, such as Norman Podhoretz, Irving Kristol, Midge Decter, Nathan Glazer, Daniel Bell, Martin Peretz, Gertrude Himmelfarb, Richard Perle, and Paul Wolfowitz, were Jews, and some had strong university affiliations. A determination to assist Israel—which many liberals and leftists had come to criticize—partially shaped their political agenda. This agenda dovetailed especially well with many evangelical Christians who believed that creation of a powerful Israel represented a critical precondition for Christ's eventual return. Cooperation with these Jewish intellectuals also provided a strong base of ideas to the conservative movement.

In 1975, alarmed by what they saw as American defeatism in the wake of the abandonment of Vietnam, a group of neocons organized the Committee on the Present Danger. The membership drew heavily from the ranks of so-called defense intellectuals, policy planners such as Paul Nitze, Paul Wolfowitz, and Richard Perle, who moved in and out of government, private think tanks, and academia. The committee lobbied for increased defense spending and a more assertive resistance to communism in the third world. Several members later served in the Reagan and Bush administrations.

POWER SHIFT: THE SPLINTERING OF THE DEMOCRATIC PARTY

As the various religious, secular, intellectual, and corporate factions of the New Right mobilized their strength in the late 1970s, the Democratic Party continued to fracture. Democrats seemed unable to staunch the losses in the southern wing of their party, which experienced continuing defections among white voters to the GOP. Disgust with Nixon and Watergate provided only temporary relief in the elections of 1974 and 1976. By 1980, major Democratic constituencies either lost faith in the party and stopped voting or actually cast their votes for Republicans. Established core groups of Democrats, including most labor union members, African-Americans, and Jews, stayed loyal to the party, but these remnants of the New Deal coalition comprised a shrinking portion of the national electorate.

The economic problems of the late 1970s hit the U.S. manufacturing sector especially hard, which also meant hitting organized labor. In 1960, almost 33 percent of nonagricultural workers belonged to labor unions. By 1978, membership declined to 23 percent and was sinking fast. The only growth in union membership occurred in service industries and among teachers and municipal workers. As overall union membership shrank, organized labor contributed less money and fewer votes to the Democratic Party. Democrats, in turn, delivered less labor-friendly legislation. As union leaders and rank-and-file members in, for example, the steel, automobile, and textile industries became more fearful of foreign competition and job losses, they focused their political efforts on getting Congress to pass narrowly targeted trade protection legislation. Organized labor devoted far less attention to promoting broader social and economic policy issues related to questions such as health care or education.

Labor's loss of clout within the Democratic Party and the nation at large occurred just as corporate managers adopted more hostile policies toward organized labor. Big business cut wages, benefits and pensions and moved in many cases to decertify existing unions. At the same time, groups such as the AFL-CIO, which had links to Democrats since the 1930s, felt excluded from the party, which now placed more emphasis on issues of race, environment, and gender and less on goals such as full employment. George Meany, head of the labor federation, voiced contempt for Democratic presidential nominee George McGovern in 1972. The AFL-CIO gave tepid support to Jimmy Carter in 1976 and 1980. One AFL-CIO leader dismissed younger Democratic Party activists as a gaggle of "kooks, crazies, queers, and feminists."

Democrats seemed to lose even the struggle for "naming rights." Influenced by Republican spinners with backgrounds in marketing, the news media often adopted GOP terminology by referring to the poor, labor unions, and minorities as "special interests" to whom the Democrats pandered. Somehow, the rich and big business were not self-serving groups. Meanwhile, those passionately opposed to abortion defined themselves as defenders of the "right to life." Abortion rights advocates, in contrast, merely defended "choice." A growing proportion of the public shared the view of neoconservatives that Democratic liberals were big-spending, high-taxing enemies of traditional values who were beholden to minorities and soft on crime.

At the close of the 1970s, a white backlash accelerated against the idea of minority preferences. Since the enactment of legislation in the mid-1960s that assured equal legal rights for minorities, the Democratic Party had promoted compensatory programs to redress historic wrongs through affirmative action and hiring and admissions quotas. Conservatives who called themselves "egalitarians" seized on this policy as a form of reverse discrimination that contradicted principles of equality and penalized hard-working whites. As the conservative sociologist Charles Murray put it, neither blacks nor whites could be blamed for their ancestors' behavior, "but all are equally responsible for what they do next."

By 1980, 69 percent of Americans identified the Democrats as the party that cared more about minorities than about whites. Between 66 percent and 75 percent of whites declared themselves opposed to "special help" for minorities and preferential college admissions or hiring practices. Less than 20 percent believed the government should make special efforts to improve the social or economic status of minorities.

Race also impinged on the public's growing concern about crime. Between 1960 and 1980, the total number of reported crimes quadrupled, and violent crime rose even faster. African-Americans comprised about 11 percent of the population in 1980 but perpetrated 30 percent of assaults and 62 percent of robberies. Conservatives blamed this problem on "permissive" judges who cared more about protecting the rights of poor and minority defendants than about crime victims. Increasingly, the public agreed. In the mid-1960s, 48 per-

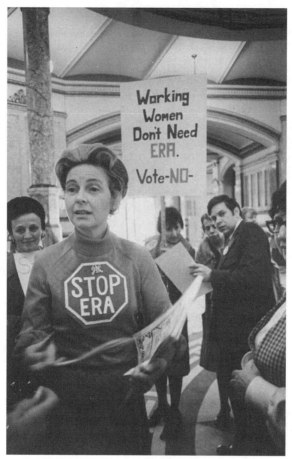

Phyllis Schlafly organized conservative women at the grassroots level in the 1970s.
Michael Mauney/Getty Images.

cent of Americans considered courts "too lenient." By 1980, the number soared
to 83 percent.

Permissiveness, conservatives charged, thrived because liberals encouraged a decadent counterculture of dependency that thumbed its nose at traditional values and personal responsibility. Liberals led the poor astray by
tolerating drug use, divorce, pornography, promiscuity, and openly gay
lifestyles. Even the Equal Rights Amendment (passed by Congress in 1972
and sent to the states for ratification), which Republican Party platforms had
endorsed for decades, was now condemned for undermining the family and
leading women astray.

Feminism, caricatured as "women's lib" by its critics, had "left behind it a
vast wreckage of broken and twisted lives," declared neoconservative Norman Podhoretz. Even though divorce, out-of-wedlock births, and single
parenting were becoming more common in all industrialized democracies,

conservatives pinned the blame on efforts to secure equality for women. Televangelist Pat Robertson summed it up in a letter to donors that blamed the "socialist" feminist agenda for encouraging "women to leave their husbands, kill their children, destroy capitalism, and become lesbians."

During the 1970s, efforts by groups such as NOW to defend abortion rights and promote ratification of the Equal Rights Amendment had spurred a "counterfeminism" among conservative women. Phyllis Schlafly, a Illinois housewife, lawyer, and Republican activist, organized the Eagle Forum, largely with the goal of stopping additional states from ratifying the ERA. In addition to voiding measures that benefited women (such as lower rates for certain insurance), she claimed the amendment would force women into military combat and promote same-sex marriage. A few years later, in 1979, Beverly LaHaye, wife of conservative activist and writer Tim LaHaye, organized Concerned Women of America (CWA), a group that lobbied against abortion, divorce, and homosexuality. CWA utilized what it called "prayer chains" to bombard politicians with the organization's messages.

The pitfalls of feminism, conservatives argued, comprised part of a larger problem. Unelected liberal elites had used courts to do an end run around state legislatures and Congress in their pursuit of a broader "rights revolution." Criminals, the mentally ill, American Indians, immigrants, youth, prisoners, and homosexuals demanded "special privileges" while hard-working Americans were overlooked and overtaxed.

Antigovernment sentiment also focused on soaring federal spending and climbing tax rates. Between 1960 and 1980, federal spending increased from $92 billion to $590 billion (unadjusted for inflation). Most Americans favored the most expensive federal expenditures, such as those for defense, Social Security, Medicare, education, home and business loans, and job training programs. When polled about programs they believed ought to be cut, average Americans named only two: foreign aid (which accounted for less than 1% of federal spending) and welfare.

"Welfare," in the minds of most Americans, did not mean the really big-ticket entitlements such as Social Security and Medicare. It meant programs that primarily helped the poor and minorities, such as Food Stamps and Aid to Families with Dependent Children (AFDC). Between 1965 and the late 1970s, the number of Americans receiving food stamps had soared from 400,000 to 17 million. The number of families on AFDC tripled. Despite these sharp increases, these two programs comprised a relatively small part of total federal social welfare expenditures. Nevertheless, by 1980, most Americans imagined that welfare for the not-so-deserving poor was a significant drain on federal coffers.

Ronald Reagan captured this resentment in anecdotes he told on the campaign trail that year. Food stamps, he claimed, allowed "some fellow ahead of you to buy T-bone steak" while "you were standing in the checkout line with your package of hamburger." Reagan often repeated an anecdote about a "welfare queen" with "eighty names, thirty addresses and twelve Social Security cards" whose "tax-free income alone is over $150,000." Although untrue, the anecdote captured public attention because it spoke to the frustration and resentment among so many working- and middle-class wage earners.

Tax Revolt

Because of deeply rooted antitax sentiment in American culture, the United States has historically taxed its citizens less than have most other industrialized democracies. During the 1970s, stagnant incomes, resentment against poor and minorities who received welfare, and inflation-induced "bracket creep" that drove up tax rates sharpened this traditional sentiment. By 1980, the proportion of Americans who viewed their federal income taxes as "too high" reached a record level. In addition, Social Security taxes and state and local income and property taxes rose sharply during the 1970s. Growing antitax sentiment among Americans of modest means dovetailed with the antitax beliefs of supply siders and other economic conservatives. The "tax revolt" that began in California in 1978 put the antitax agenda on the front burner of American politics.

Oddly, Reagan and much of the New Right were latecomers to the tax revolt. As governor of California, Reagan often cited the burden of high taxes but presided over an almost 50% rise in state sales and income taxes. The situation grew more tangled after he left office in 1975, largely because of soaring real estate values in the hot California property market. An archaic system of calculating residential property values led to steep tax increases for homeowners. Shortly before scheduled state elections in June 1978, homeowners were hit with one more spike in taxes. Public fury found an outlet in Proposition 13 (Prop 13), a plan to limit property tax increases that had been put on the ballot by Howard Jarvis, a veteran antitax campaigner. The June 1978 election stunned state officials when Prop 13 won by a two-to-one margin.

Prop 13 rolled back current property taxes and strictly limited future increases. But, in addition, it amended California's Constitution to require a two-thirds vote of the legislature to raise other state taxes and mandated a two-thirds approval by local voters to increase local taxes. In effect, this gave veto power over any future tax changes to one-third of the legislature and electorate. Over the next few years, twenty states adopted some form of tax limitation. By 1980, even Massachusetts, the bastion of liberalism, approved strict limits on property taxes.

Although he played only an observer role in the 1978 campaign, Reagan quickly recognized the symbolic power of the antitax movement. Prop 13, he declared, "triggered hope in the breasts of the people that something could be done . . . a little bit like dumping those cases of tea off the boat into Boston Harbor." *The New York Times* echoed this view, calling passage of Prop 13 a "modern Boston Tea Party" and a "primal scream by the people against Big Government." Democratic pollster Pat Caddell told President Carter that the vote represented a "revolution against government."

After 1978, high taxes became identified with big government liberalism much like sexual permissiveness, welfare spending, weakness on defense, and activist judges. Antitax rhetoric connected a large number of middle-class homeowners to the broader conservative movement and became a kind of political shorthand to attack entrenched Democrats and their expensive programs. The antitax message also entered the lexicon of racially charged code words, because it implied that if government bureaucrats would not waste so much money on welfare cheats and minorities, taxes would not be so high. Without mentioning race, politicians now called for slashing taxes and defunding programs that especially aided the poor and minorities.

TIME FOR CHOOSING: THE 1980 ELECTION

Jimmy Carter, probably the most conservative Democratic president since Grover Cleveland left office in 1897, epitomized the crisis of liberalism. Although Carter broadly supported civil rights, he believed in balancing budgets and cutting government bureaucracy. As a deeply religious southerner, he spoke openly of his faith and tried to find a middle way for "good government" to bridge the nation's social, economic, and political divides. He promoted worthy goals such as energy independence, peace between Egypt and Israel, global human rights, arms control, and environmental sensitivity. Yet, his inability either to improve the economy or resolve the Iranian hostage crisis doomed his administration. Conservatives lambasted his foreign policy as appeasement and ridiculed his domestic agenda as inept.

Carter spoke of reaching "comprehensive" solutions to problems and disdained the kind of piecemeal progress that often emerged from congressional horse trading. He appointed many talented aides but failed to outline broad policy goals that his administration could strive for. Carter often appeared consumed by details and oblivious to the "big picture." He knew in theory how government worked but not how laws actually got made. House Speaker Tip O'Neill spoke for many fellow Democrats in Congress when he declared that Carter was the most knowledgeable president he had ever worked with in terms of details but the most inept in terms of passing legislation. Carter's seriousness of purpose and talk of his own competence came across as sanctimony. When he repeated that there were no "easy answers," it sounded as if he had no answers. Even Carter's background as a nuclear engineer in the Navy seemed to haunt him. When a commercial nuclear reactor at Three Mile Island near Hershey, Pennsylvania, experienced a near-meltdown in March–April 1979, Carter's attempt to reassure Americans that they faced little danger raised rather than lowered popular anxiety. After hearing him discuss the relatively limited leakage of atomic radiation from the reactor, many wondered if their Hershey Bars would start glowing in the dark. To mix metaphors, Carter became the opposite of what journalists later called Reagan (the "Teflon president"): like Velcro, trouble stuck to him.

As one of his first acts in office, Carter pardoned all Vietnam-era draft resisters. Although he intended this act to promote reconciliation, the head of the Veterans of Foreign Wars described it as the "saddest day in American history." When Carter resumed negotiations suspended by Gerald Ford to return the Panama Canal to Panama, Reagan charged that Carter endangered national security and degraded national pride. "We built it, we paid for it, it's ours . . . and we're going to keep it," the Republican presidential aspirant declared. "We stole it, fair and square," added Senator S. I. Hayakawa, a California Republican. Even worse, conservatives accused Carter of ignoring the growing Soviet nuclear threat and rapid communist advances in the third world. Conservative criticism grew more intense following the capture of American diplomats in Iran and the Soviet invasion of Afghanistan.

The public's rage and frustration peaked following the capture of the diplomats at the American embassy in Teheran, Iran, on November 4, 1979. Revolutionary currents had swirled in Iran since 1953, when the CIA had helped to depose a nationalist regime that attempted to nationalize oil reserves and restored Shah Mohammad Reza Pahlavi to power. In cooperation with Washington, the shah modernized Iran's economy, bought billions of dollars worth of American weapons, and counterbalanced radical elements in the oil-rich Persian Gulf. But the shah's iron-fisted rule and tolerance of corruption provided an opening for Islamic fundamentalists who occupied the void created by the suppression of secular democratic reformers. In February 1979, the followers of an elderly ayatollah, or religious leader, Ruhollah Khomeini, forced the shah into exile and seized power.

The new Iranian regime forced thousands of American technicians and teachers to leave and raised oil prices steeply. In October 1979, President Carter admitted into the country the ailing shah (he suffered from a fatal cancer) for medical treatment. Khomeini denounced this humanitarian gesture as a plot by the "Great Satan" (America) to restore the shah to power. A week later, on November 4, 1979, Islamic militants overran the American embassy and, after releasing women staffers, retained fifty-three diplomats and Marine guards as hostages. For the next 444 days, this crisis mesmerized Carter, the public, and the media. It seemed to many that since its retreat from Vietnam, the United States had become the "pitiful, helpless giant" Richard Nixon had warned of. ABC TV began a late-night news program (that became *Nightline*) entitled *America Held Hostage*, a notion that enhanced popular frustration and outrage.

A month after the embassy seizure, in December 1979, the Soviet invasion of Afghanistan, where Red Army troops bolstered a tottering puppet regime, fueled conservative charges that Carter's efforts to reason with Kremlin leaders had only encouraged aggression. The nearly simultaneous toppling of the pro-American Somoza dictatorship in Nicaragua by leftist Sandinista rebels brought the specter of a Red offensive still closer to America. When Carter took office, only 25 percent of the public believed that "too little" was being spent on defense. By 1980, 56 percent of Americans called for spending more on the military.

Carter met these challenges by moving to the right. He sharply increased defense spending, threatened military action if the Soviets interfered with

Iranian students holding American hostages ridicule an effigy of President Jimmy Carter, 1980. Staff/Getty Images.

Middle Eastern oil, canceled grain sales to the Soviet Union, and withdrew American athletes from the upcoming 1980 Moscow Olympics. At home, Carter ordered reductions in welfare spending and moved against inflation. He encouraged Federal Reserve Board Chairman Paul Volcker to squeeze out inflation by driving up the prime interest rate (worsening the "misery index") from 9.1 percent in 1978 to 21.5 percent in 1980. These initiatives eventually brought down inflation and sped rearmament. But by the time they showed success, Reagan had defeated Carter and received most of the credit for what his predecessor had begun.

Even Carter's effort to demonstrate his own and America's strong commitment to human rights and disdain of communist rule in Cuba backfired badly. In March of 1980, first a handful, then several thousand Cubans dissidents sought refuge in foreign embassies in Havana. In a show of solidarity, Carter offered asylum to these dissidents. Fidel Castro trumped Carter by announcing that any Cuban who wished to could leave for the United States by departing from the small fishing port of Mariel. The U.S. government organized a flotilla of mostly private vessels to carry the so-called *Marielitos*, whose numbers reached 130,000 by the time the boatlift ended in October. However, the operation soon became a public relations fiasco when Castro opened jails and mental institutions and ordered the inmates to join those on the boats for America. Criminals and the mentally ill composed only a few thousand among the refugee exodus who made the crossing. Nevertheless, the media highlighted the impact of these hard-to-place misfits, one of whom became the model for the hyperviolent drug dealer Tony Montana in the 1983 film *Scarface*, starring Al Pacino. By the time the boatlift ended in the autumn of 1980, the media and Republican spokesmen portrayed Carter's compassion as gullibility that allowed the ever-scheming Castro to manipulate him and dump troublemakers on America.

Carter's grim, plodding style of speech eventually turned off most Americans. Even the liberal *Boston Globe* at one point characterized his delivery as "More Mush from the Wimp." Reagan, in comparison, radiated a mix of optimism, fervent anti-communism, and flag-waving patriotism that proved a perfect foil to Carter's handwringing. Among the challenger's important political achievements was success in bridging the divide between social conservatives and libertarians. In 1977, he argued that the "time has come" to "present a program of action based on political principle that can attract those interested in the so-called social issues [which he identified as "law and order, abortion, busing, quota systems"] and those interested in economic issues" such as inflation, deficit spending, and big government. He promised to "combine the two major segments of . . . American conservatism in one politically effective whole." Reagan broached few new ideas, but he proved a marvelous salesman of the New Right agenda.

A key to his political success and popularity was his ability to appeal even to those Americans who disagreed with his right-wing views. From the failed presidency of Herbert Hoover to the Goldwater campaign of 1964, many of the most prominent conservative Republicans came across as gloomy, misanthropic scolds. Reagan had an uncanny ability to project a user-friendly conservatism that enabled him to say even harsh things in a good-natured manner. He projected an aura of resolve and strong leadership without appearing mean, unfeeling, or even threatening.

Even as Carter cautioned Americans to become accustomed to limits and sacrifice, Reagan declared that "America's best days lay ahead." He scorned those who implied that "the United States has had its day in the sun." We "are too great a nation to limit ourselves to small dreams," Reagan explained. More than anything, his upbeat style, perfected in dozens of feature films and thousands of after-dinner speeches as a General Electric spokesman, captured the imagination of a public wary of scandals, government incompetence, and foreign threats. Without saying just how, Reagan convinced a majority of voters that he would tame inflation, cut taxes, and restore respect for America. Carter, he lamented, had cooked up an indigestible economic stew, "one part inflation, one part unemployment, one part recession, one part runaway taxes, and one part deficit spending seasoned with an energy crisis." The stew had "turned the nation's stomach." Looking to the future, Reagan declared, "This is the greatest country in the world. Now all we need is the leadership."

In November 1980, Reagan defeated Carter by a margin of 51 percent to 41 percent in the popular vote (running as an independent, liberal Republican Congressman John Anderson received 7 percent of the vote) and by a 489-to-49 rout of the Electoral College. Reagan's margin helped Republicans achieve a net gain of thirty-three representatives, twelve senators, and four governors.

Stalwart liberal Democratic senators, such as South Dakota's George McGovern, Indiana's Birch Bayh, and Idaho's Frank Church, were replaced by conservatives Steven Symms, Dan Quayle, and James Abdnor. These turnovers helped the GOP take control of the Senate for the first time in twenty-eight years. Although Democrats retained nominal control of the House, the GOP achieved a working majority by allying with mostly southern conservative Democrats—nicknamed "Boll Weevils." Whether Reagan's victory represented an ideological mandate or more of a "no confidence" vote against Carter (only a tenth of those voting for Reagan told pollsters they picked him because he was a "real conservative," most Reagan voters said they felt it was simply "time for a change"), conservatives had, in fact, won considerably more power and were eager to flex their new political muscle.

Sources and Further Readings

The underlying causes of the decline of the liberal consensus supporting "big government" are examined in H. W. Brands, *The Strange Death of American Liberalism* (2002); Bruce J. Schulman, *The Seventies: The Great Shift in American Culture, Society and Politics* (2001); Peter Carroll, *It Seemed Like Nothing Happened: The Tragedy and Promise of America in the 1970s* (1990); Thomas B. Edsall, *The New Politics of Inequality* (1984); Thomas B. Edsall and Mary D. Edsall, *Chain Reaction: The Impact of Race, Rights, and Taxes on American Politics* (1991); E. J. Dionne, *Why Americans Hate Politics: The Death of the Democratic Process* (1992); Thomas Ferguson and Joel Rogers, *Right Turn: The Decline of the Democrats and the Future of American Politics* (1986); William C. Berman, *America's Right Turn: From Nixon to Clinton* (1998); Ronald Radosh, *Divided They Fell: The Demise of the Democratic Party, 1964–1996* (1996).

Economic stagnation and its effects during the 1970s and early 1980s are described in Richard J. Barnet, *The Lean Years: Politics in an Age of Scarcity* (1980); Bennett Harrison and Barry Bluestone, *The Great U-Turn: Corporate Restructuring and the Polarizing of America* (1988); William Greider, *Secrets of the Temple: How the Federal Reserve Runs the Country* (1987); Frank Levy, *Dollars and Dreams: The Changing American Income Distribution* (1987); K. Newman, *Falling from Grace: The Experience of Downward Mobility in the American Middle Class* (1988); Barbara Ehrenreich, *Fear of Falling: The Insecure Life of the Middle Class* (1985); Julius Wilson, *The Truly Disadvantaged: The Inner City, the Underclass, and Public Policy* (1987); Alan Wolf, *America's Impasse: The Rise and Fall of the Politics of Growth* (1981); Robert Zieger, *American Workers, American Unions* (1994).

On the rise of the New Right, including televangelists, culture warriors, and neoconservatives, see the books listed in Chapter One, especially John Micklethwait and Adrian Wooldridge, *The Right Nation: Conservative Power in America* (2004), and Richard Viguerie, *The New Right: We're Ready to Lead* (1980); Richard Viguerie, *America's Right Turn: How Conservatives Used New and Alternative Media to Take Power* (2004); Irving Kristol, *Neoconservatism: The Autobiography of an Idea* (1995); John Ehrman, *Rise of Neoconservatism: Intellectuals and Foreign Affairs, 1945–1994* (1995); Gary Dorian, *The Neoconservative Mind: Politics, Culture, and the War of Ideology* (1993); Jean Stefanic and others, *No Mercy: How Conservative Think Tanks and Foundations Changed America's Social Agenda* (1997); Sidney Blumenthal, *The Rise of the Counterestablishment: From Conservative Ideology to Political Power* (1986); Nina J. Easton, *Gang of Five: Leaders at the*

Center of the Conservative Crusade (2000); Steve Bruce, *The Rise and Fall of the New Christian Right* (1998); Jeffrey K. Hadden and Anson Shupe, *Televangelism: Power and Politics on God's Frontier* (1988); Jeffrey D. Hunter, *Culture Wars: The Struggle to Define America* (1988).

The challenges of the Carter presidency and the Iran hostage crisis are discussed in Burton Kauffman, *The Presidency of James Earl Carter* (1993); Peter Bourne, *Jimmy Carter: A Comprehensive Biography from Plains to Post-Presidency* (1997); Kenneth C. Morriss, *Jimmy Carter: American Moralist* (1996); Gaddis Smith, *Morality, Reason, and Power: American Diplomacy in the Carter Years* (1987); Gary Sick, *October Surprise: American Hostages in Iran and the Election of Ronald Reagan* (1991); Andrew W. Busch, *Reagan's Victory: The Presidential Election of 1980 and the Rise of the Right* (2005).

3

National Politics, 1981–1992

The secret is that when the Left took over the Democratic Party, we took over the Republican Party. We made the Republican Party into the party of the working people, the family, the neighborhood, the defense of freedom, and yes, the American flag and the Pledge of Allegiance to one nation under God. So you see the party that so many of us grew up with still exists except that today it's called the Republican Party and I'm asking all of you to come home and join me.

Ronald Reagan, 1988

Standing tall and elegant in his formal attire, Ronald Reagan appeared poised for action as he took the presidential oath on January 20, 1981. As seen by millions of Americans on television, the incoming and outgoing presidents were a vivid study in contrasts. Reagan had rested well the night before he assumed power. Jimmy Carter appeared stooped, almost shrunken, with hooded eyes. Unknown to the public, he had not slept for days while he negotiated the final details for the release of American hostages from Iran. In a flourish intentionally designed to humiliate the outgoing president, the Iranians released their captives just as Reagan took the oath of office.[1]

Speaking from deep conviction and utilizing his formidable acting skill, Reagan declared that Americans were not people to dream "small dreams." The new president recalled past heroes who overcame earlier crises. Reversing the central tenet of national politics since the New Deal, Reagan declared, "In the present crisis . . . government is not the solution to our problem, government *is* the problem."

Among the new president's first official acts was temporarily freezing federal hiring. In a more personal statement, he rearranged the presidential portraits hanging in the White House, giving that of Calvin Coolidge a more prominent place in the national pantheon. Reagan's homage to "Silent Cal," the puritanical New Englander who served in the "Roaring Twenties," revealed his hope of reviving an era dominated by conservative Republicanism, traditional cultural values, limited government, and an economy

---

1. The hostage-takers described humiliating Carter as "payback" for the CIA's role in the 1953 coup against Iran's nationalist prime minister, Mohammed Mossadeg.

President Reagan took pride in leading patriotic celebrations. Courtesy Ronald Reagan Library.

controlled by corporate executives and financiers. "The business of America is business," Coolidge had proclaimed in his best-remembered phrase. Reagan certainly agreed.

During the next decade, Reagan and his successor, George H. W. Bush, worked to restore this lost horizon. Both Republican presidents promoted policies designed to halt or roll back many of the New Deal's accomplishments and legacies. Reagan proved especially adept at forging a powerful bond with the public that transcended voters' opinions about his specific policies. He tapped a popular yearning to restore a sense of community, real or imagined, that had been lost since the 1960s. With his ruddy good looks, a tremor in his voice, and a twinkle in his eye, Reagan fulfilled an ideal of what a president should be. Whether or not they agreed with his programs, people enjoyed hearing his jokes and inspirational stories—which also served to deflect criticism and serious introspection. Bush, who lacked comparable charm, was elected in 1988 largely on the goodwill he had earned as Reagan's vice president. As long as the "good times" lasted, including the "end of the Cold War" and a victory over Iraq in the Gulf War, President Bush enjoyed high levels of voter approval. But when economic troubles began in 1991, he quickly lost the trust of the American public, and Republicans suffered major setbacks.

The Republican agenda during the 1980s and early 1990s focused on reducing many "big government" programs initiated by Democrats since 1933. The Reagan and Bush administrations worked to shrink the social welfare system, limit the role of federal courts and agencies in promoting civil rights and liberties, reduce government regulation of business and protection of the environment, and slash income taxes, especially for high-end earners. Both presidents worked to foster a conservative social ethic in such areas as abortion rights, gender roles, premarital sex, drug use, and the role of religion in public life. In their view, the federal government had little business in promoting greater equality. Instead, market forces would both create new wealth and assure its equitable distribution.

THE "REAGAN REVOLUTION"

As he assumed the presidency, Reagan relied on a triumvirate of top policy advisers who served him well. In an astute move, he reached outside his inner circle of conservative Californians to appoint James A. Baker III, a close friend of Vice President Bush, as White House chief of staff. The more conservative and abrasive Edwin Meese, a close associate from Reagan's time as governor, became a presidential "counselor," an amorphous post without clear responsibility. Michael Deaver, a skilled public relations expert personally close to the president and First Lady Nancy Reagan, worked as deputy chief of staff with responsibility for managing the president's image.

Reagan's first cabinet consisted almost entirely of white, male Republicans, most of whom had served in the Nixon and Ford administrations or with him in California. Only two posts, Interior and Energy, went to members of the New Right—James Watt and James Edwards. Watt's provocative criticism of liberals and non-Christians as "un-American" as well as his effort to speed development of protected federal land, eventually forced the president to replace him. Initially, no women served in the cabinet, although U.N. Ambassador Jeanne Kirkpatrick received honorary cabinet status. In 1983, after midterm elections in which GOP candidates fared poorly among women voters, Reagan appointed Margaret Heckler as secretary of health and human services and Elizabeth Dole as secretary of transportation. The new president appointed an African-American, Samuel Pierce, as secretary of housing and urban development but cared so little about housing policy that he failed to recognize Pierce the few times they spoke. At one reception Reagan held out his hand to the HUD secretary and said, "Hello, Mr. Mayor." Reagan frequently skipped cabinet meetings and often dozed off when he attended.

Chief of Staff Baker persuaded Reagan to push Congress for two items on his agenda that were popular and that the president wanted most: tax cuts and a defense buildup. "If we can do that," Baker maintained, "the rest will take care of itself." Following this advice, the president gave token support to proposals by conservative social and religious activists to amend the Constitution to ban abortion and permit school prayer—but expended little energy or political capital on their behalf.

Reagan had long been critical of the progressive income tax. He believed that people should be rewarded for achieving wealth, not taxed at higher rates for doing so. As noted earlier, he embraced supply-side economics, the theory that cutting the tax rate would pay for itself by stimulating business activity and promoting economic growth. The Republican antitax mantra also served to limit new government programs (by reducing funding sources) and appealed to voters fed up with perceived "giveaways."

Reagan's rhetoric distinguished between taxpayers and "tax takers." Taxpayers were hard-working, mostly white Americans from whom the government took exorbitant sums of money. Tax takers were the "undeserving poor" and minorities on whom Democrats supposedly lavished federal resources. GOP calls for "fairness" in taxation had the coded meaning of reducing aid to minorities. Tax cuts also served as a substitute for wage hikes at a time when workings and middle-class incomes were stagnating.

As the keystone of his agenda, Reagan asked Congress in January 1981 to cut federal business tax rates by 25 percent over three years and to lower the top marginal income tax rate from 70 percent (although the wealthy seldom paid this much because of numerous shelters) to 50 percent. To reduce federal power and expenses, he called for shifting many social programs to state control, trimming Social Security benefits, and eliminating many business regulations and environmental protections. Several of these economic proposals reflected ideas broached by Arthur Laffer and Milton Friedman. Reagan assured the public that these measures would balance the budget, create jobs, reduce inflation, make government less intrusive, and leave the American people with more money to spend.

Reagan vehemently denied that he was secretly "trying to undo the New Deal." Rather, he noted in a diary entry, he wanted to "undo the Great Society. It was LBJ's war on poverty," he insisted, "that led us to our present mess." Reagan complained that the Democrats' excessive deficit spending had "mortgaged our future and our children's future for the temporary convenience of the present." As the national debt approached $1 trillion, he believed that by reducing government social spending, his administration would both save money and encourage people to help themselves.

Although Reagan professed faith in the supply-side nostrum that tax cuts would stimulate growth and increase tax revenue, his budget director, David Stockman, recognized that without big spending cuts Reagan's program would likely generate huge budget deficits. This was especially true because the new administration intended to increase defense spending significantly without making offsetting cuts in popular programs such as Social Security and Medicare. As a result, Stockman privately predicted a "budget hemor-rhage" with annual shortfalls of $100 billion or more for the next four years, greater than any peacetime deficits run up by any Democratic president. Rea-gan dismissed these concerns, certain that his tax cuts and other business re-forms would generate plenty of revenue. If not, he guessed (correctly) that most Americans would trade big deficits that had to be paid off by future generations for current tax cuts that they could enjoy now. Also, if the deficit mounted, he could place the blame on congressional Democrats for not cut-ting wasteful programs.

The new president appealed directly to the public for support of these ini-tiatives. Organized labor feared opposing him, especially after Reagan fired 12,000 striking federal air traffic controllers whose work stoppage in Au-gust 1981 violated their contract. Even though the air traffic controllers' union, PATCO, had endorsed Reagan's candidacy, he had no qualms about acting tough. Echoing his idol, Calvin Coolidge, who had condemned a Boston police strike in 1919 by declaring "there is no right to strike against the public safety by anybody, anywhere, anytime" and had replaced the police with members of the National Guard, Reagan denounced PATCO members as selfish viola-tors of the public trust and replaced them with military personnel. The public had little sympathy for the well-paid and arrogant-sounding controllers whom they often blamed for flight delays, and generally cheered Reagan's stand.

Reagan turned even near tragedy and personal suffering to his political ad-vantage. When a crazed gunman, John Hinckley, gravely wounded the pres-ident in March 1981, just six weeks into his first term, Reagan told his wife in the emergency room, "Honey, I forgot to duck." About to go under the sur-geon's knife, he jokingly asked if the doctor was a Republican. "We're all Re-publicans today" came the reply. Reagan's good humor and spunk evoked immense affection among Americans who had questioned the warmth of some of his predecessors.

Although holding a nominal majority in the House of Representatives, Democrats, in the view of Majority Leader Tip O'Neill, were "shell shocked" and reluctant to stand in the way of popular tax cuts. Reagan also could rely on the votes of sixty-three conservative, mostly southern Democratic "Boll Weevils." In return for the president's pledge to help get them reelected, they joined Republicans in voting for the Reagan economic program.

On August 13, 1981, Reagan signed two major laws: the Economic Recov-ery Tax Act and the Omnibus Budget Reconciliation Act. The former slashed federal income tax rates by 25 percent over three years. The budget bill cut $40 billion in domestic spending but left intact most popular big-ticket programs such as Social Security and Medicare. Funding for programs such as Amtrak, synthetic fuels, low-income housing, school lunches, and other social services for the poor received small to medium cuts. Reagan spoke of pruning additional social programs, but members of Congress from both parties balked at making unpopular reductions after this first round. In effect, the president's early big victory in reducing federal spending turned out to be his last. By June 1982, as the budget deficit ballooned, Reagan bowed to congressional pressure and quietly raised taxes (or "enhanced revenues," as he preferred to call it) for the first of several times in his administration.

Much of the positive media attention lavished on the tax cuts in 1981 obscured the fundamentals, such as how the tax rate changed for different groups and the profile of who actually paid less and who paid about the same. In fact, the wealthiest fifth of Americans received the lion's share of the benefits. Also, in spite of the hoopla, the percentage of total national income that went toward taxes stayed almost level, around 19.7 percent, throughout the decade because other tax increases balanced the federal income tax cut.

The income tax decrease received by most working- and middle-class taxpayers proved especially elusive. In April 1983, Reagan and Congress approved a bipartisan panel's plan to shore up the Social Security trust fund that paid pensions to millions of elderly Americans. The plan included a small reduction in benefits and an increase in the payroll taxes paid by workers. This added levy sucked up most of the income tax reduction that low-wage workers received in 1981. But the plan stabilized Social Security for twenty-five years and removed it from partisan debate.

Reaganomics had a wobbly beginning in 1981–1982. The nation slipped into a deep recession soon after Congress approved the president's program. The recession was partly the result of decisions made by Federal Reserve Board Chairman Paul Volcker to raise interest rates as high as 21.5 percent to stifle inflation. This increase drove unemployment rates to 10.8 percent, or more than 11.5 million jobless workers. Business failures, farm foreclosures, and homelessness increased dramatically. Conditions were especially difficult in the Midwest's Rustbelt.

The recession affected the election of 1982, in which congressional Democrats partly bounced back from their earlier losses. Reagan's approval ratings declined from 61 percent to only 41 percent by the end of 1982. Media pundits began describing him as a likely one-term president. Reagan, however, refused to alter his priorities and predicted economic recovery by 1984.

Reagan's luck and optimism triumphed. The high interest rates gradually squeezed inflation out of the economy. As inflation receded, the Federal Reserve Board reduced interest rates, lowered the cost of borrowing, and promoted economic growth. A surge in foreign oil production pushed down world oil prices, lowering the cost of imported fuel. Massive defense spending created a boom in high technology and in the aerospace industries of New England, the Southwest, and the West Coast. By the end of 1983, the worst of the recession had passed, and the subsequent economic expansion lasted until 1991.

By the end of the 1980s, supply siders boasted that their policies had created eighteen million new jobs, spurred economic growth, lowered federal tax rates, and tripled the average price of stocks. Many Americans agreed that the final six years of the Reagan administration and the first three years

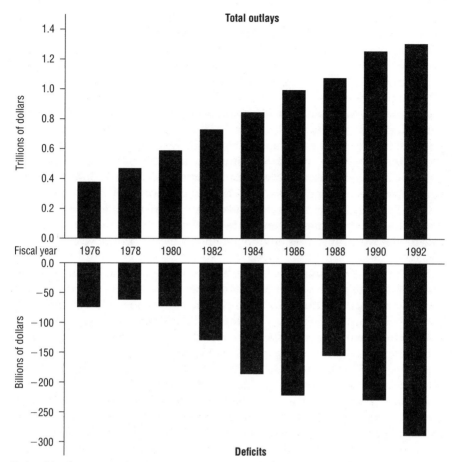

Federal budget expenditures and deficits, 1976–1992.

of the Bush administration marked a period of solid prosperity, even if some Americans benefited far more than others.

Reagan used television more effectively than any of his predecessors to gain public support for his programs. With his experience as a film star and television host, he proved a master of the electronic media, earning the nickname "the Great Communicator." Each presidential action was designed "as a one-minute or two-minute spot on the evening network news." Every presidential appearance was conceived "in terms of camera angle." Reagan possessed an uncanny ability to turn cliches into winning phrases. He fostered in his audience a sense of joint purpose even as he ridiculed the efficiency of government. In times of uncertainty, Reagan projected a reassuring decisiveness.

The large tax cuts and defense buildup laid the foundations for Republican governance in the 1980s, but the so-called Reagan Revolution and Bush aftermath reflected perception as much as reality. When Reagan left office in 1989, the federal government collected about the same percentage of the nation's GNP—just over 19 percent—in federal taxes as it had through-out the previous twenty years. Total federal spending actually increased under Reagan, rising from about 7 percent of GNP to 8.2 percent. The biggest increases occurred in defense outlays, Medicare, and Social Security. The gap between tax revenues and rising spending produced under Presidents Reagan and then Bush the largest budget deficits in U.S. history. Annual shortfalls ranged from $100 billion to over $250 billion. The cumulative national debt soared from $1 trillion in 1980 to nearly $3 trillion in 1989 to $4 trillion in 1993. To make up the shortfall, Washington turned to foreign investors—especially in Japan, Germany, and Saudi Arabia—to finance the debt by purchasing Treasury bonds and notes. These nations were able to lend so much money because they had accumulated huge dollar surpluses from their export of oil and manufactured goods to the United States. The United States began the twelve years of Republican presidential rule as the world's leading creditor; it ended the era as the world's largest debtor.

Reagan was also exceptionally persuasive in one-on-one encounters with members of Congress, whom he often charmed into voting his way. Yet, off screen or off script, Reagan often lacked focus, clarity, and direction. Un-scripted news conferences were painful to watch and were kept to a mini-mum. More than most presidents, he relied on skilled White House staff to promote his programs and manage his image. During his first administration, Chief of Staff James Baker, Baker's deputy, Michael Deaver, and Counselor Edwin Meese carefully monitored Reagan's legislative agenda and his public appearances. All three left the White House for other jobs during the second administration. Many of Reagan's most controversial actions—such as trading arms to Iran to gain the release of hostages and visiting a Nazi cemetery in Germany—took place when his second-term team gave him bad advice. In fact, during his second term, Congress passed only one piece of major legislation promoted by Reagan—a tax reform also supported by many Democrats. Mostly at Congress's initiative, the president also signed a modest immigration reform bill.

Even his closest aides found Reagan exceptionally detached from details and often had to guess at what he wanted them to do. At cabinet meetings Reagan frequently began by reading from letters and inspirational stories sent him by admirers. But typically, after a few minutes he retreated into si-lence and displayed what aides called a "glassy-eyed look." They continued discussion without his input. Reagan's friend and economic adviser, Martin Anderson, recalled that the president's aides "compensated for the fact that he made decisions like an ancient king or a Turkish pasha, passively letting his subjects serve him." Reagan told his spokesman, Larry Speakes, that he was happiest when "each morning I get a piece of paper that tells me what I do all day long." As he put it, being president was "something like shooting a script," in which characters appeared and departed and the plot advanced. Novelist John Updike's portrait of American life in the 1980s, *Rabbit at Rest*, captured this mood. Reagan, Updike's narrator observed, "had that dream distance: the powerful thing about him as president was that you never knew how much he knew, nothing or everything, he was like God that way, you had to do a lot of it yourself."

REELECTION AND THE SECOND ADMINISTRATION

By 1984, as the economy climbed out of recession and into its long expansion that lasted until 1991, Ronald Reagan loomed as a formidable opponent for any Democratic challenger. Even if economic benefits flowed mostly into the pockets of the wealthy, most voters enjoyed a few more dollars in their pockets from the 1981 tax cut, inflation had practically disappeared, and abstract difficulties such as the ballooning budget deficit were a problem for the future and had little immediate impact on individuals. Reagan's 1983 decision to invade the tiny island of Grenada (see the next chapter) was a whopping success with the public. In 1984, he even managed to share the glory of American athletes at the Los Angeles summer Olympics, where, as Soviet-bloc athletes boycotted the games, they won a large number of gold medals.

By 1984, the Democratic Party struggled to mobilize an electorate no longer attuned to the New Deal legacy. To both inside and outside observers, the Democrats often appeared a loose coalition of "special interest" groups, running the gamut from blue-collar union members to feminists to gay and African-American civil rights activists. Many party activists and members defined themselves by "identity politics," meaning they thought and acted first as gay Democrats, environmental Democrats, or feminist Democrats, lacking any unifying direction. Looked at from outside, the Democratic Party seemed like Humpty Dumpty—after the fall.

After bruising primaries, former Vice President Walter Mondale defeated rivals Gary Hart and Jesse Jackson. Mondale had worked hard to secure endorsements from organized labor, ethnic organizations, women's groups, teachers, environmentalists, and other organized elements in the party. Critics, especially among Republicans, described Mondale's celebration of the old glory days of the Democrats and his search for endorsements as pandering to "special interests" while ignoring the national interest.

After a slow and highly visible search for an "appropriate" running mate, Mondale finally selected New York Representative Geraldine Ferraro as his vice presidential candidate. As the first woman nominated for the national ticket by a major party, Ferraro excited millions of Americans. She proved a smart, articulate candidate who easily held her own in a debate with Vice President George Bush. Legal questions that surfaced about her husband's financial dealings, however, obscured her critique of the Reagan presidency. Many voters concluded that having served only three terms in Congress, Ferraro was untested. Ultimately, her presence on the ticket did not affect the election outcome.

Mondale, a thoughtful liberal who deeply believed in the virtues of good government, tried valiantly to run a campaign based on the issues. He bombarded the public with warnings about runaway spending, an out-of-control arms race, environmental disasters, and the unfairness of Reagan's economic policies. His most famous campaign line, referring to the mounting deficit, was "He'll raise taxes, so will I. He won't tell you, I just did." Commentators briefly praised Mondale's political courage in addressing the deficit issue head on, but within a week the media decided he had committed political suicide. U.N. Ambassador Jeanne Kirkpatrick, a conservative Democrat who served Reagan, dubbed Mondale "bad news Fritz," leader of the "blame-America-first crowd" who could barely wait to start raising taxes to pay for wasteful social programs.

In the first of two televised presidential debates on October 7, 1984, Reagan staggered. Even his most avid champion, Nancy Reagan, described him as "tense, muddled, and off-stride." Instead of sticking to his usual uplifting anecdotes, the president bogged down in confusing statistics that neither he nor his audience understood. Mondale told aides that up close Reagan's "eyes were wandering" and that he seemed "out to lunch." At one point Mandale worried that Reagan might actually collapse and described the president as appearing "senile." Sensing a story, the media briefly seized on the age issue, showing clips of Reagan dozing off at meetings or muddling responses to easy questions.

First Lady Nancy Reagan intervened to save her leading man. She recognized that her husband performed best when relaxed, not overly prepared. By the time the second debate took place on October 21, Reagan bounced back. Instead of statistics, he reeled off one-liners, to the delight of viewers and voters. Midway through the debate, a journalist asked Reagan if he had any concerns about his ability to serve another four years. "Not at all, Mr. Trewhitt," Reagan answered, "and I want you to know that . . . I will not make age an issue of this campaign. I am not going to exploit, for political purposes, my opponent's youth and inexperience." As the studio and national audience burst into laughter, Mondale recognized he had lost the election.

In fact, in light of his diagnosis with Alzheimer's disease a decade later, serious questions remain about Reagan's mental capacity during his second term. Close aides and journalists alike noticed his increasing difficulty in staying on task, in making decisions, and in setting an agenda. On camera, he could usually sustain the image of a vigorous, engaged leader and tossed off one-liners with aplomb. On issues dear to his heart, such as the "Star Wars" antimissile program and aid to the anti-communist contra guerrillas in Nicaragua, he still showed great interest. But, as noted later, by 1987 his chief of staff and Secretary of State George Shultz were so troubled by his mental drift that they agreed he should not be allowed to meet alone with any foreign leader.

During the remainder of the 1984 campaign, however, the public had few qualms. College students especially liked hearing talk of renewal from America's oldest serving president. On campuses where a few years before undergraduates had hurled insults and rocks at Lyndon Johnson and Richard Nixon, twenty-year-olds now screamed "U.S.A.! U.S.A.!" in response to

Reagan's proclamation that it was "morning again in America," an advertising slogan he borrowed from the Chrysler Corporation.

The president's speeches and campaign advertisements emphasized the themes of redemption, patriotism, and family. In 1980, Reagan had run against government; in 1984 he *was* government, but it made little difference. His campaign theme, summarized by the media as "don't worry, be happy," carried him to a landslide victory in forty-nine states. At the congressional level, however, Democrats did much better, retaining their majority in the House and pecking away at the slim Republican majority in the Senate.

Reagan's second term got off to a slow start, with the president giving his aides little policy direction. In fact, over the next four years, Congress passed only two major bills, one dealing with immigration reform (discussed later) and the other with taxes. In both cases, Democrats played key roles in drafting the legislation, often over the objections of conservative Republicans. Reagan pushed for passage of both bills even though they seemed at variance with his conservative views.

In the summer of 1986, as the stock market surged to record highs, Congress passed a major tax reform bill, the economic centerpiece of Reagan's second-term legislative agenda. The new tax law, a modification of the flat-rate income tax system proposed by Democrats Bill Bradley and Richard Gephardt, was presented as "revenue neutral," simply a way to restore simplicity and fairness to the complex tax code. To attract Democrats, the law closed many tax loopholes exploited by the wealthy. Republicans stressed that it reduced the tax code's multiple brackets to just three, at rates of 15, 28, and 33 percent. But the tax remained progressive, rather than a flat tax that many conservatives favored. Ultimately, most taxpayers ended up paying about the same total as before. With scant justification, Reagan claimed it reduced middle-class taxes. Neither he nor most Republicans acknowledged that by closing loopholes, such as those on real estate investments, the new law actually *increased* collections from wealthy tax avoiders. As we will see, this reform also had the unintended effect of wrecking the savings and loan industry, taking an immense toll on the economy.

On July 4, 1986, the president hosted a celebration in New York Harbor that showed him at his best. The extravaganza featured a newly renovated Statue of Liberty, the biggest fireworks display ever assembled, and Ronald Reagan. Leslie Stahl, a White House reporter for CBS, commented that, "Like his leading lady, the Statue of Liberty, the president, after six years in office, has himself become a symbol of pride in America." However, despite Reagan's immense popularity, he failed to achieve a realignment in national politics. In the November 1986 congressional elections, even as Reagan rode high in the polls, the Democrats actually regained control of the Senate and increased their majority in the House. With their dual majorities and renewed confidence, Democrats blocked administration proposals to make further cuts in social programs, to expand defense spending, or to intervene more directly in Central America's civil wars.

By late 1986, the Iran-contra scandal—which involved illegal weapons-for-hostage deals with Iran and arms transfers to a group of Central American "freedom fighters"—was becoming public, and during the next year it proved a profound embarrassment to the administration. A year later, in October 1987, a collapse in stock prices jolted the confident economic mood that had prevailed since 1983. After the Dow Jones Industrial Average hit a record high of 2,700 points in August, it slumped. In mid-October it fell six hundred points in a few days, losing almost a fourth of its value and reviving memories of the 1929 stock market crash that had ushered in the Great Depression. Although Wall Street soon recovered most of its losses, the crash created economic anxiety that proved difficult to shake.

The combined impact of the Iran-contra scandal and Wall Street jitters in 1987 might have proved to be Reagan's undoing and the most memorable disappointments of his administration. But the president's ability to adjust to circumstances once again surprised Americans. During 1987–1988, as relations between the United States and the Soviet Union improved dramatically, the public proved willing to overlook the Iran-contra scandal. Reagan left office with an overall 68 percent approval rating, higher than that of any president since Franklin D. Roosevelt.

George H. W. Bush, Michael Dukakis, and the 1988 Election

As Ronald Reagan approached the end of his second term, Democrats once again hoped to win back control of the White House by restoring the New Deal coalition that had splintered in the late 1960s and 1970s. But the Democratic Party's divisions had not healed, and a majority of the public still viewed the party's agenda with suspicion.

Despite serving eight years as vice president, George Bush remained relatively unknown to the public. Not personally close to Reagan, he told one interviewer that during his eight years of vice presidential service he had never even been invited to the family wing of the White House. Nor had Bush played much of a part in setting the domestic or foreign policy agenda. Until being tapped as Reagan's running mate in 1980, Bush had stood with Republican moderates in support of abortion rights and had disparaged Reagan's budget plan as "voodoo economics." These past lapses, along with his "preppy mannerisms," grating voice and tortured grammar that made many listeners wince, and what some saw as a wimpy "Mr. Rogers" personality, made Bush the object of mistrust and derision among the Republican right wing. In the contest to succeed Reagan, more conservative challengers, such as Reagan aide Patrick Buchanan, televangelist Pat Robertson, Delaware Governor Pete DuPont, Congressman Jack Kemp, and Senator Robert Dole, accused Bush of being an unauthentic conservative, more "eastern establishment liberal" than rugged individual. One wag dismissed Bush's claim to being a Texan as "all hat and no boots."

In fact, Bush was a skilled and ambitious politician who had long sought the presidency. The son of a wealthy Republican senator from Connecticut,

Bush left Yale University during World War II to become the youngest fighter pilot in the U.S. Navy. A photo of a young, smiling Bush being plucked from the Pacific after his plane went down was used with devastating impact in the 1988 campaign. After the war, Bush had returned to Yale and graduated, moved to Texas, and made a fortune in the oil business. As a moderate in an increasingly conservative Republican Party, he served two terms in the U.S. House of Representatives from 1967 to 1971. His steadfast support for funding family-planning programs earned him the nickname "Rubbers" among House members. Until his selection as Reagan's vice president in 1980, Bush continued to support a woman's right to choose an abortion as well as the proposed Equal Rights Amendment to the Constitution. After Bush lost his 1970 bid for a Texas Senate seat, first President Nixon and then President Ford appointed Bush to a number of posts, including chairman of the Republican National Committee, U.S. representative in China, and director of the CIA.

As the GOP presidential candidate in 1988, Bush reached out to conservatives. He selected Senator Dan Quayle of Indiana, a favorite among the Christian right but otherwise considered a lightweight, as his running mate. At the Republican convention, Bush brought delegates to their feet by paraphrasing a line spoken by actor Clint Eastwood. "Read my lips," he declared, "no new taxes." Despite this nod to Reagan, which came back to haunt him, Bush never won the respect or trust of the GOP right. Conservatives especially bristled at a line in his acceptance speech at the convention in which he pledged to be president of a "kinder and gentler America." Kinder and gentler than who?, they wondered.

Once again, Democrats approached the 1988 election factionalized and uncertain. Eight candidates battled for their party's nomination, and by the spring just two remained in play. The Reverend Jesse Jackson, the first African-American presidential candidate to win a substantial following, led what he called a "Rainbow Coalition" that championed a variety of traditional liberal causes. But Massachusetts Governor Michael Dukakis, a relative unknown, eventually outpolled Jackson, who was dogged with a "radical" image. Dukakis shunned the "liberal" label and promised to achieve nationally the rapid economic growth that his state had experienced during his efficient governorship. In hope of attracting at least some white southern males back to the Democratic fold, Dukakis selected Texas Senator Lloyd Bentsen as his running mate. Ultimately, this so-called Boston/Austin axis attracted few such voters.

Television coverage of the 1988 campaign introduced the public to phrases formerly used only among professional consultants. Describing the issues and divisions between candidates like a horse race, TV pundits made the terms *spin control, sound bite,* and *handler,* common parlance. When opinion polls in the summer of 1988 showed Bush running seventeen points *behind* Dukakis, the GOP candidate took the advice of aide Lee Atwater to trash the public's generally positive view of Dukakis as a capable technocrat sensitive to the needs of ordinary people. Republicans first circulated a rumor that Dukakis had been treated several times for depression. When asked for his

Running for president in 1988, George Bush visits a flag factory to stress his patriotism. Diana Walker/Getty Images.

opinion of the Democratic candidate, Reagan (who otherwise sat out the campaign) gave credence to the slur by telling a journalist, "I'm not going to pick on an invalid."

To energize skeptical conservatives, Bush reemphasized his opposition to abortion and promised to cut taxes, promote prayer in public school, and get even tougher on drug users. He demonized Dukakis as a "high-tax, high-spending, pro-abortion, card-carrying member of the American Civil Liberties Union." Bush lambasted his opponent for his veto of a Massachusetts law requiring school teachers to lead students in the Pledge of Allegiance to the

---

2. Dukakis based his veto on a 1943 Supreme Court decision, *Barnette v. West Virginia*, which barred states from compelling school children to salute the flag or to recite the Pledge of Allegiance.

American flag[2] and blamed him personally for granting a prison furlough to convicted murderer Willie Horton, who while on release raped a woman. In fact, the Massachusetts furlough program resembled that in thirty-three other states and produced very few problems. But "independent" pro-Bush committees flooded the air waves with advertisements that blamed Dukakis for the crime and that emphasized the fact that Horton was African-American and his victim white. Without making overt racial statements, the Bush campaign linked Dukakis to white fear of black crime and sexual assaults. At one point in the campaign Bush actually visited a flag making factory and declared "I don't understand the type of thinking that lets first degree murderers . . . out on parole so they can rape and plunder again, and then isn't willing to let teachers lead the kids in the Pledge of Allegiance."

Dukakis proved to be a wooden candidate, slow to respond to Bush's charges or to articulate a program designed to regain the support of conservative Democrats who had voted for Nixon and Reagan. When challenged in a presidential debate to explain how he would react if someone murdered his wife, Kitty, Dukakis offered a stilted and wordy discourse on research that showed the failure of the death penalty to deter murder. Dukakis had the facts on his side, but in the aftermath of the Willie Horton incident the public wanted to hear him roar that he would personally tear the perpetrator apart, limb by limb. Instead, the public heard a policy wonk flub the easiest question of the debate.

Bush won the election with 54 percent of the popular vote and majorities in forty states. He secured an even larger share of the self-identified evangelical vote (81 percent) than had Reagan and ran especially strong among white men and white southerners. Yet, Bush was also the first candidate since John F. Kennedy to win the presidency while his party lost seats in the House of Representatives. Democrats made a net gain of two House seats for a majority of 260–175. In the Senate, Democrats won nineteen of thirty-three contested seats and retained their 55–45 majority. In state elections, Democrats picked up one governorship and made substantial gains in several state assemblies. The results showed that Republican domination of national politics still centered on the presidency and that at the local and state level conservatives had not established dominance.

THE BUSH PRESIDENCY AT HOME

As a candidate, Bush had pledged to preside over a "kinder and gentler America," an implication that he intended to govern from the center and with more concern for meeting people's needs than for achieving ideological purity. His talk of "public service as the highest and noblest calling," along with his promise to be the "environmental" and "education" president, won over many moderate voters but infuriated conservative Republicans, especially in Congress. Soon after taking office, Bush purged many Reagan appointees from rank-and-file federal positions and severed White House ties to several right wing groups. As one Bush aide explained his outlook, "We don't have

President George Bush signs the Americans with Disabilities Act into law. George Bush Presidential Library.

ideologies, we have mortgages." In other words, the administration wanted to get on with the work of government rather than use its authority to transform the nation's ideology.

From 1989 through 1991, continued economic expansion, the collapse of the Soviet Union, and quick military successes in the Panama intervention and Gulf War sustained Bush's popularity. Even while the president's abrasive chief of staff, former New Hampshire Governor John Sununu, worked to keep the White House on good terms with the religious right, Bush generally cooperated with the Democratic majorities in both houses of Congress. Working with the president, the Democratic Congress passed several important pieces of legislation for the environment and the disabled.

The Americans with Disabilities Act of 1991 was designed to assure that government, business, and educational institutions provided equal access to the physically handicapped. It expanded opportunities—and often physical access—in private employment, schools, public services, and travel to a broad class of people who had often been excluded from participating fully in public life. The act required the redesign of many commercial and government buildings as well as public transport to accommodate the handicapped. The Supreme Court, however, limited the scope of the act in a series of rulings in the late 1990s and in 2001–2002 that narrowed the definition of "disability" and made it easier for employers to deny certain kinds of jobs to the disabled.

Revisions of the Clean Water Act and the Clean Air Act, laws first enacted in the 1970s, enhanced federal and state standards for water and air purity, regulated automobile and industrial emissions, and funded sewage treatment systems. The Radiation Exposure Compensation Act provided monetary payments to thousands of victims of atomic mining and testing during the Cold War. These victims included Navajo miners from Arizona, technicians at Oak Ridge, Tennessee, and other weapons assembly sites, and tens of thousands of veterans of the armed services who were exposed to radiation from bomb blasts as part of their training in the 1950s. The Native American Graves Repatriation Act required that museums return certain looted bones and cultural artifacts to Native American tribes. In 1991, Bush signed a civil rights bill that permitted racial and gender goals (but not strict quotas) in hiring. He also cooperated with a group headed by Arkansas Governor Bill Clinton who called for federal initiatives to raise local education standards. Support for these "good government measures" infuriated more conservative Republicans. Dick Armey, a Texas House member, complained that instead of "finishing off liberalism," Bush had orchestrated a "reversal of the Reagan Revolution."

Anger among congressional conservatives intensified when economic pressure forced Bush to retreat from another pillar of the Reagan Revolution—his commitment not to raise taxes. Faced with a staggering federal deficit climbing toward $300 billion per year and complaints from foreign creditors worried about the future value of the dollars owed to them, the president and the Democratic congressional leadership agreed to a budget deal late in 1990. It called for modest tax hikes along with small spending cuts in social programs and defense. The deal would boost revenues by a relatively paltry $130 billion over five years by increasing "sin taxes" on tobacco and alcohol and by raising the top income tax bracket from 28 percent to 31 percent.

Conservative Republicans led by Georgia Representative Newt Gingrich condemned Bush for breaking his "no new taxes" pledge. Gingrich saw tax cuts as a critical tool in his plan to overthrow what he disparaged as "the liberal welfare state." He boasted to colleagues of his "enormous ambition." "I want to shift the entire planet," Gingrich declared, "and I am doing it." In an odd twist, liberal Democrats joined Gingrich in opposing higher sales taxes on beer and cigarettes, arguing that this unfairly hammered the poor. This unlikely left-right coalition blocked the budget deal, humiliated Bush, and forced a three-day shutdown of the federal government in October 1990.

Congress soon approved a reconfigured budget that included small tax hikes for high-income Americans and a small reduction in spending. Nevertheless, Bush's compromise in raising taxes had outraged Gingrich and his right-wing followers. The president never regained their trust. Democrats expressed their own contempt for Bush, charging that his waffling on taxes and spending proved that he was ineffective and lacked principles.

By now it was clear that Bush, unlike Reagan, did not really believe that "government" or even the Democrats were the "enemy." Unlike the president, however, Gingrich and a group of younger, more conservative House Republicans advocated a "take no prisoners" strategy of politics, denouncing all Democratic motives and opposing everything Democrats attempted to accomplish in Congress. As the newly selected Republican whip (a party officer charged with enforcing discipline) in the House, Gingrich favored confrontation as the best way to undermine the Democrats built-in advantage of incumbency.

In contrast to more pragmatic GOP governors, congressional Republicans assumed an unyielding conservative posture during the 1980s and 1990s. Except for a handful of northeastern senators and a somewhat larger group of House members, moderate or "accommodationist" Republicans became an endangered species in Congress. Reflecting the changing voting base of the party, conservative southern and southwestern Republicans, such as Gingrich and Mississippi Senator Trent Lott, dominated the GOP leadership by the 1990s.

In 1989, Democrats provided unintended assistance to Gingrich when the Senate rebuffed Bush's nomination of former Texas Senator John Tower as secretary of defense. Tower, whom many senators from both parties personally disliked, faced embarrassing criticism about his problems with alcohol, womanizing, and questionable business ethics. Gingrich used Tower's rejection to rally House Republicans and justify his own blistering attack on the ethics of House Speaker Jim Wright, Democrat of Texas. Wright, a flamboyant personality who had violated House procedures by making a large profit from a sweetheart book deal, resigned under pressure in 1989.

In contrast to Wright, Democrat Thomas Foley of Washington, the new House speaker, was a model of probity. Nevertheless, he had to defend himself against charges of homosexuality spread by Republican National Committee Chairman Lee Atwater. GOP leaders peddled a report entitled "Tom Foley: Out of the Liberal Closet," which implied that the speaker was both a big government liberal and gay, two grave faults in the opinion of much of the New Right. Bush, who liked Foley personally and hoped to cooperate with him in passing legislation, apologized for the smear and reprimanded Atwater. This effort at conciliation further angered Gingrich. During the next two years, members of Congress from both parties frequently accused the other side of numerous ethical and legal transgressions.

Despite growing partisan rancor in Congress, voters returned nearly all incumbents on election day in November 1990. Only one of thirty-two Senators seeking reelection—Republican Rudy Boschwitz of Minnesota—lost his seat, and nearly all House incumbents won reelection. Democrats held an increased 56–44 majority in the Senate and an eight-seat gain to 267–165 in the House, once again demonstrating the party's residual appeal at the state and local levels.

Nevertheless, public distaste for congressional feuding expressed itself in other ways. Colorado became the first state to impose term limits on federal officeholders. Voters in California, Colorado, and Oklahoma placed similar limits on service by state legislators. The balance of Republican and Democratic governors changed little in 1990, but fourteen state house majorities switched from one party to the other, and more incumbent governors were defeated than in any election since 1970.

Bush's success in toppling Manuel Noriega in Panama and in mobilizing a twenty-eight-nation coalition to liberate Kuwait from Iraq made him an extremely popular president through mid-1991. He also won respect for his cooperation with the Soviet reformer Mikhail Gorbachev and then Boris Yeltsin in their effort to steer the Soviet Union toward democracy. But as the excitement of victory in the Gulf War faded, and as the fear of the Cold War lapsed with the dissolution of the Soviet Union in December 1991, Americans refocused their concern on the deteriorating economy. President Bush, who appeared so dynamic and resourceful in managing foreign military ventures, came across as lethargic and disengaged from domestic problems. After first denying that the nation faced a recession, he insisted that economic problems would solve themselves. But certainly on issues of their economic livelihood, Americans preferred an activist president. This set the stage for a political transformation as the 1992 election neared.

GEORGE BUSH, BILL CLINTON, AND THE 1992 ELECTION

In spite of the president's boast that the United States had finally "kicked the Vietnam Syndrome," the glow of victory in the Gulf War and popular faith in conservative leadership proved fragile. In Iraq, coalition forces had halted their push on Baghdad before driving Saddam Hussein from power. Bush and his advisers feared that if the Iraqi tyrant were toppled, he might be replaced by even more threatening Islamic fundamentalists. Although the terms of the ceasefire stipulated that Saddam agree to permit U.N. inspectors to make sure he did not possess nuclear, chemical, or biological weapons of mass destruction (WMDs)[3], he continued to threaten his neighbors and to harass international monitors. By 1992, a growing number of Americans criticized Bush for his failure to "finish off" Saddam. Over the remainder of the decade, this lack of follow-through in Iraq undermined GOP claims of being better able than Democrats to manage foreign policy and safeguard the nation.

The "new world order" that President Bush had predicted would emerge from victory in Iraq and the end of the Cold War seemed to slip away even before it began. Now that many of the restraints imposed on client states by the terms of the decades long U.S.-Soviet rivalry had disappeared, bloody ethnic and religious violence erupted in parts of Africa, the Balkans, and the Middle East.

The lack of clear direction after the end of the Cold War and the murky outcome of the Gulf War were somewhat abstract problems. The onset of a steep economic recession in 1991 proved to be far more tangible and damaging

---

3. Saddam behaved erratically and sometimes impeded inspections. But, as became clear after President George W. Bush invaded Iraq in 2003, the dictator had actually destroyed most of his pre-1991 arsenal and possessed no new WMDs, the ostensible justification for the U.S. attack.

to the Bush administration and GOP fortunes. Conservative Republicans angrily attributed the 1991–1992 downturn to the reversal of Reagan's tax policies. Bush, who privately called the recession an economic "free fall," felt trapped between the massive federal deficit of almost $300 billion and GOP conservatives eager to denounce him for any display of moderation. Afraid to raise taxes (to reduce the deficit) or to boost spending (to stimulate the economy), the president appeared paralyzed. Democrats charged that Bush's lethargy proved that he was ineffective and that Reaganomics was a failure.

As the recession extended into 1992, politicians, the media, and the public placed responsibility for it on a variety of villains. With the unifying demon of the Soviet Union gone, some Americans condemned the nation's traditional allies as well as third world upstarts for unleashing a barrage of automobiles, electronic gadgets, and cheap textiles against the United States. While America had devoted its industrial resources to "winning" the Cold War, foreign beneficiaries of this largesse, such as Japan and Germany, repaid their benefactor by pursuing export strategies that overwhelmed the U.S. market and stripped the nation of well-paying jobs.

By early 1992, the fading glow of the Gulf War victory and the worsening recession tarnished Bush's halo. His proud use of the phrase "new world order" became an object of derision. Criticism by Democrats of the president's apparent apathy toward domestic issues, along with harsh denunciations by conservative Republicans of his breaking his 1988 "Read my lips, no new taxes" pledge, drove down Bush's job approval rating from about 91 percent in March 1991 (immediately following the Gulf War) to 44 percent in February 1992. That spring, over 80 percent of Americans told the Gallup Poll that they worried that the U.S. was headed in the wrong direction.

Despite his plummeting popularity, Bush won renomination for a second term in the summer of 1992. Former Reagan aide and TV pundit Patrick Buchanan mounted another spirited conservative attack on Bush's foreign and domestic record. Weighing in against the Gulf War, Buchanan charged that even though many things were worth fighting for, saving "an extra ten cents on a gallon of gasoline" was not one of them. He accused Bush of betraying Reagan's economic legacy and promised that if he became the GOP candidate he would wage a "culture war" against liberal influence in government, schools, churches, and Hollywood. Even though Buchanan collected fewer than one hundred delegates, he wounded Bush by portraying him as an insincere conservative and an incompetent administrator.

To make matters worse, Bush consented to have Buchanan deliver an opening speech at the GOP's nominating convention. Instead of graciously endorsing the president, Buchanan turned the occasion into a mean-spirited prime-time attack on both Bush and the Democrats. Anticipating themes that came to dominate politics a decade later, Buchanan declared that, "There is a religious war going on in our country for the soul of America." Gay-bashing his opponents with glee, Buchanan characterized the Democratic presidential and vice presidential candidates as the "most pro-gay and pro-lesbian ticket in history." He ridiculed the recent Democratic convention as the "greatest single exhibition of cross-dressing in American political history." Vice President Dan Quayle's wife, Marilyn, followed up with a slashing attack on moderates within Republican ranks. She demanded that the GOP purge these apostates and return to its conservative roots. Many viewers and voters recognized that these criticisms were directed as much at President Bush as at the Democrats.

Since 1968, Democratic presidential candidates had lost five of six elections, including three straight landslide trouncings in the 1980s. Political pundits and academic specialists speculated that the GOP had secured a "lock" on the White House, given Republican strength in the southern and southwestern Sunbelt states, the Rocky Mountain region, and the upper Midwest. These states possessed about 250 electoral votes, just 20 fewer than the 270 needed for victory. A related argument held that a majority of voters was strongly attracted to symbolic and cultural positions held by GOP candidates. These positions included the espousal of patriotic nationalism and "traditional moral values"—shorthand for issues such as abortion, gay rights, and school prayer—along with opposition to taxes that paid for government programs for the poor and minorities. Democrats, in contrast, seemed beholden to minorities, labor unions, feminists, and secular "liberal values."

Beginning in 1985, a small but influential group of Democrats worked to reshape its party's positions on issues of patriotism and moral values, challenging the perceived GOP advantage. Calling themselves "New Democrats," these reformers organized the Democratic Leadership Council (DLC). Most DLC members came from the moderate and conservative wings of the party; many were from the South; and most had close ties to large corporations. DLC ranks included such rising stars as Senators Al Gore of Tennessee, Joseph Lieberman of Connecticut, Sam Nunn of Georgia, Joseph Biden of Delaware, as well as Governor Bill Clinton of Arkansas, who assumed leadership of the DLC in 1990.

New Democrats worked to distance the party and its candidates from their traditional embrace of liberal policies and their close identification with labor unions and racial and ethnic minorities. Past efforts by Democrats to satisfy these constituencies, they argued, had alienated a much larger group of white voters, especially males, who lived in the nation's suburbs and in the South. To win the presidency, a Democratic candidate would have to reconnect with these "Reagan Democrats" by adopting relatively conservative or "hawkish" positions on issues such deploying of military force, reducing welfare rolls, supporting the death penalty, and being "tougher" on crime. By supporting free trade agreements and by distancing themselves from labor unions, New Democrats hoped to obtain vital corporate campaign contributions. Traditional party leaders such as Jesse Jackson dismissed New Democrats as GOP clones and joked that the initials DLC stood for "Democrats for the Leisure Class."

Yet, New Democrats, unlike conservative Republicans, still believed that the federal government should play a major role in many areas of public life. These areas included support for job training and national service programs, environmental protection measures, and increased investments in education, health, transportation, and housing. In marked contrast to the New Right and conservative Republicans, New Democrats supported a woman's right to choose an abortion. Since Reagan, Republicans had identified the federal government as "the problem" and had called for turning many public functions over to state and local officials or "privatizing" them entirely by relying on the private sector and religious charities to provide services. New Democrats, on the other hand, spoke of "reinventing government" to make it smaller, more efficient, and more responsive to local needs.

As governor of Arkansas, as DLC chairman, and as a candidate for president, Bill Clinton embraced these themes. As one student of his campaign noted, he "stressed economic mobility rather than wealth transfers, took a tough-minded line on crime, welfare dependency, and international security issues, and called for a new ethic of personal responsibility to temper demands for entitlements."

Lee Atwater, who devised Bush's slashing attacking on Michael Dukakis in 1988, recognized as early as 1990 the threat posed by Clinton. In hope of sabotaging Clinton's reelection as governor of Arkansas that year, Atwater organized a Republican campaign "to throw everything we have to at Clinton." Recognizing some of Clinton's weaknesses, Atwater instructed an aide to tempt the Democrat with "drugs, women, whatever works." In spite of this effort, Clinton won reelection. The effort to block Clinton's reelection as governor failed, but the attack strategy resurfaced in the 1992 presidential campaign and beyond—funded in part by wealthy conservative donor Richard Mellon Scaife—even though by then Atwater had died of cancer.

Confounding many journalists and party traditionalists, as well as his Republican critics, Clinton won most of the Democratic state primaries in 1992 and secured the Democratic presidential nomination despite persistent rumors—some true, many false—of marital infidelity, drug use, financial chicanery, and "draft dodging" during the Vietnam War. As the "Bush recession" worsened, Clinton skillfully added an element of economic populism to his campaign. This element appealed to organized labor, liberals, and nonunion working-class Americans who felt ignored both by Bush and many of the issues promoted by the New Democrats. Clinton got Democrats to unite and focus on an economic message. In reply to questions asking what the election was about, his campaign declared, "It's the economy, stupid."

Clinton heaped scorn on "savings and loan crooks" (including the president's son Neil) who profited while "workers were losing their jobs." At the same time, Clinton appealed to conservative, white Democrats by making a point of condemning the rap artist Sister Souljah, whose song lyrics lamented black-on-black violence by asking, "Why not have a week and kill white people?" By taking this stand, Clinton sent the message that he was both tough

During the 1992 presidential debates, Bush was challenged by Bill Clinton and Ross Perot. David Ake/Getty Images.

on crime and not beholden to "special interests," meaning African-American Democrats.

In contrast, Bush's ineffectual attempts to connect with working people often backfired and made him appear even more detached. This happened, for example, when he made a well-publicized visit to a supermarket to buy milk and bread. Upon reaching the checkout counter he marveled at the "new fangled" optical price scanner and asked the perplexed cashier what happened to the cash register. No "spin doctor" could obscure the message that Bush had not gone shopping for quite some time.

In another strange political twist, Ross Perot, a flamboyant Texas billionaire who personally disliked Bush, entered the presidential race as a self-funded independent. Perot began his career as a salesman for IBM before founding a company named "EDS" that processed Medicare claims. Although he made his fortune as a government contractor, he portrayed himself as a small-time businessman from Main Street, U.S.A., whose success lay entirely in the private sector. Perot had first dabbled in politics during the Nixon administration when he investigated unresolved cases of missing servicemen in Vietnam. Saying little about contentious social issues, Perot promised to slash the soaring deficit and shake up government by applying his business management skill. His mercurial candidacy (Perot quit the race, charging that agents of Bush had threatened his family, then reentered) attracted slightly more Republican than Democratic voters. On balance, his candidacy helped Clinton.

President Bush ran a lethargic reelection campaign. Clinton's relatively conservative position on issues such as the death penalty and crime made it hard to paint him as a bleeding-heart liberal. The collapse of the Soviet Union at the end of 1991 also muted the effectiveness of the standard GOP charge that Democrats were soft on communism and defense. In place of these accusations, Bush unleashed a relentless attack on Clinton's character, including his rumored womanizing, youthful marijuana use, and avoidance of the Vietnam-era draft. But to Bush's surprise, Clinton was no Dukakis, and he gave as good as he got. Ultimately, the personal attacks fell flat as the public responded enthusiastically to Clinton's pledge to improve the economy.

On Election Day, voters turned Bush out of office. Clinton carried thirty-two states, won 370 electoral votes, and received forty-three percent of the popular vote, compared with Bush's 38 percent and Perot's 19 percent—the most for a third-party candidate since 1912. Just as George Wallace's candidacy in 1968 had drawn the votes of conservative Democrats and had given Nixon an edge over Hubert Humphrey, in 1992 Perot's appeal to moderate Republicans helped put Clinton in office.

The outcome of congressional races also showed a desire for change. Record numbers of women, African-Americans, and Hispanics were elected. Four women, including one African-American, won Senate seats, contributing to the Democrats' 55–45 majority. Retirements, redistricting, and voter discontent led to a 25 percent turnover in the House, where Republicans scored a net gain of ten seats, leaving the Democrats with a still-substantial 258-to-176 majority. Few governorships changed hands, but voters in fourteen states imposed congressional term limits, which the Supreme Court later held were unconstitutional.

Clinton's victory and the return of Democratic majorities to both houses of Congress dashed GOP hopes of institutionalizing the Republican ascendancy begun under Nixon and solidified during the Reagan and Bush administrations. Despite the apparent setback, some conservatives appeared almost relieved by Bush's defeat. As Texas Congressman Tom DeLay saw it, Bush's exit spared "real" conservatives such as himself "four years of misery." A mock postelection wake held by staff of the Heritage Foundation featured a plastic replica of Bush's head on a platter covered with blood-red crepe paper. Clinton's victory, conservatives reassured themselves, represented merely a speed bump along the path of the nation's political transformation.

Clinton owed a great deal to the high jobless rate during the 1992 recession that followed twenty years of stagnant incomes for 80 percent of families. Defying the pattern begun in the 1960s, Clinton won six southern and border states and swept the Pacific West, becoming the first Democrat since 1964 to secure California's fifty-four electoral votes. As a moderate southern Democrat, Clinton appeared to have patched up the tattered but resilient New Deal coalition. Reduced racial tensions, the end of the Cold War, and economic recession brought millions of working-class, southern, and Catholic white voters back to the Democratic fold. Whether Democrats had reversed the long-term decline in their political fortunes was less clear. As James Carville, Clinton's perceptive and tart-tongued campaign strategist, acknowledged, "We didn't find the key to the electoral lock . . . we just picked it."

Sources and Further Readings

Neither Reagan's ghostwritten memoir, *An American Life* (1990), nor his authorized, partly fictional biography by Edmund Morris, *Dutch, Memoir of Ronald Reagan* (1999), sheds much useful light on the man or his ideas. However, readers can get a feel for Reagan's populist style and ideas by reading some of his radio commentaries from the 1970s. See Kiron Skinner and others, eds., *Reagan in His Own Hand* (2001). Journalists and historians have written several excellent overviews of the Reagan presidency. See, for example, Haynes Johnson, *Sleepwalking through History: America in the Reagan Years* (1991); Lou Cannon, *President Reagan: The Role of a Lifetime* (1991); Jules Tygiel, *Ronald Reagan and the Triumph of American Conservatism* (2005); William Pemberton, *Exit with Honor: The Life and Presidency of Ronald Reagan* (1998); Robert Dallek, *Ronald Reagan: The Politics of Symbolism* (1984); Michael Schaller, *Reckoning with Reagan: America and Its President in the 1980s* (1992), Stephen F. Hayward, *The Age of Reagan: The Fall of the Old Liberal Order* (2001); Garry Wills, *Reagan's America* (1985); Michael Rogin, *Ronald Reagan, the Movie and Other Episodes in Political Demonology* (1987); John Ehrman, *The Eighties: America in the Age of Reagan* (2005); Godfrey Hodgson, *More Equal than Others: America from Nixon to the New Century* (2004); Gil Troy, *Morning in America; How Ronald Reagan Invented the 1980s* (2005).

For overviews of the Bush presidency and family, see: John Robert Greene, *The Presidency of George Bush* (2000); Michael Duffy and Don Goodgame, *Marching in Place: The Status Quo Presidency of George Bush* (1992); Herbert S. Parmet, *George Bush: The Life of a Lone Star Yankee* (1998); Bill Minutaglio, *First Son: George W. Bush and the Bush Family Dynasty* (2001); Kevin Phillips, *American Dynasty: Aristocracy, Fortune, and the Politics of Deceit in the House of Bush* (2003).

The presidential campaigns of 1984 and 1988 are artfully described in Jack Germond and Jules Witcover, *Wake Us When It's Over: Presidential Politics of 1984* (1985); Jack Germond, *Whose Broad Stripes and Bright Stars: The Trivial Pursuit of the Presidency* (1988); Sidney Blumenthal, *Pledging Allegiance: The Last Campaign of the Cold War* (1990).

On national politics and general policies during the 1980s, see the biographies of Reagan listed earlier as well as John A. Farrell, *Tip O'Neill and the Democratic Century* (2001); Richard S. Conley, ed., *Reassessing the Reagan Presidency* (2003); Sidney Blumenthal, *Our Long National Daydream* (1986); Mark Hertsgaard, *On Bended Knee: The Press and the Reagan Presidency* (1988); Rob Schieffer and Gary Paul Gates, *The Acting President* (1989).

Among the more interesting family and political memoirs of the Reagan era are Patti Davis with Maureen Strange, *Home Front* (1986); Michael K. Deaver with Mickey Herskowitz, *Behind the Scenes* (1987); Peggy Noonan, *What I Saw at the Revolution: A Political Life in the Reagan Era* (1990); Martin Anderson, *Revolution* (1988); Joan Quigley, *"What*

Does Joan Say?": My Seven Years as White House Astrologer to Ronald and Nancy Reagan (1990); Nancy Reagan with William Novak, *My Turn: The Memoirs of Nancy Reagan* (1989); Maureen Reagan, *First Father, First Daughter: A Memoir* (1989); Michael Reagan, *On the Outside Looking In* (1988); Donald T. Regan, *For the Record: From Wall Street to the White House* (1988); Larry Speaks with Robert Pack, *Speaking Out: The Reagan Presidency from inside the White House* (1988); David Stockman, *The Triumph of Politics: How the Reagan Revolution Failed* (1986); James Watt with Doug Wead, *The Courage of a Conservative* (1985); Caspar Weinberger, *Fighting for Peace: Seven Critical Years in the Pentagon* (1990); Edwin Meese, *With Reagan* (1992); George P. Shultz, *Turmoil and Triumph: My Seven Years as Secretary of State* (1993).

4

FROM THE NEW COLD WAR
TO THE NEW WORLD ORDER

My fellow Americans, I'm pleased to tell you today that I've just signed
legislation that will outlaw the Soviet Union forever. We begin bombing
in five minutes.

RONALD REAGAN, "JOKING" ON RADIO IN 1984

During the first half of the 1980s, America's confrontation with the Soviet
Union reached a fever pitch before abating almost completely. By the time the
Soviet Union dissolved in December 1991, Washington and Moscow had become tacit allies. For many Americans, President Reagan's celebration of patriotism and determination to "rearm" the United States not only made the
nation proud and safer but also, in the words of British Prime Minister Margaret Thatcher, won the Cold War "without firing a shot." Conservative leaders came to admire Reagan not only as a man of firm principle, but also as a
brilliant strategist. When the former president died in June 2004, Texas Congressman Tom DeLay praised Reagan as an "intellectual warrior" who "marshaled ideas like troops" and freed the world from the threat of communism.
Reagan's once-ridiculed naivete was recast as sincerity; his laziness presented as inner calm; his disinterest in details proof of his mastery of the big
picture. George Bush, by contrast, appeared as little more than a foot soldier,
tidying up the details of America's Cold War triumph.

Shortly before Reagan left office in 1989, Robert McFarlane, the third of
Reagan's six national security advisers, wrote his former boss that the transformation of the Soviet system represented a "vindication of your seven-year
strategy." Confronted by the "renewal" of American economic, military, and
spiritual power, Soviet leaders understood that "they simply had to change
their system or face inevitable decline." One adoring presidential chronicler,
Peter Schweizer, argued this point even more forcefully. Unlike presidents
before him, Reagan made the defeat of communism a primary goal. Dwight
D. Eisenhower and Richard M. Nixon *talked* a tough game but valued stabil-
ity over confrontation and compromised with the Kremlin. Reagan, in contrast, considered communism both a moral evil and an inherent threat to
peace. By not only *talking* but also *acting* tough, by rearming America and

challenging Soviet power globally, the "so-called bumpkin" as Schweizer put it admiringly, "won the Cold War." Perhaps the shrillest praise of Reagan's foreign policy accomplishments came from conservative media pundit Ann Coulter. Liberals, she wrote, "lie about Reagan's victory because when Reagan won the Cold War, he proved them wrong on everything they had done and said throughout the Cold War. It is their last defense to fifty years of treason."

Without doubt, Reagan expanded U.S. military power and restored public confidence in presidential leadership. His rhetoric uplifted the spirits of Americans—and many foreigners—who during the 1970s saw themselves as victims in an unfriendly world of hostage-taking, nuclear threats, rising oil prices, and third world insurgencies. Yet, as in his domestic policy, a gulf persisted between the idealism, self-assurance, and occasional bluster of Reagan's calls to action and his administration's actual accomplishments.

Reagan oversaw the largest military buildup in peacetime history and played a critical role in transforming the Soviet-American relationship. However, the cause-and-effect connection between spending on arms and talking tough and transforming Soviet policy remains uncertain. Several of Reagan's initiatives, such as using covert force in Central America, the Middle East, and Africa, had unintended and sometimes dire consequences. U.S. intervention did not cause the violence endemic to these regions, but it did little to alleviate it or to enhance American security. For example, the CIA's program from 1982 to 1988 of arming Islamic fighters resisting Soviet forces in Afghanistan not only helped drive out the invaders, but also unintentionally promoted the rise of an Islamic terror network led by Osama bin Laden. Elsewhere, Reagan's support for pro-American dictatorships in countries such as Haiti, the Philippines, and Pakistan and in Central America, along with a willingness to negotiate secretly with Middle Eastern terrorists, marked some his administration's worst failures.

Background

Long after he rejected Franklin Roosevelt's New Deal liberalism, Ronald Reagan continued to admire his childhood idol's spirit and style. To Reagan, the inspirational FDR remained a "soldier of freedom" who rallied dispirited Americans against the heartbreak of the Great Depression at home and the threat of Axis aggression abroad. Above all, he led when others faltered. Just as fascism threatened Roosevelt's America, Reagan saw communism as a challenge to global freedom after 1945.

Like millions of Americans his age, Reagan recalled with special fondness Roosevelt's use of the radio to communicate his thoughts on everything from banking reform to foreign affairs. In October 1964, when Reagan delivered his first nationally broadcast political speech, on behalf of Republican presidential candidate Barry Goldwater, he lifted verbatim one of FDR's most famous lines, declaring that Americans "have a rendezvous with destiny." Reagan often declared his belief that God had selected Americans as his

President Reagan shows Nancy the guns of the U.S.S. *Iowa*. Courtesy Ronald Reagan Library.

chosen people. The United States was, as Puritan visionaries proclaimed, a "city on a hill" with a special mission.

During the 1970s, as his ambition turned toward the White House, Reagan broadcast hundreds of short, inspirational radio talks that placed his name and ideas before a national audience. A typical commentary in May 1975 described communism as a "form of insanity" that "will one day disappear from the Earth because it is contrary to human nature." Anticipating his later assertion as president that Soviet leaders would "commit any crime" to advance their cause, Reagan depicted communists as willing to carry out any crime "if it advances the cause of socialism."

Once elected president, Reagan revived the lapsed practice of delivering regular radio commentaries. In August 1984, while he engaged in banter with technicians before delivering a Saturday morning radio talk, Reagan spoke into a microphone that he did not know was activated. "My fellow Americans," he began, "I am pleased to tell you today that I've just signed legislation that will outlaw the Soviet Union forever. We begin bombing in five minutes." Critics were appalled by his making a joke of nuclear war. Soviet officials took the off-the-cuff remark seriously enough to instruct KGB agents in Washington to report signs of war preparation. The president simply laughed off criticism of his words as if it were something his friend John Wayne might have said while swaggering in a Hollywood western.

Remarkably, less than eight years later, legislation *was signed* abolishing the Soviet Union. On Christmas Day 1991, Soviet President Mikhail Gorbachev issued a decree dissolving the fast-crumbling communist empire. With this final act, Gorbachev turned over authority to the elected leader of the Russian Republic, Boris Yeltsin. Reagan's admirers and even some skeptics credited "the Great Communicator," as journalists dubbed him, for the leadership and determination that culminated in America's Cold War victory.

Reagan spoke forcefully about the division he saw between the peaceful democratic world of America and its allies and the aggressive web of communist dictatorships controlled by Moscow. As a candidate in 1980 and often thereafter, he remarked that the Soviet Union "underlies all the unrest that is going on" in the world. If "they weren't engaged in this game of dominos, there wouldn't be any hotspots in the world." Reagan stressed his deep religious antipathy for communism in an address to the National Association of Evangelicals on March 8, 1983. The Soviet Union, he declared, was "the focus of evil in the modern world," truly an "evil empire."

Reagan perceived a simple truth: the Soviet Union was doomed to fall. In addressing the British Parliament on June 8, 1982, the president dismissed the Soviet Union as a force that "runs against the tide of history." With its economic, political, and social system all "astounding" failures, he consigned communism to the "ash heap of history." Although Reagan's knowledge of the Soviet Union might be "primitive," as CIA Deputy Director Robert Gates described it, his gut instinct coincided with reality. The president's clarity of vision, Gates and others argued, allowed him to see the future in ways that eluded more sophisticated thinkers.

While campaigning for the White House, Reagan insisted "there are simple answers to complex questions." He told a gathering of veterans in August 1980 that under incumbent President Jimmy Carter America suffered from what he called the "Vietnam Syndrome," an unwillingness to use force to resist Soviet pressure or to defend foreign friends and interests against Soviet-inspired threats. This syndrome explained why American diplomats in 1979 had been seized and held as hostages in Iran while Soviet troops occupied Afghanistan and Cuban- and Soviet-backed insurgents made a play for power in Central America and Africa. Reagan traced the problem to the failure to win a military victory in Vietnam and a guilt complex left over from that war. "It's time," he told the cheering veterans, "we recognize that ours, in truth, was a noble cause." Alexander Haig, whom the newly elected Reagan named secretary of state in 1981, echoed this theme. The American people were ready to "shed their sackcloth and ashes." Taking a cue from the president's call in his inaugural address to "dream heroic dreams," the new administration moved to bolster the nation's military superiority, defend allies, and, in what was later informally called the "Reagan doctrine," assist anti-communist movements throughout the world. Not by coincidence, the president's aides explained, did Iran release its long-held American captives just as Reagan took the presidential oath on January 20, 1981.

Reagan's approach to world affairs rested upon a key assumption: since the Nixon administration, the United States had pursued a misguided policy of détente toward the Soviet Union. This effort to reduce superpower rivalry relied upon arms control agreements, expanded East-West trade, and an acceptance by each side of the other's legitimate security interests. At his first press conference, on January 29, 1981, Reagan echoed the complaints of conservative strategists that détente had become a "one-way street," little more than a smoke screen behind which the Soviets had expanded their strategic nuclear arsenal, cheated on arms control treaties, and supported communist insurgents in the third world. The Soviet Union, he warned, was on track to dominate the third world and isolate the United States. Reagan saw his historic mission as reversing this flow of power and delegitimizing the Soviet Union.

Although he never said so publicly (and his aides claimed this as a strategy only *after* he left office), Reagan believed that the inherent weakness of the communist system made the Soviet Union vulnerable to American economic pressure. By blocking access to Western technology and markets, Washington could cripple the inefficient Soviet economy. Meanwhile, rising American defense expenditures would overstress Soviet industry as it tried to match the rapid U.S. buildup. According to several high officials who spoke out after 1989, the plan to cripple the Kremlin through an arms race and economic warfare formed the centerpiece of Reagan's strategy to win the Cold War.

In addition to bringing military and economic pressure to bear directly on the Soviets, Reagan, prodded by CIA Director William Casey, set about confronting Soviet proxies in places such as Poland, Afghanistan, Lebanon, Angola, Mozambique, El Salvador, Grenada, and Nicaragua. By winning these proxy wars, Reagan and his advisers believed, the United States would undermine the appeal of communism and unravel Soviet self-confidence, creating a sort of Vietnam Syndrome in reverse. Ultimately, the Soviet Union would have no choice but to fundamentally alter its foreign and domestic policies. Diplomacy and negotiations with the Soviets would, at most, be an afterthought to certify American supremacy.

During his first five years in office, Reagan justified his refusal to talk with Soviet leaders by insisting on the need to first rearm and achieve military superiority. Also, he quipped in response to a journalist's question, how could he meet his Soviet counterparts when "they keep dying on me." This reference to the decrepit health of Kremlin leaders—and, implicitly, to his own vitality despite age—deflected public criticism. But at a basic level, Reagan found himself pulled in different directions by advisers who disagreed on fundamentals and disliked each other almost as much as they hated communism.

Administration Infighting

Reagan's senior foreign policy advisers shared his antipathy toward the Soviet Union and his determination to build up American military strength. But that was about *all* they agreed upon. Alexander Haig, who served as Reagan's first secretary of state, described the White House as "mysterious as a ghost ship. You heard the creak of the rigging and the groan of the timbers and sometimes even glimpsed the crew on deck." But he had no idea "which of the crew was at the helm." Haig considered the president a "cipher" who virtually never discussed foreign policy with him. Haig's difficulty in guessing Reagan's mind had a domestic counterpart. Treasury Secretary (and Second-term White House Chief of Staff) Don Regan reported that the president had never discussed economic policy with him!

Many successful presidents, such as Franklin Roosevelt and Dwight Eisenhower, played off contentious aides to achieve a policy consensus. This "hidden hand" approach of allowing subordinates to take the credit—or blame—provided valuable political cover. But Reagan's distance from policy details was of a wholly different order. Even his closest aides, such as CIA Director Casey, were taken aback by their boss's passivity. With few exceptions, such as missile defense (Strategic Defense Initiative [SDI]), arms sales to Iran, and aid to the contra guerrillas in Central America, Reagan initiated nothing and issued few orders. The president who came across so forcefully in scripted television speeches lost focus off camera. Reagan seldom contributed more at cabinet and National Security Council (NSC) meetings than telling a few stories and reading letters sent by admirers. If his staff reached a policy consensus, he endorsed it. If not, he deferred deciding. Reagan's aides kept his attention at meetings by putting on a slide or video show that presented simple, sometimes simplistic, alternatives. After initiating a policy, Reagan seldom followed up on implementation.

The president's three closest aides during his first term, Chief of Staff James Baker, Deputy Chief Michael Deaver, and Counselor Edwin Meese, carefully controlled the domestic and diplomatic agendas. The so-called "troika" met each morning to review the past day's events and current day's plans. One of the three men sat in with Reagan on virtually every meeting.

Baker, Deaver, and Meese wanted to prevent the emergence of a powerful national security adviser in the mold of Henry Kissinger under Nixon. Thus, the first four national security advisers, Richard Allen, William Clark, Robert McFarlane, and John Poindexter, were relatively marginal figures in the administration. Secretary of State Haig, who barely knew his boss, also remained outside Reagan's inner circle during his short tenure. George P. Shultz, who succeeded Haig in June 1982, ultimately emerged as the most influential and respected member of Reagan's cabinet. But his role remained muted during the first term while his two principal rivals, Defense Secretary Caspar Weinberger and CIA Director William Casey, often undercut him.

Broadly speaking, "pragmatists" and "ideologues" competed for Reagan's attention. Pragmatists, including Haig, Shultz, Baker, Deaver, and Nancy Reagan, believed that when the United States assumed a position of dominant military strength, it should resume arms control and other negotiations with the Soviets. Hardliners within the administration, including Weinberger, Casey, U.N. ambassador Jeanne Kirkpatrick, and Pentagon adviser Richard Perle, rejected entirely the notion of bargaining with the Soviets at any point. Better to rearm and challenge Moscow on all fronts.

James Baker, the president's chief of staff, described the foreign policy apparatus during Reagan's first six years as often "a witches brew of intrigue" and competing agendas made worse by the fact that no one knew precisely what the boss wanted. Reagan's fifth and sixth national security advisers, Frank Carlucci and Colin Powell, were forced to decide on their own fundamental arms control questions because they could not get the president to make a decision. As Powell recalled, a frustrated Carlucci "moaned as we left" an Oval Office meeting, " 'My God, we didn't sign on to run this country.' "

Defense Secretary Weinberger, an unwavering opponent of negotiations with Moscow, pushed continuously for increased military spending. At the same time, he opposed committing American forces to regional conflicts. Taking casualties in murky causes, Weinberger worried, would erode public support for rearmament. Secretary of State Shultz, in contrast, believed that a powerful military would induce the Soviets to talk on American terms and allow Reagan to meet communist challenges in places such as Central America. At one cabinet meeting an exasperated Shultz snapped at the defense secretary, "If you are not willing to use force, maybe we should cut your budget." Reagan declined to overrule either man, asking his contentious aides to settle their differences among themselves, a solution that National Security Adviser Robert McFarlane described as "intrinsically unworkable." The standoff between Shultz and Weinberger permitted CIA Director Casey to win Reagan's backing for risky covert operations, at least one of which— the Iran-contra Scandal—nearly sank the administration.

The Military Buildup and Star Wars

In explaining his determination to boost the arms budget, Reagan declared that "defense is not a budget issue . . . you spend what you need." Surprisingly, Jimmy Carter had agreed. In contrast to complaints that Carter babied the Soviets, Carter's final defense budget had proposed a 5 percent increase annually for the next five years. Reagan's military buildup rested on the base set out by his supposedly wimpy predecessor.

Budget Director David Stockman realized that the new administration's plan for increased defense spending contained a mathematical error that would boost military outlays for the next few years by $200 billion more than Reagan had approved. But when Stockman attempted to correct the error, Defense Secretary Weinberger balked and took his case to the White House.

Weinberger stressed "how awesome the Soviets were and how far behind we were." Anyone cutting a nickel out of the military budget, he implied, "wanted to keep us behind the Russians." Weinberger's show-and-tell slide show superimposed Soviet defense plants on a map of Washington. Other illustrations depicted Soviet nuclear and conventional forces dwarfing those of the free world. "Sir, our B-52 planes are older than their pilots," the defense secretary remarked gravely while the president nodded in agreement.

As Stockman gazed in disbelief, Weinberger displayed a cartoon depicting three soldiers. The first, a pygmy carrying no weapon, represented the Carter budget. The second, a bespectacled wimp resembling Woody Allen, carried a tiny rifle and represented Stockman's military budget. The third, "GI Joe himself, 190 pounds of fighting man, all decked out in helmet and flak jacket, and pointing an M-60 machine gun," represented Weinberger's plan, which Reagan happily endorsed.

During Reagan's first term, the military share of the GNP grew from 5.7 percent to 7.4 percent. In dollar terms, military spending increased 50 percent, totaling $1.5 trillion. With $300 billion budgeted in 1985, the Pentagon spent more than $30 million per hour. Most of this went for new weapons such as neutron bombs designed to irradiate attacking Soviet forces; one hundred MX intercontinental missiles, each capable of carrying ten nuclear warheads with pinpoint accuracy; the B-1 intercontinental bomber to replace the aging B-52; radar-avoiding "stealth" bombers and fighter planes; new D-5 submarine-launched missiles; intermediate-range cruise and Pershing II missiles; a six hundred ship Navy; and SDI antimissile research.

Many of these expensive weapons caused unintended problems. No one, including Reagan's most loyal congressional supporters, wanted the new MX missiles based in his or her state because they tempted a Soviet "first strike." Ultimately, the new missiles were housed in existing Minuteman rocket silos whose supposed vulnerability to Soviet attack had been Reagan's justification for building the new missiles! The expensive B-1 bomber had so many technical problems that it remained grounded most of the time and never replaced the B-52. (In fact, the venerable B-52 remained the workhorse of the Air Force right through the invasion of Iraq in 2003.) Stealth technology proved difficult to perfect, and planes that utilized it were notoriously hard to maintain. By the time stealth aircraft were ready to fly combat missions in the 1990s, there was no Soviet air defense to avoid.

Although Reagan had denounced existing arms control agreements with the Soviets as "fatally flawed," he did not abrogate them. During his first term, the Joint Chiefs cautioned Reagan that the Strategic Arms Limitation Treaty II (SALT II), negotiated by President Carter but never ratified, actually *enhanced* U.S. security. Even if, as Reagan claimed correctly, the Kremlin cheated at the margins, SALT II imposed limits on the number of nuclear missiles the Soviets actually deployed. Reagan continued to criticize the SALT II framework, but, in private, he generally adhered to the treaty.

One of Reagan's most cherished military innovations—the Strategic Defense Initiative—represented an effort to beat the Soviets technologically and, perhaps, bankrupt them. Despite much criticism of the scheme in the 1980s and beyond, Reagan's defenders, such as British Prime Minister Thatcher, argued that the president's "original decision" to support missile defense "was the single most important of his presidency."

Shortly before he took office, Reagan expressed shock to learn that in a nuclear war more than half of all Americans might quickly perish. The president blamed this terrible dilemma on the policy of mutual assured destruction (MAD), comparing it with two rivals (say, the U.S. and Soviet Union) pointing loaded guns at each other and hoping that neither would pull the trigger. But this scenario misrepresented defense strategy. In fact, MAD presumed that neither side would fire first because to do so would bring certain retaliation from surviving weapons remaining in the hands of Soviet and American forces, no matter who shot first.

Initially the Reagan administration tried to dampen fears of a nuclear holocaust by claiming that a revived fallout shelter program, like that promoted in the 1950s, could save millions of lives. But when Pentagon spokesman T. K. Jones told a startled audience that most Americans could survive a nuclear war if only they took time to "dig a hole, cover it with a couple of doors, and then throw some dirt on top," the shelter campaign became an object of derision.

Although most Americans supported Reagan's overall tough stand, during 1982 and 1983 as many as 70 percent of Americans, including a number of clergy and members of Congress, questioned Reagan's nuclear buildup. Many voiced approval of a "nuclear freeze movement" that called for capping these weapons at current levels. A best-selling book by Jonathan Schell, *The Fate of the Earth* (1982), depicted in chilling detail the effect of a single hydrogen bomb dropped on New York City. Catholic bishops issued a pastoral letter that decried nuclear weapons as "immoral" and the arms race as "robbery of the poor." These public misgivings troubled the president and his pollsters.

In the late 1970s, physicist Dr. Edward Teller and retired Air Force General Daniel Graham, who headed a lobbying group called "High Frontier", told Reagan of the possibility of building an antimissile shield. At an Oval Office meeting early in 1983, Teller described progress (bogus, it turned out) in creating a nuclear-powered X-ray laser that if based in space could generate energy beams powerful enough to shoot down Soviet missiles shortly after their launch. This "space shield" concept may have rekindled Reagan's memories of his role in a 1940 movie entitled *Murder in the Air* that featured an "inertia projector," which could stop enemy aircraft in flight.

The president latched on to the concept of a space shield and made it an intense personal cause. Nuclear war, he told friends, might be Armageddon, the biblically prophesized battle before Christ's return. Perhaps SDI could prevent it. Just how a technological fix would prevent a cataclysm ordained by God to purge the world of sinners was theologically unclear. But SDI promised material as well as spiritual rewards.

The Joint Chiefs of Staff privately doubted the practicability of building a leakproof umbrella but thought it might be possible to devise a limited system to protect a small number of American nuclear missile launchers—not cities—from Soviet attack. This system would enhance, not eliminate, MAD by assuring that the United States could retaliate against even a Soviet first strike. Defense contractors, university physicists, and computer and optical scientists relished the prospect of massive research and development contracts that would flow from funding such a program. Some arms control experts thought the threat of SDI (in contrast to actually building it) might prod the Soviets into a new round of strategic arms control negotiations on terms more favorable to the United States. Administration hardliners such as Secretary of Defense Caspar Weinberger, who opposed any dealings with

Moscow, hoped SDI would outrage the Soviets and clear the way for the United States to act even more forcefully and unilaterally.

Reagan alone clung to the idea of creating a leakproof shield that would protect all Americans. With this in mind, he latched on to a statement by Army Chief of Staff General John W. Vessey that it would be "better to protect the American people than to avenge them." On March 23, 1983, he shared what he called his "vision" in a televised speech that spoke of rendering Soviet missiles "impotent and obsolete" by destroying them before they "reached our own soil or that of our allies." Reagan, as SDI chronicler Frances Fitzgerald, noted, "appropriated the language of the antinuclear movement" even as he endorsed a plan to expand the nuclear arms race to outer space.

Like Margaret Thatcher, some of Reagan's advisers later described his fixation with SDI—or "Star Wars", after the recently released George Lucas film, as his critics promptly dubbed it—as a brilliant deception. Deputy CIA Director Gates argued that SDI did not even need to work because the mere concept inspired terror in Moscow. SDI represented the triple threat of superior American technology, managerial skills, and wealth harnessed to a project that the Soviets could not possibly hope to match. In fact, Gates argued, the only true believers in SDI were Reagan and the old men who sat on the Soviet Politburo. Reagan, Gates and Thatcher implied, intuitively sensed that SDI was a "symbolic threat" to the Soviets, a sort of "perfect storm" that would cripple the regime.

Gates justified SDI in part because the Soviets themselves invested heavily in antimissile research. But, as he admitted, they lacked the requisite technology to achieve much of value. Gates interpreted strident Soviet opposition to SDI as evidence of Soviet frustration over the prospect of having spent billions of rubles on building a nuclear arsenal that might be rendered obsolete by American technology.

But even Gates recognized that Soviet hostility toward SDI stemmed from several sources. Aside from Reagan, virtually no one believed that the U.S. could soon deploy an antimissile system capable of neutralizing a Soviet attack. The Pentagon estimated it might require several thousand flights of America's unreliable space shuttle to boost SDI components into orbit. Because the shuttle flew only a few times each year, at this pace deployment of the system could take a century. It might be possible to more quickly deploy a "leaky" system capable of shooting down a small number of enemy rockets. From the Soviet perspective, this system could enable the United States to launch a first strike against the Soviet Union and sit back with enough antimissile capacity to deflect a weak Soviet retaliation—thus neutralizing MAD.

Some of Reagan's advisers later argued that SDI comprised part of the secret "bankrupt the Soviets" strategy hatched in 1981–1982. But most officials closely involved with SDI dispute this argument. CIA Deputy Director Gates found little evidence to suggest that Soviet efforts to counter SDI overstressed the Soviet economy. Arms control negotiator Lt. General Edward L. Rowny doubted that scholars would discover in the archival record "any serious talk about [spending the Soviets into the ground] at all." Rowny, along with National Security Adviser Robert McFarlane, argued that Reagan pushed the plan primarily because he believed it would counter Soviet missile strength and secondarily because he thought it might actually save the U.S. money in its ongoing arms competition with the Soviets. They saw no indication that Reagan expected SDI to bankrupt the Soviets or become a first step toward ridding the world of nuclear weapons.

Although Reagan offered little beyond generalities in defense of SDI, his talk of abandoning the concept of mutual assured destruction and pulling out of the 1972 Anti-Ballistic Missile Treaty (ABM) aroused grave anxiety in Moscow. As discussed later, his tough talk may have actually delayed, rather than accelerated, Soviet-American cooperation. During Reagan's two terms, the United States spent nearly $20 billion on antimissile research. Under Presidents George H. W. Bush, Bill Clinton, and George W. Bush (through 2005), over $60 billion more went toward this project. In 2001, President George W. Bush put antimissile defense back on the fast track. In 2004, he ordered rapid deployment of a largely untested missile defense system in Alaska designed to intercept a handful of rockets that might be launched by North Korea or another "rogue state." Technologically, this program was unrelated to the Reagan-era SDI. Nevertheless, conservatives argue that Reagan's dream—or bluff—not only helped break the Cold War stalemate but also set the stage for future defense of the nation.

THE ECONOMIC COLD WAR

In addition to bulking up American military strength, Reagan implemented related efforts to undermine the Soviet economy. He later explained that during a March 1982 briefing he learned that the Soviets were "in very bad shape and if we can cut off their credit they'll have to yell 'uncle' or starve." CIA Director Casey identified Soviet vulnerabilities that were targeted for economic warfare. Assuring Reagan "we can do them in," Casey's "vulnerability assessments" became part of the regular intelligence data given to the president.

For a man who had long considered the Soviet system inherently unstable, this information was music to his ears. In a May 1975 radio commentary, for example, Reagan had declared that "communism is neither an economic or a political system—it is a form of insanity." In radio remarks of September 1979, he had endorsed the notion that "given our industrial superiority," America "could not possibly lose . . . an unrestrained arms race." Although the president and his aides shared a general belief in a weak and vulnerable Soviet economy, they disagreed on what, if anything, they should do about it. National Security Adviser Robert McFarlane recalled that "many in Reagan's own cabinet . . . didn't agree with him" that "a more energetic competition could impose such burdens as to bring down the Soviet Union."

Douglas MacEachin, director of the CIA's Office of Soviet Analysis from 1984 to 1989, voiced strong doubts about the efficacy of economic warfare.

Experts in and out of government, he recalled, were "virtually unanimous" in agreeing that the Soviet system had reached a "near critical" mass of social and economic problems. But the same rigid central controls that caused these problems also made it likely that the Soviet Union would muddle along in slow decline, perhaps for several decades. Although some actions taken by Reagan "imposed costs" on Moscow, former National Security adviser McFarlane believed that "80 to 90 percent of what happened to the U.S.S.R. was because Marxism was a dumb idea" rather than the result of American pressure.

After the Soviet collapse, strident ideologues such as Pentagon adviser Richard Perle and NSC staff member and Harvard scholar Richard Pipes took credit for implementing an economic warfare strategy. But the two advisers who ultimately influenced Reagan's most important Soviet initiatives from 1983 onward, career diplomat Jack Matlock and Secretary of State George Shultz, dispute the claim that Reagan pursued a master plan to "bring down" the evil empire. "None of the key players," Matlock remarked in 1998, "were operating from the assumption that we were going to bring them down. . . . That's all thinking after the fact." The goal was always "to give the Soviets incentives to bring the Cold War to an end." Shultz made this point to Reagan in a 1983 report that predicted a long period of ongoing competition. The best way to bring about "actual improvement" in relations with Moscow, Shultz insisted, was for the administration to quit "name calling" and open a dialogue with Moscow. The communist regime had "serious weaknesses," Shultz affirmed, "but it would be a mistake to assume that the Soviet capacity for competition with us will diminish at any time during your presidency."

The Soviet economy confounded friends and foes. Rising from the ashes of World War II, it had become one of the biggest producers of steel, cement, fertilizer, tractors, machine tools, and weapons. To achieve these levels in what nearly all observers recognized were grossly inefficient factories, Soviet industry relied upon and often squandered the nation's vast natural resource base. Chronic agricultural shortfalls required Moscow to import food, often from the United States, by exporting hard currency-earners such as oil and precious metals.

By 1980, however, the system had reached the point of diminishing returns. The Soviet growth rate began declining, and the quality of life, as measured by infant mortality, longevity, rates of alcoholism, and so forth, markedly deteriorated. The long-standing technology divide between the Western economies and Japan on the one hand and the Soviet bloc on the other had become a yawning chasm by the time Reagan took office. Dynamic market economies surged ahead by utilizing computers and new ways to manage information. The archaic Soviet command system could mobilize labor and natural resources but had little capacity to promote creativity or innovation. Soviet officials so feared losing control of the political and economic spheres that they jealously restricted access to such basic technology as photocopiers and personal computers. As one Kremlin official acknowledged to his colleagues in the early 1980s, "the Soviet economy is not in much better shape than that of Poland."

Early in his presidency, Reagan moved to sever Soviet access to U.S. technology and credit, although whether he did so in the belief that the enemy was on the verge of collapse is unclear. Reagan also pressed American allies in Europe and Japan to cancel or restrict sales of oil- and gas-drilling and pipeline technology to the Soviet Union. One secret U.S. initiative permitted the Soviets to steal flawed computer programs that contributed to a massive pipeline explosion. CIA Director Casey and Defense Secretary Weinberger encouraged U.S. arms sales to Saudi Arabia as an incentive to the desert kingdom to expand oil production.

In 1980, Saudi Arabia produced nearly nine million barrels per day, almost all for export. By 1985, output declined to around three million barrels. After the United States convinced the Saudis to resume pumping nine million barrels daily, global prices declined from around $30 per barrel in mid-decade to half that in 1989–1990. American drivers enjoyed the savings, but, more significantly, the hard currency the Soviets earned from their own substantial petroleum exports fell sharply.

Several Reagan aides later attributed the collapse of the Soviet Union to these sorts of economic strategies. However, the facts don't match up neatly with the rhetoric. For example, as early as 1984, barely three years after first imposing sanctions, a year and a half before reformer Mikhail Gorbachev assumed power, and seven years before the Soviet collapse, Reagan actually began *lifting* these much-heralded sanctions. He acted as it became clear that the economic offensive had produced unintended consequences. For example, the heavy pressure put on U.S. allies to stop selling gas- and oil-drilling and pipeline technology to Moscow infuriated the British, French, Germans, and Japanese who, unlike the Americans, strongly desired to import Soviet energy supplies. To appease the allies, Reagan relaxed many of the more onerous restrictions.

America's partners were also livid at Reagan's decision to permit U.S. exporters to resume selling the Soviets their biggest product. In 1980, President Carter had responded to the Soviet invasion of Afghanistan by placing an embargo on U.S. grain sales to Moscow—even though this angered midwestern farmers and hurt the Democrat's reelection prospects. Reagan, who charged that Carter had babied the Soviets, *resumed* grain sales to Moscow, largely to placate farmers, soon after taking office.

Even the use of oil as a weapon proved to be a two-edged sword. The Saudi decision to boost production in 1985 drove down the price of petroleum by more than 50 percent, cutting deeply into the foreign currency earned by Soviet oil exports. At the same time, the U.S. energy sector also paid dearly for this strategy. Falling prices devastated many small and medium producers in the "oil patch" states of the American West. By the late 1980s, tumbling property values in the region sped the collapse of the shaky savings and loan (S&L) industry. The scope of these losses—over $300 billion to American taxpayers—became apparent only after Reagan left office.

To finance the huge military buildup while also cutting taxes, and to prevent the already record budget deficit from growing larger, the U.S. Treasury under Reagan borrowed massively from foreign investors and governments. Reagan inherited a cumulative national debt of just under $1 trillion in 1981. Over the next twelve years, annual budget shortfalls under Reagan and Bush ranged from $128 billion to nearly $300 billion. Federal indebtedness had tripled, to nearly $3 trillion, by 1989 and rose to $4 trillion in 1992.

Increasingly, Japanese, Saudi, German, and other foreign sources purchased Treasury notes and bonds that financed the deficit. By the end of Reagan's presidency, foreign creditors held nearly 20 percent of the national debt, a historic high. Under Reagan, the nation's foreign trade imbalance also grew dramatically. The cumulative foreign trade deficit of the United States totaled nearly $1 trillion by 1989 and kept on growing. As discussed later, the Japanese, Germans, and Saudis financed the Reagan-Bush-era arms buildup and tax cuts by lending back to the U.S. Treasury the dollar surpluses they earned by selling manufactured goods and oil to Americans. The global dollar flow from 1980 to 1992 transformed the United States from the world's biggest creditor nation to the world's biggest debtor nation in record time. When a journalist asked Reagan to comment on this seismic change, he simply denied it was so. If, as Reagan boosters sometimes claim, he "spent" the Soviets into defeat, he did so largely with borrowed money, the cost of which is being borne by succeeding generations.

Terrorism, Democracy, and Covert Warfare

The Reagan administration portrayed terrorism in the Middle East and against American interests elsewhere as among the gravest threats confronting the United States. In speeches delivered within days of taking office, the president and his new secretary of state issued clear warnings. "Let terrorists beware," Reagan declared, "our policy will be one of swift and effective retribution." In 1985, he repeated that "America will never make concessions to terrorists" and condemned Iran and Libya as "outlaw states . . . run by the strangest collection of misfits, Looney Tunes, and squalid criminals since the advent of the Third Reich."

In a reversal of President Carter's approach, Reagan abandoned the policy of putting pressure on pro-American dictatorships to improve their human rights performance. Reagan praised the ideas of Jeanne Kirkpatrick (whom he named as ambassador to the United Nations), voiced in an article she wrote for the conservative journal *Commentary* in 1979. Kirkpatrick berated Carter's failure to support friendly "right-wing autocracies" such as those of the shah of Iran or the Somoza family of Nicaragua. Unlike left-wing regimes, she argued, pro-American dictatorships "sometimes evolve into democracies." Secretary of State Haig declared that the struggle against "international terrorism will take the place of human rights in our concern because it is the ultimate abuse of human rights." Reagan's support for anti-communist despots such as Ferdinand Marcos in the Philippines and Jean-Claude "Baby Doc" Duvalier in Haiti—even in the face of popular uprisings against their rule—reflected these priorities.

A terrorist attack destroyed the U.S. embassy in Beirut, 1983. AP/Wide World Photos.

To further mobilize public opinion against the Soviets, CIA Director Casey and his deputy, Robert Gates, tried to prove that the Kremlin masterminded the 1981 attempt by a Turkish criminal to assassinate Polish-born Pope John Paul II. They cited claims by journalist Claire Sterling that the gunman worked for Soviet-controlled Bulgarian intelligence. Several career State Department and CIA analysts (who, unlike Casey, believed the Soviets considered the pope something of a *moderating* force in Polish politics) recognized that Sterling's case relied largely on disinformation fed to her by other U.S. intelligence agents who hoped to discredit the Soviets. But Casey would not relent, and over the next four years he and Gates doggedly pursued evidence of Soviet complicity.

Despite efforts to portray terrorism as either madness or a Soviet plot, the Reagan administration sometimes bent its own rules barring support for or negotiations with groups linked to terror. Reagan personally approved the sales of weapons to two nations he publicly condemned as terrorist states (Iraq and Iran), authorized giving weapons to anti-communist guerrillas linked to terrorism in Lebanon, Afghanistan, Africa, and Central America, and secretly bargained for the release of American hostages held by terrorists in Lebanon.

Terrorism, sometimes described as "the atomic bomb of the weak," was as often a symptom as a source of instability. The kidnapping of a handful of Americans in Lebanon, occasional aircraft and ship hijackings, and the bombing of several airliners were despicable and unsettling but rare acts in the larger world arena. In aggregate during the 1980s, about as many American civilians were killed by lightning while playing golf as died at the hands of terrorists. Terrorism became a popular obsession partly because the media hyped it and partly because Reagan made it so. Until September 11, 2001, the two deadliest foreign terrorist attacks against Americans occurred during the Reagan administration. In two bombings in Lebanon during 1983, nearly three hundred Marines and embassy personnel died. The December 1988 bombing of a Pan-Am flight over Scotland killed almost 280 people.

Although conservatives caricatured Jimmy Carter as a "wimp," during 1979–1980 he not only initiated a major arms buildup but also initiated several of the covert operations credited to his successor. As CIA Deputy Director Gates admitted, the Soviets "saw Carter as a committed ideological foe as well as a geopolitical adversary." He "prepared the groundwork for Reagan in the strategic arena, in confronting the Soviets" in the third world.

CIA Director Casey, with help from the National Security Council, served as the administration's coordinator of policies on terrorism and covert challenges to the Soviet Union. Casey, a veteran of the World War II–era Office of Strategic Services (OSS), a wealthy Wall Street investor, and Reagan's campaign manager in 1980, deeply admired the president. But, a top aide recalled, in private even Casey "would complain about the president's lack of interest in specifics, his unwillingness to take hard decisions . . . and his rather simplistic view of the world." Reagan's inner circle, James Baker, Edwin Meese, and especially Michael Deaver, worried that the spy chief "played to Reagan's dark side." Casey's habit of mumbling, along with the president's impaired hearing, often left White House staff unsure what the two men discussed or agreed upon during their closed-door discussions. After Casey met with Reagan, Deaver debriefed his boss. If the CIA director had sold the president on some wild scheme, Deaver passed word to Baker, who spoke with Nancy Reagan and arranged for the first lady to talk the president out of it.

Casey called for arming anti-communist groups around the world because of his belief that the Soviet Union was "tremendously overextended and vulnerable." If America challenged the Soviets everywhere and defeated them in just one place, he argued, "that will shatter the mythology . . . and it will all start to unravel." Reagan endorsed this argument, sometimes called the "Reagan Doctrine," in several internal policy papers and in a speech delivered at his alma mater, Eureka College, on May 9, 1982, where he promised active support for people fighting communism, wherever they were. He put his words and beliefs into action, but with mixed results.

For example, Reagan inherited an unstable, violent Middle East and left the region in pretty much the same condition. Conflicts between the Israelis and Palestinians, among Lebanese factions, within Afghanistan, and between Iraq and Iran continued during the 1980s and set the stage for future problems, some involving terrorism aimed directly at the United States.

In the early 1980s, Lebanese religious and political factions resumed their periodic civil slaughter, with Israel and Syria backing armed rivals. When the White House criticized Secretary of State Haig's June 1982 support for an

Israeli invasion of Lebanon, Haig quit in a huff. George Shultz, named as Haig's successor, had no more success in stabilizing the area.

As chaos engulfed Lebanon, the United States dispatched Marines to join French and Italian troops as peacekeepers. The Marines assisted Christian militias fighting Muslim forces backed by Syria. In response, on April 18, 1983, a suicide squad blew up the U.S. embassy in Beirut, killing sixty-three people. U.S. Navy ships off Lebanon then bombarded several Islamic strongholds. On October 23, a Muslim suicide bomber retaliated by driving a truck filled with explosives into a U.S. Marine barracks near the Beirut airport, killing 241 Americans.

Reagan offered a stirring tribute to the fallen Marines but no credible explanation of their mission or the reason for their deaths. A few months later, in his 1984 State of the Union message, he described the Marine presence in Beirut as "central to our credibility on a global scale." Two weeks later, without explanation, he withdrew all American forces and seldom spoke of the subject again.

Public reaction to the disaster in Beirut was muted in part because of lavish media attention focused on Grenada, a tiny Caribbean island. Although it had been ruled by Marxists since 1979, neither the Carter nor Reagan administration had paid much attention to the island. The only American presence consisted of five hundred students enrolled in a private medical college. Close by, a contingent of armed Cuban laborers was building an airport designed to either boost tourism (as Grenada claimed) or to serve as a Soviet-Cuban air base (as the CIA asserted).

A more militant Marxist faction seized control of Grenada on October 12, 1983. Immediately after the October 23 catastrophe in Beirut, Reagan declared that the Soviets intended to turn Grenada into an "outpost of communism" and terrorism and that the American students on Grenada might become hostages, although none had been threatened. On October 25, he ordered thousands of Marines and amphibious Army troops to liberate Grenada and the American students from a "brutal gang of thugs."

In an action that resembled a comic opera more than a war, U.S. troops quickly secured the island. The students were flown home. As if to compensate for the Beirut debacle, the Pentagon awarded an unprecedented eight thousand medals to members of the assault force, more than the number of soldiers in the invasion! Free elections restored representative government to the island. News coverage of the invasion alerted many Americans to Grenada's lovely beaches and eventually sparked a tourist boom, facilitated by the Cuban-built airport.

Most Americans approved of the invasion, telling pollsters they were pleased that the United States had "won one for a change." Scenes of the "rescued" medical students falling to their knees and kissing American soil obscured the fact that they had never been threatened. Reagan's reelection team used film of the grateful students, with devastating effect, in the 1984 campaign against Walter Mondale, the Democratic nominee, who had called the invasion a violation of international law.

The celebration of victory in Grenada coincided with a growing wave of nationalism that Reagan both stimulated and skillfully rode. During the 1980s, several popular films and novels portrayed American heroes who exacted revenge in Vietnam and defeated Soviet troops and their allies in the third world. Often, these celluloid and print heroes returned to Vietnam to rescue American POWs left to rot by cowardly politicians. Although no responsible U.S. officials actually believed any POWs remained in Southeast Asia, Reagan's aides found it politically useful to hint that by taking a tough stand, some might yet be found. As the film character John Rambo, actor Sylvester Stallone (who had avoided service in Vietnam) beat Russian and Vietnamese communists in guerrilla warfare. Before being sent back to the jungle in *Rambo II*, he plaintively asked "Do we get to win this time?" Kung fu champion Chuck Norris similarly karate-chopped his way to victory in Southeast Asia. In the film *Top Gun*, Tom Cruise blasted Libyan and Soviet pilots out of the sky with a grin and a swagger. Tom Clancy novels, such as *The Hunt for Red October*, revealed how American technical and moral superiority could defeat the Soviets. Fiction merged with politics in the appearance of "RONBO," a popular poster of the mid-1980s on which Reagan's head sat atop Stallone's buff torso.

A determination to "win" assumed new meaning during the 1984 Olympic Games held in Los Angeles. Partly because of a boycott by the Soviet Union and its allies, American athletes triumphed in an unusually large number of events. Stadium crowds waved banners proclaiming "We're #1" as they chanted "U.S.A., U.S.A." Television coverage of the games often skipped victory ceremonies in which non-American athletes took top honors and sometimes declined to broadcast the foreign national anthems. Reagan's reelection commercials in 1984 included substantial Olympic footage.

Washington focused much of its antiterrorist sentiment during the 1980s on Libya's demagogic and oil-rich strongman, Muammar Qaddafi. Flush with cash, he purchased Soviet weapons and funded several terrorist groups. To contain the threat, the U.S. Navy deployed ships close to Libya and engaged Qaddafi's air force in several dogfights. In April 1986, after Libyan agents were implicated in the bombing of a Berlin nightclub frequented by GIs, Reagan condemned Qaddafi as the "mad dog of the Middle East." He ordered American planes to bomb targets in Tripoli, including Qaddafi's residence, where his infant daughter was killed.

Following these attacks, Libya and the United States engaged mostly in verbal warfare. Reagan's aides boasted that his tough stand had put Qaddafi "back in his box." In fact, the same plunging oil prices that hurt the Soviets, as well as feuds between Libya and its north African neighbors, constrained Qaddafi as much as anything. Two years later, however, in December 1988, Libyan agents planted a bomb aboard a Pan-Am jet that exploded over Scotland, killing 279 mostly American passengers and crew.

The bloodiest violence in the Middle East occurred during a nine-year war between Iraq and Iran that started in 1980. Fought over regional influence, oil, and access to deep-water ports, the war claimed nearly two million lives before it ended in 1988. The war put the American government in an awkward position. U.S. officials disliked and feared both sides. No one wanted to see the influence of Iran's Islamic zealots expand. Nor did they savor the prospect of Iraq's dictator, Saddam Hussein, dominating the Persian Gulf.

To prevent either side from gaining the upper hand, Reagan authorized military assistance to both nations, shifting aid back and forth as the battlefield balance fluctuated. At one point the United States provided Saddam with detailed photo intelligence of Iranian positions. In the mid-1980s, Reagan dispatched Pentagon aide Donald Rumsfeld on a goodwill mission to Iraq, where the future architect of the 2003 war against Iraq provided Saddam with offers of assistance. Neither Rumsfeld nor Reagan criticized Saddam's brutal use of poison gas to kill tens of thousands of dissident Kurds and invading Iranian soldiers. By 1988, war-weary Iran and Iraq agreed to a ceasefire, with both condemning the United States.

Among the several Reagan-era interventions, Afghanistan is usually hailed as the most successful. In 1979, the Soviets invaded that bleak land on their southern border in an effort to save a shaky local communist régime established a few years earlier. Soon over 100,000 Soviet troops were trapped in a vicious guerrilla war against mujahideen, or freedom fighters, many of whom were inspired by fundamentalist Islam.

President Carter had initiated aid to these anti-Soviet guerrillas. The Reagan administration expanded aid. In 1982, CIA Director Casey, among other Americans, fell under the sway of Pakistani strongman Mohammed Zia ul-Haq. Zia convinced these Americans that the Soviets had revived a nineteenth-century czarist strategy (known as "the Great Game") aimed at dominating the Persian Gulf, Pakistan, and India via Afghanistan. Casey's decision to transform the mujahideen into a serious fighting force won support from a flamboyant Texas congressman, Charlie Wilson, who persuaded his Democratic colleagues to fund a major military aid program. By 1986, the Afghan guerrillas received U.S. antiaircraft missiles and other advanced weaponry that took a heavy toll on Soviet forces.

To deliver these weapons, Washington worked closely with Afghanistan's neighbors, China and Pakistan. Chinese communist leaders resented the Soviets almost as much as did Reagan. Their helpful attitude convinced the president, a longtime supporter of Taiwan, to temper his criticism of the People's Republic. Pakistan drove a harder bargain. Zia insisted that Washington provide his repressive regime with substantial military, economic, and political support. With tacit U.S. approval, Pakistan began creating a nuclear arsenal, and some of its scientists transferred nuclear technology to other nations. Pakistan also served as a training camp for Islamic fundamentalists from throughout the world who were drawn to the fight in nearby Afghanistan. Among those arriving was Osama bin Laden, a wealthy Saudi who viewed the anti-Soviet struggle as the first phase in a broader war against Western infidels. At the time, few Americans in or out of government questioned the beliefs or ultimate goals of these allies so long as they fought the Soviets.

During the 1980s, Reagan authorized several other CIA covert operations. These ranged from providing money to sustain the peaceful Solidarity labor movement challenging Soviet domination of Poland to arming anti-Vietnamese guerrillas—including remnants of the bloody Khmer Rouge—operating in Cambodia. The CIA also supported guerrilla armies in Angola and Mozambique who battled Cuban-backed movements. Although aid to Solidarity and the Afghan resistance enjoyed broad support among Americans and Europeans, the operations in Cambodia and Africa were largely kept secret. This secrecy reflected the fact that in these struggles the United States had allied itself with several brutal and antidemocratic groups. The few "victories" in these covert operations came in Poland and Afghanistan, places where the United States allied itself with popular movements resisting direct Soviet domination. The administration's most controversial interventions occurred in Central America, where Reagan's personal interest in supporting anti-communist forces nearly brought down his presidency.

From Banana Wars to Iran-Contra

Throughout his presidency, Reagan and his closest aides appeared obsessed by what they called a Soviet and Cuban threat to the Western Hemisphere. To counter this threat and to erase the humiliating memory of Vietnam, the president revived the tradition of U.S. muscle-flexing in Latin America. Administration rhetoric often sounded like a replay of warnings from the early Cold War. Officials spoke of a "Moscow-Havana" axis (replacing the Moscow-Beijing alliance of the previous era) that conspired to spread revolution in both Latin America and Africa. U.N. Ambassador Jeanne Kirkpatrick called Central America and the Caribbean "the most important place in the world for us." Reagan warned that Moscow and Havana intended to set up puppet regimes in Latin America as part of a plan to sever the U.S. "lifeline to the outside world."

As a candidate, Reagan had criticized Carter for abandoning Nicaraguan dictator Anatasio Somoza, whose family had ruled the country since the 1920s. As president, Reagan claimed that the leftist Sandinista movement that had toppled Somoza had turned Nicaragua into a Soviet outpost and a "safe house and command post for international terror." In one especially vivid speech, he conjured up a vision of Sandinistas driving a convoy of armed pickup trucks north into Harlingen, Texas, a town on the Mexican border. Cartoonist Garry Trudeau parodied this warning in his *Doonesbury* comic strip that depicted a group of "good ol' boys" from Harlingen peering through the sights of their hunting rifles, prepared to repulse an invasion.

Democratic critics of this rhetoric, such as Connecticut Senator Christopher Dodd, countered that Reagan and his advisers knew "as much about Central America" in the 1980s "as we knew about Indochina in 1963." As a former Peace Corps volunteer in Latin America, Dodd insisted that if the region "were not wracked with poverty, there would be no revolution." To dampen criticism and build support for his policies, Reagan asked Henry

Kissinger to assess the situation. In 1984, a commission led by the former secretary of state acknowledged that many of Central America's problems could not be blamed on Soviet meddling. Nevertheless, Kissinger urged providing increased military aid to anti-communist regimes such as El Salvador and to guerrillas fighting in Nicaragua.

In spite of Reagan's passion on the subject, the U.S. public responded apathetically to Latin American events. Pollsters found that most people did not care very much who dominated, say, Tegucigalpa or Managua. At the same time, the public deferred to Reagan as long as Americans were not killed in combat. As a result, the administration openly supplied economic and military assistance to friendly governments in the region but limited its direct involvement to training troops, using small numbers of special forces and providing covert aid to anti-communist guerrillas. These operations put few American lives at risk and minimized public debate.

During the 1980s, Reagan authorized spending nearly $5 billion to shore up the government of tiny El Salvador, a nominal democracy controlled by hardline militarists who had been battling a left-wing rebellion since 1979. A terribly poor nation in which 2 percent of the population owned nearly everything, El Salvador had been wracked by rural rebellions for most of the twentieth century. In spite of this massive U.S. aid, the Salvadoran army could not defeat the leftist rebels and their civilian allies. The army squandered much of the money while government troops and paramilitary death squads, some trained by Americans, killed about seventy thousand peasants, teachers, union organizers, and church workers during the 1980s. Congress placed a cap on the number of U.S. military advisers in El Salvador but otherwise asked few questions. The brutal civil war continued until 1992, when a truce restored a semblance of representative government.

The moral morass of El Salvador seemed crystal clear compared with the hole that Reagan dug for himself in neighboring Nicaragua. Nothing the president did in eight years so tarnished his reputation or called into question his judgment so seriously as his decision to sell weapons to Iran as part of a scheme to ransom U.S. hostages in Beirut while funding anti-communist fighters in Central America.

Reagan condemned Nicaragua's Sandinista leaders as Marxists who harassed opponents, blocked free elections, disliked the United States, and received aid from Cuba and the Soviet Union. The president spoke truthfully but misrepresented the meaning of these facts. Violent rights abuses by the Sandinistas never approached the scale and scope of the brutality inflicted on civilians and indigenous Indians by pro-U.S. regimes in El Salvador, Guatemala, and Honduras. Nicaragua, a tiny nation with fewer residents than many American cities, did not appear as much of a threat to U.S. survival.

Nevertheless, both Reagan and CIA Director Casey saw global stakes at risk. Casey, according to his deputy, "became obsessed with Central America" and believed that if the United States could defeat a Soviet proxy in just one place, the entire evil empire would "unravel." "Nick-a-wog-wha," as he pronounced it, "is that place."

In 1981, Reagan ordered Casey to organize an anti-Sandinista force called the *"contra-revolutionarios,"* or "contras." The president praised them as "freedom fighters" and later called them "the moral equal of our founding fathers." With U.S. aid, contra ranks swelled to between ten thousand and twenty thousand men. Most of the contra leaders were veterans of the old Somoza dictatorship, not incipient Thomas Jeffersons.

When Congress raised questions concerning CIA funding of these guerrillas, Casey assured the lawmakers that the contras did not intend to overthrow the Sandinistas. Rather, he said, U.S. aid enabled them to interdict Sandinista weapons going to leftist rebels in El Salvador. This was a blatant lie, however, because Casey knew that in December 1981 Reagan had signed a secret order authorizing contra aid for the purpose of deposing the Sandinistas. When media reports surfaced in 1982 linking contra attacks to thousands of civilian deaths in Nicaragua, Congress passed a resolution named for Representative Edward P. Boland that capped CIA assistance to the rebels at $24 million and ordered that none of the funds be used to overthrow the Nicaraguan government. In October 1984, after learning that the CIA and contras had illegally mined Nicaraguan harbors, Congress passed an even stricter version of the Boland resolution that barred *any* U.S. government funds going to the contras for any purpose.

These restrictions infuriated Reagan, who disparaged Congress as a committee of busybodies. He told National Security Adviser Robert McFarlane and his deputy, Admiral John Poindexter, as well as NSC staffer Lt. Col. Oliver North, "to do whatever you have to do to help these people keep body and soul together." For a president who seldom issued clear instructions to subordinates, this was a definitive order.

After conferring with Casey and several State Department officials, McFarlane, Poindexter, and North devised a scheme to "privatize" contra aid by soliciting funds from friendly foreign governments and wealthy American conservatives. North opened Swiss bank accounts into which he deposited money donated by Israel, Saudi Arabia, South Africa, South Korea, Taiwan, and Brunei as well as from Nelson Bunker Hunt and Joseph Coors. Some of the foreign funds actually originated as U.S assistance to the countries that "donated" them to the contras. Reagan also permitted his aides to deal with Panamanian strongman Manuel Noriega. Although Noriega had turned Panama into a money-laundering and transportation haven for Colombian cocaine dealers, U.S. officials gave him a stamp of approval when he permitted the CIA to use Panama as a conduit for aid to the contras. Reagan did not know—or want to know—all the details of contra aid, but McFarlane and his successor as national security adviser, John Poindexter, kept him informed of their general activities and received his blessing.

Although some two dozen CIA, State Department, and White House officials were linked to the illegal scheme to aid the contras, Secretary of State Shultz considered the operation foolhardy. In June 1984, he warned Reagan that soliciting funds to circumvent Congress might constitute an "impeachable offense." The president clearly understood Shultz's meaning because he

Marine Lt. Colonel and former presidential aide Oliver North testifies to Congress about the Iran-contra scandal, 1987. Chris Wilkins/Getty Images.

quipped to aides that if the story of his assisting the contras ever got out, "we'll all be hanging by our thumbs in front of the White House."

In March 1986, even while Soviet-American relations were beginning to improve, Reagan delivered a dramatic televised speech warning that the Soviets and Cubans had turned Nicaragua into a base to sever U.S. access to South America, the Panama Canal, and vital Caribbean sea-lanes. Moscow and Havana, he declared, had implemented the "old communist slogan" that "the road to victory goes through Mexico." As it often did, Congress bowed to Reagan's urgent plea to resume limited aid to the contras. By then, however, Reagan had approved yet another illegal scheme.

Unbeknownst to Congress or the public, in the previous year the illicit contra aid scheme had merged with another secret project with Iran. Reagan had several times publicly condemned the Iranian regime as an "outlaw state." U.S. law barred selling or giving Iran any military equipment unless the president notified Congress in writing of a compelling reason to do so. Reagan found a reason but told no one.

For some time Reagan had been moved by the plight of seven Americans who had been kidnapped in Beirut and held as hostages by Islamic militias linked to Iran. With the exception of one hostage, CIA agent William Buckley, all were private citizens who had remained in Lebanon despite official warnings to leave. Recalling public disgust with Carter's handling of the Iranian hostages, Reagan acted boldly. In mid-1985, an Iranian businessman contacted National Security Adviser Robert McFarlane and claimed that he could secure the hostages' release in return for U.S. arms sales to "moderate" elements in Iran who might take power following the death of Ayatollah Khomeini.

Despite his pledge "never to negotiate with terrorists," Reagan told Mc-Farlane, "Gee, that sounds pretty good." In his diary, the president indicated he liked the idea of a deal to get "our seven kidnap victims back." He said nothing about building a new relationship with Iran. Over the next year, Reagan authorized several secret arms sales to Iran valued in the hundreds of millions of dollars. Three hostages were released, but three more were taken as replacements. Reagan not only had broken his pledge by dealing with terrorists and defied American law, but also had created a lucrative market for seizing Americans.

This scheme took an even more bizarre turn when Oliver North conceived what he called a "neat idea." Why not overcharge the Iranians for the American weapons they wanted and use profits from the sales to support the Nicaraguan contras whom Congress had cut loose? As North joked, the Iranians would unknowingly make a "contra-bution." At one point North and McFarlane tried to expand the deal by actually flying to Iran to meet with the supposed "moderates." Like other elements of the scheme, this, too, violated federal law because profits from any sale of U.S. government property— including weapons—had to be returned to the Treasury, not given to the president's favorite guerrilla charity in defiance of Congress.

The tangled scheme began to unravel in October 1986 when Sandinista gunners shot down a CIA-chartered plane carrying weapons to the contras. A surviving American crew member told interrogators all he knew about the secret U.S. contra aid program. In early November, just as American voters returned control of the Senate to the Democrats, the other shoe dropped. Iranian officials revealed the sordid tale of the arms sales-for-hostages scheme. U.S. weapons, they explained, had not gone to "moderates," but rather to Khomeini loyalists who had hoodwinked the Reagan administration from the start.

Reagan, CIA Director Casey, North, and other participants tried at first to cover up the scandal by shredding documents and lying about their actions to the press, to Congress, to a special prosecutor, and to the American public. Despite compelling evidence of his active role, Reagan insisted that he knew nothing about any arms-for-hostages deal or illegal funding of the contras. The public did not believe him, and by December 1986, Reagan's approval rating plummeted to 36 percent.

Under pressure to come clean, the president appointed a blue-ribbon inquiry commission chaired by former Senator John Tower. After hearing misleading and confused testimony from Reagan (who first admitted, then denied, then said he could not recall anything about trading arms for hostages and diverting funds), the Tower Commission concluded in its February 1987 report that the Iran arms sales had devolved into a sordid ransom scheme designed to illegally fund the contras. Reagan's actions ran "directly counter" to his public promise to punish terrorists. The report portrayed the president as disengaged, uninformed, and easily manipulated. Reagan sidestepped the criticism by firing several of his aides linked to the Iran-contra scheme and by giving a speech on March 4, 1987, in which he appeared to accept responsibility without actually doing so. The "facts" might suggest he permitted ransom payments and other illegal acts, Reagan asserted, but in his "heart" he never meant to break the law. Several congressional probes and criminal trials over the next few years led to a dozen convictions of Reagan-era officials for their role in the scandal. Several co-conspirators confirmed that the president had approved their actions and had impeded full disclosure.

Despite talk among some Democrats of impeachment, Reagan survived the scandal. The competing House, Senate, and special prosecutor investigations into Iran-contra often lacked focus. Although the public strongly disapproved of his actions in the Iran-contra affair, Reagan retained an important quotient of goodwill. But perhaps the most important reason why the scandal faded was the striking improvement in Soviet-American relations. During 1986, a Cold War thaw had begun between Moscow and Washington. By 1987, fundamental changes had occurred inside the Soviet Union, and the president rushed to embrace them. Ironically, improved relations with the "evil empire" salvaged Reagan's legacy.

Reagan, Gorbachev, and the End of the Cold War

As his supporters argued, even if the president erred in "small things" such as Iran-contra, he steered a true course on the most important issue, engineering the demise of the Soviet Union. As Alaska Senator Ted Stevens remarked at Reagan's funeral in June 2004, at the time of Reagan's inauguration in 1981, the Soviet Union was "winning the Cold War." A decade later, it collapsed. Most historians, however, dispute the claim that the Soviets were on a victory roll in 1981 or that Reagan's policies buried them.

The Reagan administration's relationship with the Soviet Union started badly and soon got worse. At his first presidential press conference in 1981, the president condemned détente and branded Soviet leaders as liars and criminals committed to world domination. It would no longer be business as usual with Moscow. Yet, even as he spoke, Reagan asked Secretary of State Haig to inform Soviet Ambassador Anatoly Dobrynin that his harsh language was not meant to offend anyone "but was just an expression of his deep convictions." The clarification, Dobrynin responded, "only made things worse."

This pattern persisted into Reagan's second term. The president condemned the Soviet Union as the "focus of evil in the modern world" and a rotten system ready to be shoved onto the ash heap of history. Yet, he typically followed these rhetorical bombshells by sending warm personal letters to Soviet leaders, including Leonid Brezhnev, who died in November 1982, Yuri Andropov (who served from November 1982 to February 1984), Konstantin Chernenko (from February 1984 to March 1985), and then Mikhail Gorbachev. These letters contained pleas for cooperation and mutual understanding. Reagan frequently remarked that if he could talk one-on-one to a

Soviet leader, he could convince him of America's good intentions and the corresponding evils of communism.

Yet, in spite of these personal messages, Reagan refused to speak with *any* Soviet official for nearly two years. He met his first high-level Soviet representative only in February 15, 1983, when, on his own initiative, Secretary of State Shultz brought Ambassador Dobrynin to the White House for an impromptu chat. Reagan took the opportunity to voice concern for seven Siberian Pentecostals holed up in the U.S. embassy in Moscow since 1978. Two months after this conversation, the religious dissidents were permitted to emigrate. In apparent response, Reagan agreed to sell the Soviets $10 billion worth of grain over the next five years, despite his pressure on allied nations to cut off their trade with the Kremlin.

Many of Reagan's Soviet policies, including those related to nuclear weapons and trade, were inconsistent. He spoke somberly of nuclear war as possibly the biblically prophesized Armageddon. He confided to his closest aides that he hoped to abolish nuclear weapons. Yet, he expanded America's arsenal of around ten thousand nuclear bombs to counter the Soviets' eight thousand. After this rapid buildup, in 1984 Reagan called publicly for abolishing nuclear weapons. In 1987, he and Gorbachev agreed to eliminate several hundred shorter-range nuclear-tipped missiles. But during his last year and a half in office Reagan spurned efforts by the Soviet reformer to slash nuclear arsenals more dramatically.

Frosty relations with the Soviet Union hit new lows during 1983. On September 1, U.S. intelligence officials learned from electronic intercepts that a Soviet fighter plane had the previous day downed Korean Airlines Flight 007 carrying 269 people (including a member of Congress). The KAL plane had strayed into Siberian airspace near a missile test site. Evidence later revealed that a navigational error caused the intrusion. At the time, Soviet spokesmen (uncertain of the facts and preoccupied by the disabling illness of Communist Party chief Yuri Andropov) first denied the shootdown, then insisted the airliner was a spy plane and a legitimate target. From intercepted messages, U.S. intelligence analysts quickly realized that the Soviets sincerely, although mistakenly, believed that KAL 007 had been on a spy mission. In spite of this confusion, Reagan condemned the attack as an intentional, unprovoked massacre and a "crime against humanity."

Also in September, the imminent deployment of American Pershing II and cruise missiles to western Europe infuriated Soviet leaders. Reagan insisted that the new missiles only redressed earlier Soviet deployments of similar weapons capable of hitting western Europe—which Moscow had justified as needed to balance the U.S. advantage in other weapons systems. From his hospital bed, Andropov condemned the deployment of the new U.S. missiles as dispelling "any illusion" that Reagan favored improving bilateral ties. The Soviets then canceled a planned round of disarmament talks. In October 1983, after the U.S. invasion of Grenada, the Soviet press compared Reagan to Hitler, calling him a madman "making delirious plans for world domination." That December, when U.S. forces conducted a secret war game called "Exercise Able Archer," Soviet intelligence warned Andropov that the war game might be a cover for a real nuclear attack, perhaps requiring a Soviet first strike.

Reagan viewed the deployment of the intermediate-range missiles in Europe, along with the Grenada invasion and arms buildup, as among his most significant achievements. At the same time, pollsters warned the president that nearly half of all Americans voiced concern over rising tensions with the Soviet Union. Secretary of State Shultz, National Security Adviser Robert McFarlane (who replaced the more conservative William Clark when Clark replaced James Watt as secretary of the interior), along with White House Deputy Chief of Staff Michael Deaver and Nancy Reagan, urged the president to take a more flexible approach. He agreed, and on November 11 in a speech in Japan Reagan declared, "My dream is to see the day when nuclear weapons will be banished from the face of the Earth." In December, at Shultz's prompting, the president sent another conciliatory letter to Andropov. Then, on January 16, 1984, Reagan made a speech in which he described a coming "year of opportunities for peace." The United States and U.S.S.R. should resume a dialogue based on "realism" and a "spirit of compromise." He added a coda about how wonderful it would be if ordinary Russians such as "Ivan and Anya" could meet their American counterparts, "Jim and Sally."

Soviet leader Andropov's lingering terminal illness and death on February 9, 1984, precluded a response. His successor, Konstantin Chernenko, held power for barely one year, until March 1985. A plodding party functionary, Chernenko suffered from emphysema that limited his activities. The succession of decrepit leaders in Moscow reduced pressure on Reagan to justify to the world his own tough approach.

In the run-up to the 1984 U.S. presidential election, Reagan carefully modulated his anti-Soviet rhetoric, backing off from his early confrontational line. He denied harboring a desire or plan to overthrow the communist regime. "We made it plain we're not out to change" the Soviet system, Reagan declared. "We're certainly not going to let them change ours." But "we have to live in the world together." This hardly sounded like a man who planned to topple the U.S.S.R. Reagan's conciliatory tone, combined with an improving American economy, soothed voters' fears and assured the president's reelection by a landslide in November 1984.

The Soviet-American dynamic changed dramatically on March 11, 1985, when the relatively young (age fifty-four), vigorous, and well-educated Mikhail Gorbachev was chosen by Communist Party officials to lead the Soviet Union. As the best-educated, most urbane, well-traveled, media-savvy, and articulate Soviet leader since Lenin, Gorbachev impressed nearly all Western leaders who met him, including Secretary of State Shultz and British Prime Minister Thatcher. Thatcher, whom Reagan respected deeply, declared that she "could do business" with Gorbachev. Shultz and Thatcher (along with astrologer Joan Quigley, consulted by the president and first lady) encouraged Reagan to sit down with the new Soviet leader.

A "getting-to-know-you" encounter at Geneva in November 1985 proved helpful, even if no formal agreements emerged. Reagan found Gorbachev's openness and lack of doctrinaire rhetoric appealing. During their initial chat, the president startled Gorbachev by breaking into what Reagan aides called his "little green men speech." Achieving peace would be simpler, Reagan explained, "if there was a threat to this world from some other species, from another planet, outside this universe." If so, Soviets and Americans would "forget all the little local differences that we have between our countries, and we would find out once and for all that we really are all human beings here on this Earth together." Whatever Gorbachev made of this parable, Reagan's easy charm overcame any awkwardness. Meanwhile, the Russian turned out to be a fan of American films and enjoyed hearing the president tell colorful stories about Hollywood celebrities from the 1940s and 1950s.

The two leaders also broached substantial issues at Geneva, including the idea of deep cuts in a variety of strategic nuclear weapons. Gorbachev wanted to explore details, but Reagan ended the discussion by insisting that any reduction in nuclear weapons must be linked to Soviet acceptance of American development and deployment of the SDI antimissile system—despite the prohibitions on this in the existing ABM treaty. When Gorbachev described SDI as a dangerous escalation of the arms race, Reagan countered with his mantra that the antimissile scheme was intended as a "shield, not a spear."

Reagan's rigidity on SDI puzzled some of his aides as much as it did Gorbachev because no workable system existed or would likely be developed for a decade or longer. In effect, Reagan's refusal to discuss serious arms reductions until the Soviets consented to U.S. testing and deployment of SDI blocked most progress toward Reagan's stated goal of a "nuclear-free world."

Gorbachev's desire to end the Cold War stemmed primarily from forces and ideas within the Soviet system. As one of the best-informed scholars of the period, Raymond Garthoff, observed, America's so-called victory in the Cold War "came when a new generation of Soviet leaders realized how badly their system at home and their policies abroad had failed." Gorbachev, unlike his predecessors, recognized the "interdependence of the world," the priority of "all human values over class values," and the indivisibility of common security. In spite of claims by Reagan and his conservative admirers, the Soviets did not "lose" the arms race because of America's faster pace. Rather, Gorbachev simply called it off. Reagan had the good fortune—and good sense—to respond to these changes even if he had only a small part in initiating them.

During 1986, Gorbachev, along with his new foreign minister, Eduard Shevardnadze, initiated dramatic changes in Soviet domestic and foreign policy. Gorbachev resolved to save communism by reforming it. He began by lifting press restrictions, releasing political prisoners, and easing emigration by religious and political dissidents. To jump-start the economy, he introduced

President-Elect Bush, President Reagan, and Soviet President Mikhail Gorbachev celebrate U.S.-Soviet cooperation in New York City, 1988. Courtesy Ronald Reagan Library.

market mechanisms in agriculture and industry. Implementing these reforms required reductions in global tension and lower arms expenditures along with expanded ties to capitalist nations. Gorbachev's initiatives coincided with American goals but were not forced on him by Reagan.

The length to which the Soviets were prepared to go became clear as the two leaders met a second time in Reykjavik, Iceland, in mid-October 1986. Gorbachev stunned American delegates by proposing 50 percent cuts in the number of heavy missiles along with substantial reductions in other weapons systems. In turn, he wanted the United States to adhere to the ABM treaty for ten years, confining SDI to laboratory testing. Reagan again balked.

As proposals flew back and forth, teams of negotiators proposed even deeper and wider cuts of nuclear arsenals. However, several critical issues remained unclear, including the status of British and French missiles, the size of future conventional armed forces, and whether the reductions applied only to delivery systems (missiles, planes, etc.) or also to the nuclear warheads they carried. Reagan ultimately proposed eliminating *all* nuclear weapons (not just delivery systems). Gorbachev agreed, so long as the U.S. did not deploy an antimissile system for at least a decade. Angrily declaring that he "promised the American people" he would "not give up SDI," Reagan broke off discussions and returned home.

In retrospect, Reagan's supporters believe that the president's unbending commitment to SDI broke Gorbachev's resistance and set the stage for a general Soviet retreat. Just why they believe this is unclear because aides to both Gorbachev and Reagan, including George Shultz, recognized that SDI deployment was, at best, many years away. Why not move *now* toward meaningful nuclear disarmament and proceed with SDI *research*, which Gorbachev did not oppose? Conversely, why did Gorbachev give up the chance to win arms cuts he desperately wanted when all he had to do was give a nod of approval toward a largely imaginary SDI program that had a lock on Reagan's mind? Both leaders' rigidity doomed the summit. Several of Reagan's more conservative aides expressed relief at the failure to reach a deal because real questions existed about exactly what the president had proposed or agreed to.

Three weeks after the confused Reykjavik summit, the Iran-contra scandal broke. In the November 1986 election, Republicans lost control of the Senate. As the scandal deepened and as the public expressed growing disillusionment with the president's behavior and ability, Reagan replaced many of his hardline advisers with moderates. Frank Carlucci took over as national security adviser from the disgraced John Poindexter; former Senator Howard Baker replaced the abrasive Don Regan as White House chief of staff; FBI Director William Webster took charge of the CIA from the ailing William Casey; and later in 1987 Caspar Weinberger resigned as defense secretary. Carlucci took over the Pentagon post, opening the NSC slot for Gen. Colin Powell. Secretary of State Shultz, long the lone voice advocating negotiations with Moscow, now enjoyed the backing of a much more pragmatic group.

During 1987, events pushed both Gorbachev and Reagan toward a more cooperative relationship. Gorbachev's economic and social reform program ran into roadblocks created by Communist Party bureaucrats. As the Soviet public grew frustrated at his inability to deliver a better life, Gorbachev hoped to slash defense spending (an estimated 25 percent of Soviet GNP, as compared with 3 percent in the U.S.) to free resources for economic restructuring. He counted on democratic reforms to mobilize support for his leadership and win concessions from Washington.

To this end, in 1987 Gorbachev proposed to Reagan a deal eliminating most intermediate-range nuclear missiles while leaving the Americans wiggle room for SDI. The Soviet leader's proposal reflected advice given him by a recently freed dissident, physicist Andrei Sakharov. The "father of the Soviet H-bomb" convinced Gorbachev that SDI either would not work or could be neutralized by relatively cheap Soviet countermeasures. Shultz and other moderates now advising Reagan saw this development as something of a lifeline for a president who was floundering in the Iran-contra scandal and whose public approval had fallen sharply. Yet, Reagan refused to bargain.

Despite his frustration with Reagan's unwillingness to compromise, Gorbachev pressed forward and eventually decided to ignore completely the SDI issue. In late 1987 and early 1988, he announced that all Soviet troops would leave Afghanistan within one year, and he offered to help broker peace deals in Nicaragua and Africa, where Soviet and American proxies had been fighting for years.

Reagan once again ignored these initiatives. The administration even reneged on its earlier pledge to halt military aid to the Afghan guerrillas once Soviets forces pulled out. Rejecting peaceful mediation in Nicaragua, Reagan instead called on Congress to boost contra aid in order to "prevent consolidation of a Soviet military presence" on the American mainland. Defense Secretary Weinberger's final report from the Pentagon, released in January 1988, called for increased defense spending because (in contradiction to what nearly everyone else could see) there was "no slackening of the growth of Soviet military power or abandonment of expansionist aspirations."

But now Democrats had regained a Senate majority and felt bold enough to defy a weakened president. In short order, Congress blocked new aid to the contras, modestly reduced defense spending, and warned the administration not to weasel out of the traditional interpretation of the ABM treaty that limited SDI deployment.

Despite Reagan's half-hearted retreat from the Cold War, his own needs and those of Gorbachev again pushed them closer. In December 1987, the two leaders signed a treaty, largely on American terms, to eliminate all of their intermediate-range nuclear forces (INF). Although the INF treaty cut only about 4 percent of the twenty thousand or so nuclear weapons contained in the U.S. and Soviet arsenals, it marked the first time the two rivals had agreed to completely eliminate a class of weapons. Ironically, when the Soviets agreed to ironclad verification rules, some Pentagon officials objected to foreign intrusion into their secret weapons sites.

Unfortunately, the INF treaty represented the first and last significant arms reduction agreement of the Reagan administration. Gorbachev hoped to build on the momentum by moving toward major cuts in long-range missiles and again offered to accept U.S. testing of SDI, which, as he told Reagan, he now considered more a waste of money than a threat. Reagan, who appeared so confident when confronting hostile Soviet leaders, lost his bearings when he got "yes" for an answer. During Gorbachev's December 1987 visit to Washington for the INF treaty signing, the Soviet leader and president met at the White House. As Gorbachev proposed further cuts to their nuclear arsenals and cooperation to bring peace to Africa, Latin America, and Afghanistan, the president appeared confused. He responded to Gorbachev's appeal by telling old, off-color anti-Soviet jokes. A visibly furious Secretary of State

Shultz took Reagan aside to berate his "terrible performance." Shultz and White House Chief of Staff Howard Baker agreed to closely monitor Reagan's future discussions with foreign leaders, sensing that his mental faculties were no longer adequate for conducting negotiations. By this point more Americans (65 percent) held a favorable view of Gorbachev than of Reagan (61 percent) and *Time* magazine named Gorbachev "Man of the Year" for 1987. When Reagan retired in January 1989, Gorbachev's approval rating topped the president's, 80 percent to 70 percent.

Reagan's passivity during his final months in office halted the momentum to move beyond the Cold War. In both public and private settings, Reagan boasted that his hard line had forced a Soviet retreat. He appeared to lose interest in antinuclear initiatives after some of his more conservative supporters complained that his misguided "rush to disarm" made him appear like a "useful idiot" for the Kremlin. When Soviet forces departed Afghanistan ahead of schedule, Reagan again spurned Moscow's call for jointly backing a moderate regime. Instead, Washington continued to arm Islamic fighters, some of whom later formed the core of the extremist Taliban.

In June 1988, the president traveled to Moscow for something like a victory lap. In a remarkable "photo op," the old Cold Warrior spoke to a crowd while standing on Lenin's tomb in Red Square. When asked by an American reporter how he felt about visiting the heart of the "evil empire," Reagan answered, "I was talking about another time, another era." But when Gorbachev once again tried to engage him in discussions on reducing arms and solving regional conflicts, Reagan did little more than smile.

Near the end of the Reagan era, Mikhail Gorbachev sardonically asked the president's sixth national security adviser, Colin Powell, "What are you going to do now that you've lost your best enemy?" Powell, like Reagan, had no easy answer. In the wake of the Reagan presidency, the United States faced a range of unanticipated challenges. The anti-Soviet fixation of the 1980s did not prepare the nation for such problems as the rise of Islamic-inspired terrorism, the proliferation of nuclear weapons, the emergence of regional economic and political blocs, growing dependence on imported energy, a ballooning foreign trade deficit, and the accelerating loss of American manufacturing jobs, especially to Asia.

In 1989, State Department analyst Frances Fukuyama published an article (later expanded into a book) entitled "The End of History" in the conservative journal *National Interest*. Fukuyama celebrated what he described as the complete triumph of free market economics and democracy over communism and other political systems. Society, he implied, had reached perfection. Conservative intellectuals hailed this insight as a milestone just as important as George Kennan's 1947 "X" article that symbolically initiated the Cold War by calling for "containment" of the Soviet threat.

Fukuyama's self-congratulatory tone seemed already dated by the time the Soviet Union dissolved in December 1991. By then, a variety of new challenges, regional conflicts, and ethnic violence had emerged in the post–Cold

War world. Kennan, the architect of containment, spoke to this fact in 1992. It was "simply childish" to say that Reagan's policies achieved victory. The United States had not "won" the long struggle that cost both sides so dearly. A far "mellower" Kennan than the one writing in 1947 now observed that each side bore some responsibility for the inception and duration of the Cold War. He urged politicians to think twice and consider the world's complexities before congratulating themselves on the obvious superiority of the American system.

The most respected novelist of the Cold War, John Le Carre, offered a similar caution against American "triumphalism" in his book *The Secret Pilgrim* (1991), which surveyed a world in which drug dealing, money laundering, arms peddling, and ethnic cleansing followed the Soviet collapse. Veteran spymaster George Smiley, the fictional narrator, observes, "We won. Not that the victory matters a damn. And perhaps we didn't win anyway. Perhaps they just lost. Or perhaps without the bonds of ideological conflict to restrain us any more, our troubles are just beginning."

Toward a New World Order

Improved Soviet-American relations eased Vice President George Bush's path toward the White House. The years of his presidency, from 1989 through January 1993, witnessed dramatic changes in world politics. As the Cold War waned, the United Nations began to function as a forum for global cooperation for the first time since its creation in 1945. The end of Soviet-American rivalry hastened the collapse of satellite regimes in eastern Europe and, ultimately, led to the demise of the Soviet state.

Bush's foreign policy team included National Security Adviser Brent Scowcroft, Secretary of Defense Richard Cheney, Secretary of State James Baker III, and Gen. Colin Powell, chair of the Joint Chiefs of Staff. All had served during the Ford and Reagan administrations and generally favored the pragmatic policies that Reagan adopted in his final two years. But Bush's most notable foreign policy accomplishments were more passive than active. He had the good fortune to preside over the peaceful collapse of communism in Europe and claimed credit for the good things that happened on his watch. In some ways, he resembled his Soviet counterpart, Mikhail Gorbachev. Both leaders tried to move their nations beyond the limits of the Cold War. Much like Bush, Gorbachev did not so much push change as decline to resist internal pressures for reform.

During 1989, Gorbachev stunned nearly everyone by permitting free elections to the Soviet parliament. In July, he told communist leaders in eastern Europe that he would not use force to defend pro-Soviet regimes. The satellite states were free to run their own affairs, even if this freedom led to radical change. Boisterous but largely peaceful demonstrations brought down nearly all the communist governments imposed after World War II. Only in Bulgaria and Romania did the old guard put up futile armed resistance.

Both Soviet and American leaders seemed stunned by the pace of change. For several months after taking office, Bush and his advisers hesitated to respond to ferment within the communist world. Should they work with Gorbachev or remain observers? Was Gorbachev a real partner or, as Secretary of State Baker said derisively, only a "dime store cowboy," all flash and no substance? When the president toured eastern Europe in 1989, he advocated a go-slow approach. There was, he told local leaders, "big stuff, heavy stuff going on." Pushing too quickly to depose communist regimes or to unify Germany might "be more than the market can bear." But his cautious words had little impact.

Germany, long at the heart of the Cold War, hurtled toward unification. In November 1989, after months of street protests, East German authorities opened the hated Berlin Wall. Soon wrecking balls and sledgehammers wielded by exuberant Germans battered down this icon of East-West division. Street vendors hawked pieces of the wall as mementos. With Moscow's tacit assent, Germany reunited on October 2, 1990, and remained a pillar of the NATO alliance.

Even the Soviet heartland experienced upheaval. Gorbachev hoped that he could nudge the Soviet Union toward political democracy and a market economy while preserving the guiding role of the Communist Party. But most Soviets lost faith in the old order, and the demand for change was even stronger among the many ethnic groups who comprised the nearly twenty republics under Soviet control. In 1990, the Baltic republics of Lithuania, Estonia, and Latvia proclaimed their independence. Soon the Ukraine, Belarus, Moldova, Armenia, Azerbaijan, Georgia, Turkmenistan, Tajikistan, Kazakhstan, Kyrgyzstan, and Uzbekistan demanded sovereignty. Communist hardliners blamed Gorbachev for unleashing chaos, whereas reformers, such as Boris Yeltsin, accused him of moving too slowly. Yeltsin, a former communist official, won election as president of the huge Russian republic in June 1991 and challenged Gorbachev's authority.

Initially Bush had been slow to embrace Gorbachev. But during 1990 he threw his support and U.S. economic aid behind Soviet reform efforts. Bush met with Gorbachev six times before the end of 1991. In November 1990, they released a joint statement declaring what was already clear—a formal end to the Cold War. The president lavished praise on Gorbachev, criticized Yeltsin's attempt to undermine the Soviet government, and urged the restive republics to remain under Moscow's umbrella.

Despite American support, Gorbachev's hold on power grew steadily weaker. In August 1991, after he dissolved the Warsaw Pact alliance, Gorbachev proposed granting substantial autonomy to Soviet republics. Communist hardliners struck back on August 18, arresting Gorbachev and proclaiming a new government. The ill-planned coup collapsed three days later after Yeltsin led huge demonstrations in defense of democratic reform. Gorbachev survived as head of a largely powerless Soviet government. During the final months of 1991, Yeltsin and leaders of the republics all but ignored him. On Christmas Day, Gorbachev bowed to reality by signing a decree dissolving the Soviet Union. He resigned as president and transferred control of the government and Soviet nuclear weapons to Yeltsin, whose Russian Republic comprised about 75 percent of the territory of the former Soviet Union.

The People's Republic of China underwent nearly as profound a transformation as did the Soviet Union. During the 1980s, China's de facto leader, Deng Xiaoping, steered the world's most populous nation toward a market economy even while the Communist Party maintained a firm hand on political power. In May 1989, frustrated students and other advocates of political reform held huge protest rallies in Beijing's Tiananmen Square. Ignoring orders to disperse, the protesters erected a "goddess of democracy," modeled on the Statue of Liberty, partly in a bid to attract attention. On June 4, Deng ordered military units to clear the square and restore unchallenged communist authority. Between one thousand and three thousand civilians were shot or crushed by tanks. Vivid televised images of the violence appalled Americans. But President Bush, like Nixon, Ford, Carter, and Reagan before him, believed that China's growing importance in Asia and its surging economy outweighed calls to sever ties or even to impose harsh sanctions. Bush placed some mild trade restrictions on China but quietly passed word to Deng through a secret envoy that the United States. intended to remain a close ally regardless of domestic oppression. Many Americans ridiculed what they saw as Bush's coddling of the "butchers of Beijing."

The end of Soviet-American rivalry did not, unfortunately, initiate a golden age of peace and reason. Much of the world remained dangerous and unstable, sometimes because the old balance of power imposed by the Cold War rivals had disappeared. American military interventions continued, now justified as a defense of human rights, as humanitarian aid, as a counter to ethnic violence, as protection of energy supplies, or as suppression of the drug trade.

In Central America, the United States under Bush backed away from its hardline support for military regimes and anti-communist guerrillas. In Nicaragua in 1990, Washington ended assistance to the contras. Bush endorsed a plan for free elections devised by Latin American mediators. The resulting election accomplished what almost a decade of U.S.-supported violence had failed to—the defeat of the Sandinistas and a peaceful transition to democracy. In neighboring El Salvador, the Bush administration also encouraged a political compromise that ended the civil war in 1992.

Washington acted more forcefully in Panama, a strategically located nation ruled by a greedy despot. Manuel Noriega, a military officer and longtime CIA informant, had assumed power in 1983 after the death of Omar Torrijos, a local hero who had negotiated the treaty returning control of the canal to Panama. At various times, Noriega had cooperated with Fidel Castro, the CIA, Colombian drug lords, and foreign bankers eager to stash cash and launder drug money in Panama. During the 1980s, he assisted U.S. efforts to topple the Sandinistas. In return, the Reagan administration ignored his drug running. But as the Cold War ebbed, Noriega became an embarrassment to his American patrons.

Shortly before he left office, Reagan made a half-hearted and unsuccessful effort to push the dictator into exile. Bush, who initiated a new "war on drugs," found Noriega even more unsavory and backed several plots to remove him. Then, in 1989, Noriega voided the results of an election won by his opponents and sent thugs into the streets to beat his critics, including some Americans living in Panama. Declaring "enough is enough. This guy's not going to lay off," in December 1989 Bush dispatched twenty seven thousand American soldiers to Panama to arrest Noriega and install as president the winner of the voided election. In three days of fighting, twenty-three Americans and several hundred Panamanian civilians who got caught in the crossfire died. Put on trial in Miami, Noriega argued that Reagan had long been his silent partner in drug running. Unmoved by this defense, in 1992 a jury found him guilty, and he received a life sentence.

Iraq's invasion of the tiny but oil-rich sheikdom of Kuwait in August 1990 posed a far more serious challenge to American interests. Iraqi dictator Saddam Hussein had long coveted his wealthy neighbor, calling it a "lost province." By adding Kuwait's oil reserves to those in Iraq, Saddam could become a powerful player in the world economy, not just a local strongman. During the long Iraq-Iran war of the 1980s, the Reagan administration had partially backed Iraq while overlooking Saddam's use of poison gas against enemy soldiers and civilians. Because of its fear of Iran, the government of Kuwait had also lent money to Saddam. In 1989, to cultivate ties with Baghdad, Bush expanded the grant of generous U.S. trade credits to Iraq. American diplomats also informed Saddam that the United States did not favor either Iraq or Kuwait in their ongoing boundary dispute. The expansion of American aid, coupled with a promise not to take Kuwait's side against Iraq, may have persuaded Saddam that the Bush administration tacitly approved his plan to grab his oil-rich neighbor. By taking Kuwait, Saddam would acquire oil wealth and evade repayment of Kuwait's wartime loans.

Nevertheless, the Iraqi assault roused Bush's ire. Although Kuwait was no democracy, the Bush administration would not permit Iraq to control its oil reserves or to intimidate nearby Saudi Arabia, another major oil supplier. Calling Saddam a new Hitler who threatened the rule of law in the world, the president prevailed on the United Nations to impose an economic blockade on Iraq and sent nearly a half-million U.S. troops to the Persian Gulf region as part of a twenty-eight nation coalition force. Even the Soviet Union, formerly an arms supplier to Iraq, joined the collective effort. By mid-January 1991, diplomatic pressure had failed, and a U.N. deadline for Iraqi withdrawal passed. By a narrow margin, Congress authorized Bush to undertake military action against Saddam, who threatened to destroy all invaders in what he dubbed the "mother of all battles."

American and coalition planes began striking Iraqi targets on January 17. In launching what he dubbed "Operation Desert Storm," Bush paraphrased the words of President Woodrow Wilson, who had entered World War I with a declaration that "we have before us the opportunity to forge for ourselves a new world order." After five weeks of air attacks, the ground campaign

President Bush and First Lady Barbara Bush visit U.S. troops who liberated Kuwait, 1991. George Bush Presidential Library.

began on February 23. With Saddam's beleaguered forces putting up minimal resistance, U.S. and coalition forces quickly liberated Kuwait and pushed halfway toward Baghdad in less than one hundred hours. When Bush granted Saddam's plea for a ceasefire on February 27, only 223 coalition troops (including 148 Americans) had been killed, compared with as many as 100,000 Iraqis. Nearly all Americans—90 percent in some polls—applauded Bush's actions.

Not only had the U.S.-led coalition achieved its goal, but also it appeared to have mastered the art of low-casualty warfare. The Bush administration also tightly controlled press coverage of the fighting. It confined most journalists to headquarters in Saudi Arabia, where authorized spokesmen such as the commanding general, Norman Schwarzkopf, provided them with carefully prepared news releases and selected video footage such as that showing "smart" laser-guided bombs always hitting intended targets.

Although pleased by the quick success in freeing Kuwait from the Iraqi boot, many Americans were confused by the president's decision to leave Saddam Hussein in power. Bush and his advisers feared that removing the Iraqi strongman might open the path to power for Islamic fundamentalists within Iraq or from neighboring Iran. These religious zealots might pose an even greater threat to American interests in the region and to moderate Arab regimes than did Saddam. Whether justified or not, leaving Saddam in power created a host of later problems—for the United States and Iraq's neighbors. Many Americans came to resent Bush for leaving a job half done. Meanwhile,

" CONGRATULATIONS.... YOU WON THE COLD WAR! "

The end of the Cold War ushered in a period of uncertainty in the early 1990s. © Jim Borgman. Reprinted with permission of King Features Syndicate.

Saddam vented his wrath on thousands of Iraqi dissidents, who were slaughtered in the wake of the ceasefire.[1]

The triumph in the Cold War, along with the easy victories in Panama and Iraq, boosted Bush's popularity to unprecedented levels. Yet, just eight months after the war, polls showed only 39 percent of Americans approving of Bush's leadership. His 90 percent positive rating had vanished in record time. By 1992, continued violence in the Middle East, turmoil in parts of the old Soviet empire, chaos in Africa (where Bush dispatched a military relief column to Somalia), and a sharp economic recession at home overshadowed recent victories. Bush's two best-known phrases, "read my lips, no new taxes," and "new world order," became objects of derision. Conservative Republicans such as Patrick Buchanan mocked Bush as both a wimp and an unworthy successor to Reagan. The post–Cold War world seemed nearly as dangerous and certainly as unpredictable as before.

As a growing number of Americans questioned the value of the partial victory in Iraq, they also discovered some unpleasant side effects to the end of the Cold War, especially the "peace dividend" of reduced military spending. The decline in high-technology defense orders in the early 1990s sent painful jolts through the economy. Southern California, the center of so much defense contracting, received an especially hard hit as orders for big-ticket

---

1. Although speculative, President George W. Bush's determination in 2003 to invade Iraq and depose Saddam may have reflected a desire to rectify his father's unpopular decision a decade earlier and to avenge Saddam's unsuccessful plot to kill the elder Bush in the wake of the Gulf War.

weapons systems diminished. The sense of despair felt by some mid-career defense workers who lost their jobs was graphically portrayed in the 1993 film *Falling Down*, starring Michael Douglas. It told the story of an anonymous aerospace engineer who on one awful day loses his job, his marriage, his hope, and ultimately his life. The laid-off hero abandons his car on a jammed Los Angeles freeway and begins a violent trek through an urban underworld that culminates in a fatal shootout with police outside the home of his estranged wife. The film's plot seemed to echo a bitter joke told by presidential hopeful Senator Paul Tsongas, Democrat of Massachusetts: the "good news is that the Cold War is over; the bad news is that Germany and Japan won."

In the run-up to the 1992 presidential election, as budget and foreign trade deficits reached record levels and as millions of workers feared that foreign competition from high-tech producers such as Japan or low-wage exporters such as Mexico might soon displace them, George Bush unleashed a barrage of personal attacks upon Democratic presidential candidate Bill Clinton. He denounced Clinton's avoidance of military service during the Vietnam War as well as his admitted marijuana smoking in his youth and his alleged womanizing. Similar accusations had torpedoed past Democratic candidates. This time, as Bush discovered to his regret, they were duds.

SOURCES AND FURTHER READINGS

Among the general evaluations of Reagan-Bush-era foreign policies, several stand out for their depth, balance, and innovative research: Raymond Garthoff, *The Great Transition: American-Soviet Relations and the End of the Cold War* (1994); Don Oberdorfer, *From the Cold War to a New Era: The United States and the Soviet Union, 1983–1991* (1998); Beth Fisher, *The Reagan Reversal: Foreign Policy and the End of the Cold War* (1998); John L. Gaddis, *The United States and the End of the Cold War* (1992); Jack Matlock, *Reagan and Gorbachev: How the Cold War Ended* (2004); Michael Beschloss and Strobe Talbot, *At the Highest Levels: The Inside Story of the End of the Cold War* (1993); Philip Zelikow and Condoleeza Rice, *Germany United and Europe Transformed: A Study in Statecraft* (1995).

The argument that Reagan had a "secret plan" to win the Cold War, centered on "Star Wars," is made by Paul Lettow, *Ronald Reagan and His Quest to Abolish Nuclear Weapons* (2005); Peter Schweizer, *Reagan's War: The Epic Story of His Forty-Year Struggle and Final Triumph over Communism* (2002); Peter Schweizer, *Victory: The Reagan Administration's Secret Strategy that Hastened the Collapse of the Soviet Union* (1994); this argument is debunked by Frances Fitzgerald, *Way Out There in the Blue: Reagan, Star Wars, and the End of the Cold War* (2000); William Broad, *Teller's War: The Top Secret Story behind the Star Wars Deception* (1992). See also Michael Rogin, *Ronald Reagan, the Movie and Other Episodes in Political Demonology* (1987).

The Soviet shootdown of KAL flight 007 and its impact are discussed by Seymour Hersh, *The Target Is Destroyed: What Really Happened to Flight 007* (1987).

Among those who served as foreign policy experts in the Reagan-Bush era, the most informative personal accounts include George P. Shultz, *Triumph and Turmoil: My Years as Secretary of State* (1993); Caspar Weinberger, *Fighting for Peace: Seven*

Critical Years in the Pentagon (1990); George Bush and Brent Scowcroft, *A World Transformed* (1998); James Baker III, *The Politics of Diplomacy: Revolution, War and Peace, 1989–1992* (1995); Robert M. Gates, *From the Shadows: The Ultimate Insider's Story of Five Presidents and How They Won the Cold War* (1996); Jack Matlock, *Autopsy of an Empire: The American Ambassador's Account of the Collapse of the Soviet Union* (1995); Alexander Haig, *Caveat: Reagan, Realism, and Foreign Policy* (1984); Caspar Weinberger, *Fighting for Peace* (1990); Colin Powell with Joe Perscio, *My American Journey* (1996).

On the Soviet side, see Anatoly Dobrynin, *In Confidence: Moscow's Ambassador to America's Six Cold War Presidents, 1962–1986* (1995). Both the Garthoff and Oberdorfer books described earlier contain substantial material from Soviet sources.

For a general discussion of covert operations during the 1980s, see Steve Emerson, *Secret Warriors: Inside the Covert Operation of the Reagan Administration* (1988); Bob Woodward, *Veil: The Secret Wars of the CIA* (1987); Jonathan Kwitny, *Crimes of Patriots: A Tale of Dope, Money, and the CIA* (1987). Two outstanding accounts of operations in Afghanistan are George Crile, *Charlie Wilson's War: The Extraordinary Story of the Largest Covert Operation in History* (2003), and Steve Coll, *Ghost Wars: The Secret History of the CIA, Afghanistan, and Bin Laden, from the Soviet Invasion to September 10, 2001* (2004). Central American policies are discussed in Raymond Bonner, *Weakness and Deceit: U.S. Policy and El Salvador* (1984); Roy Gutman, *Banana Diplomacy: The Making of Policy in Nicaragua, 1981–1987* (1988); Mark Donner, *Massacre at El Mozote: A Parable of the Cold War* (1994); John Dinges, *Our Man in Panama: How General Noriega Used the United States and Made Millions in Drugs and Arms* (1990); Frederick Kempe, *Divorcing the Dictator: America's Bungled Affair with Noriega* (1990). Reagan's treatment of Philippines strongman Ferdinand Marcos is analyzed in Raymond Bonner, *Waltzing with a Dictator* (1988).

The Iran-contra scandal is the subject of several excellent books, including Jane Mayer and Doyle McManus, *Landslide: The Unmaking of the President, 1984–1988* (1988); Theodore Draper, *A Very Thin Line: The Iran-Contra Affairs* (1991); Leslie Cockburn, *Out of Control: The Story of the Reagan Administration's Secret War in Nicaragua, the Illegal Arms Pipeline, and the Contra Drug Connection* (1988); John Tower and others, *The Tower Commission Report* (1987); Lawrence E. Walsh, *The Iran-Contra Conspiracy and Coverup* (1997). Two accounts by participants are colorful but not terribly reliable. See Oliver North with William Novak, *Under Fire: An American Story* (1991) and Robert McFarlane, *Special Trust* (1994); for a sympathetic account of Reagan's role, see David Abshire, *Saving the Reagan Presidency* (2005).

Events and policies leading up to the 1991 Gulf War are discussed in Gary Sick, *October Surprise: The American Hostages in Iran and the Election of Ronald Reagan* (1991); Bruce Jentelson, *With Friends Like These: Reagan, Bush, and Saddam* (1994); Alan Friedman, *Spider's Web: The Secret Story of How the White House Illegally Armed Iraq* (1993); Rick Atkinson, *Crusade: The Untold Story of the Persian Gulf War* (1993); Stephen R. Graubard, *Mr. Bush's War: Adventures in the Politics of Illusion* (1992); Sandra Mackey, *The Reckoning: Iraq and the Legacy of Saddam Hussein* (2002).

5

WHO WANTS TO BE A MILLIONAIRE?

Law, Economics, and Society in the 1980s

> Greed is all right, by the way. I want you to know that. I think greed is healthy. You can be greedy and still feel good about yourself.
>
> IVAN BOESKY, 1986

From 1983 forward, economic recovery, swift military victories in Grenada, Panama, and Kuwait, and the eventual waning of the Cold War gave the impression that the nation's troubles had been vanquished by a combination of supply-side theory, patriotic pride, and presidential optimism. Reagan's remarkable success at communicating his ideas and faith in America created a triumphal mood that prevailed into the Bush administration. Although material life improved for some Americans, and many more were buoyed by the resurgent national spirit of the times, reality did not always match either president's glowing rhetoric. Some old problems deepened, and some disturbing new economic and social trends arose. Yet, through 1991, political leaders and the mass media often ignored or minimized these issues.

During the 1980s and beyond, conservatives pointed to economic growth—along with "winning" the Cold War—as their signal accomplishment. Consumer spending (along with consumer debt) boomed with the rise of new discount giants such as Wal-Mart. Annual sales by this Arkansas upstart grew from $1.6 billion in 1980 to $20.6 billion in 1988. Other innovative retailers such as Circuit City and Home Depot captured more specialized market niches.

Traveling along the nation's interstate highways, motorists discovered a Wal-Mart strategically located within an hour's drive of clusters of small towns whose own main street businesses had often been driven out by "big box" competition. Some considered this development a triumph of discount marketing that made inexpensive goods widely available. Others mourned the lost sense of community as main street shopping districts disappeared from both small towns and many urban downtowns. Wal-Mart shelves bulged with products made mostly in low-wage foreign factories, contributing to the further erosion of U.S. manufacturing jobs.

Some economists and many labor leaders warned about the erosion of the nation's manufacturing base, but workers had difficulty stopping this juggernaut. Only a few unionized industries, such as automobile manufacturing, retained enough clout to bring pressure on national leaders to intervene on their behalf. For example, in 1981 members of the United Automobile Workers (UAW) rallied near Chicago to protest the growing share of the domestic market taken by Japanese car makers. Under a banner that read "If You Sell in America, Build in America," UAW members mugged before TV cameras as they demolished a Toyota with sledgehammers. In this instance, Reagan got the message and convinced Japan to cap for several years the number of cars exported. This "voluntary export restraint," really a quota, bought some time for U.S. automakers but had little impact on the overall growing trade imbalance between America and the rest of the world.

As a candidate for president, Reagan ridiculed Carter's "runaway" deficit of nearly $80 billion and the cumulative national debt of almost $1 trillion. Addressing Congress in 1981 shortly after his election, Reagan charged that liberal Democrats had mortgaged the nation's future to finance big government's voracious appetites. Yet, over the next twelve years the Reagan and Bush administrations ran up annual deficits that ranged from $128 billion to nearly $300 billion. The national debt tripled to almost $3 trillion by 1988 and grew by $1 trillion more during the Bush presidency. Paying the annual interest tab of over $200 billion became the third-largest item in the federal budget. "Tax-and-spend liberals" had been replaced by "borrow-and-spend conservatives." Borrowed money, of course, would *eventually* have to be repaid, either by tax increases or program cuts, but that would occur on someone else's watch.

Reagan and Bush dodged responsibility for any of this. Instead, they accused Democrats in Congress of squandering funds on new and wasteful social programs. In fact, new social spending programs were few and far between during the 1980s and early 1990s, and neither president ever submitted a balanced budget proposal to Congress. Most of the tide of red ink flowed first from Reagan's insistence on increasing defense spending while reducing tax rates and then from Bush's embrace of tax cuts. When both Reagan and Bush endorsed proposed constitutional amendments mandating a balanced budget, they stipulated that it should apply only to their successors. Proclaiming the virtue of a balanced budget while driving the deficit ever higher resembled, as one Washington wag put it, "a drunk preaching temperance."

To be sure, when Reagan had pushed large tax cuts and massive defense increases through Congress, lawmakers had balked at making countervailing cuts in popular entitlement programs such as Social Security and Medicare. But Reagan and later Bush, like Congress, happily placated the public's wish to *both* pay lower taxes and still receive generous benefits. Inevitably, this policy compounded the deficit problem. The executive and legislative branches gave the appearance of austerity by making numerous small cuts to programs that primarily aided the poor.

Because the Treasury had to borrow so much money to fund the deficit, fewer public and private dollars were available for investment in research, new plants, and machinery. Although the country began the 1980s with a positive trade balance in manufactured goods, the flow soon turned negative. The foreign trade deficit grew dramatically, surpassing $150 billion per year by the second half of the decade. On average, every week during the Reagan-Bush years, American consumers purchased about $2 billion more on imported goods than foreigners spent on American goods. To see this inequity practice, one merely had to walk down any aisle in a Wal-Mart or Circuit City and view the country of origin for most of what lay on the shelves. The cumulative trade imbalance for the decade approached $1 trillion and kept growing after 1990. This imbalance put pressure on the dollar as well as on domestic manufacturers, who could not compete with the influx of lower-cost foreign goods. They, in turn, cut jobs at American plants.

One area in which the Reagan administration did cut costs was aid to states. The president spoke of a "new federalism" in which local government would assume greater power and responsibility. In reality, Reagan and then Bush shifted costs, not power, to the states. Washington imposed new and often expensive "unfunded mandates" on the states to perform duties such as monitor air and water pollution, remove asbestos from school buildings, and supervise nursing homes. The federal government also deferred scheduled maintenance and repairs of the national highway system. All told, during the 1980s, federal allocations to states fell by almost 13 percent in real dollars. To pay for vital and mandated services, many states raised taxes, negating a large part of the federal income tax reduction at the heart of Reaganomics.

THE CULTURE OF GREED

In 1986, financier Ivan F. Boesky addressed graduating business students at the University of California at Berkeley. Boesky, celebrated for his success at buying shares of stock in companies about to be acquired in lucrative mergers, told his audience on a campus once renowned for its social activism that "greed is healthy." This child of immigrant parents explained that earning and flaunting great wealth (he made $100 million in 1985) were the driving force of capitalism, the key to growth and prosperity. After hearing him celebrate the free market, students rushed to read his new book, *Merger Mania*, which stressed the "tried and true virtues of hard work, common sense and luck." That autumn, however, the Justice Department charged Boesky with multiple violations of security laws. He pleaded guilty to buying inside information from corporate officials, which he used to manipulate stock prices and acquire companies cheaply, pocketing huge sums in ill-gotten gains. Boesky's experience mirrored the ambiguities of the new economic environment.

Film director Oliver Stone chronicled the rise and fall of Gordon Gecko, a Boesky-like tycoon played by actor Michael Douglas in the 1987 movie *Wall Street*, a cautionary tale about the era's glitter and deceit. Like his real-life prototype, Gecko specialized in acquiring companies through "leveraged buyouts," a fancy term for borrowed money. He then sold off or "stripped" assets of the acquired company to repay the loans and to bag a profit. Often, however, little remained of the original company or its jobs. In one of the film's key sequences, Gecko proclaims at a company pep rally that "greed is good, greed is healthy" because it promotes growth and success. Ultimately, in this case of art imitating life, Gecko is unmasked as a crook who built a fortune on deceit and lawbreaking.

For all the talk of new prosperity, the economic expansion of the 1980s was highly selective. Prosperity and wealth tended to flow to both coasts, partly because of heavy defense spending, technological innovation in those areas, and real estate speculation fueled by easy loans. The Northeast and California boomed. After severe doldrums in the 1970s, cities such as Boston and Manhattan blossomed again during the 1980s as real estate prices skyrocketed for both residential and commercial property.

At the same time, much of the upper Midwest experienced a loss of high-paying industrial jobs, continuing the decline that began in the 1970s. For example, employment in the steel industry fell by 58 percent during the 1980s as foreign competitors flooded the world with cheaper steel. In addition, farm states and energy-producing states staggered. Small farmers abandoned the land in accelerating numbers, while cities such as Houston, buffeted by falling energy prices, faced economic disaster. As Reagan spoke of "morning in America," the sun set on many traditional industries and small farms, and the Southwest experienced a prolonged recession.

Viewed in aggregate, the economy certainly improved from 1981 to 1991. As measured in current dollars (not counting for inflation), both the gross domestic product and per capita income doubled. Reagan and his aides also pointed out that they did not destroy what they called the "safety net" for the old, sick, poor, and disabled. They noted that changes in tax law allowed six million low-wage earners to avoid paying any federal income tax. As for the rich, by 1990 they paid a higher percentage of total income tax than they had paid in 1980. All told, conservatives argued, Reaganomics had achieved a trifecta: it tamed inflation, stimulated growth, and created a rising tide that raised all ships. Although they acknowledged that income inequality increased, Reagan's boosters stressed that per capita income (a measure of the average per person—that is, a millionaire and homeless person in a room together had a per capita income of $500,000) grew by 18 percent even when adjusted for inflation. Despite the rocky early 1980s, the economy added over eighteen million jobs during the decade. Reagan's pollster, Richard Wirthlin, boasted that "growth is the best alternative we can offer to the Democrats' state welfarism."

When examined more closely, however, the long economic expansion of the Reagan-Bush years was less impressive than it appeared. The record from 1982 to 1992 showed a marked improvement only when compared to the period

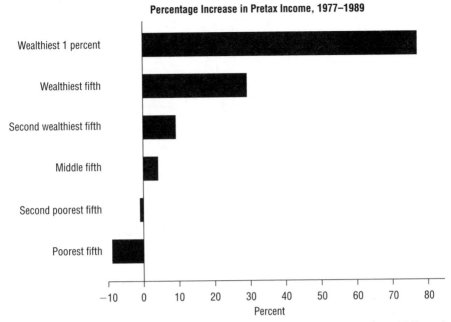

Percentage Increase in Pretax Income, 1977–1989

During the 1980s, the wealthiest Americans got richer, while those in the middle and lower classes fared poorly.

1978–1982. When placed beside the entire period from 1945 to 1980, the achievement appeared more modest. During most of the 1980s the inflation rate was twice as high as the average for the years from 1947 to 1967. Unemployment also remained higher than in most years between 1947 and 1973. Overall, the economy grew no faster and created no more jobs during the 1980s than it had during the 1960s and 1970s or would during the 1990s. Despite tax incentives and other breaks for the well-to-do, the rates of personal savings and investment—supposedly a prerequisite for growth—did not improve.

Continuing a trend of the 1970s, real wages (earnings adjusted for inflation) remained stagnant; in fact, salaries declined slightly on average during the 1980s, although the impact was hidden by an increase in the number of working wives and mothers whose earnings boosted total family income. About half of the 18.5 million jobs created between 1981 and 1990 paid minimum or low wages, often without medical and other benefits.

Meanwhile, incomes soared for the richest Americans. Between 1945 and 1973, one of the notable achievements of the economy was its fairly even distribution of steadily rising incomes. In contrast, from 1981 to 1991, the richest 20 percent of Americans realized most of the income gains, with the top 1 percent doing best of all. In 1980, a typical corporate chief executive officer (CEO) made about forty times the income of an average factory worker; nine years later the CEO made ninety-three times as much.

For several reasons, including lower tax rates on the rich and rising stock prices, the number of people who earned salaries of at least $1 million

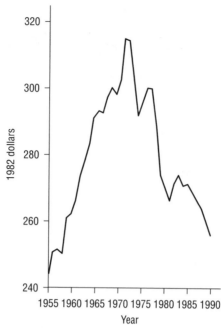

Real average weekly wages, 1955–1990.

annually increased dramatically. About 4,400 Americans occupied this elite category in 1980. Their ranks swelled to almost thirty-five thousand in 1986 and to almost sixty-five thousand by 1994. Reagan-Bush-era policies nearly doubled the share of national income going to the wealthiest 1 percent of Americans, from 8.1 percent to about 15 percent. Over 60 percent of income growth during the 1980s went to this top 1 percent. Wealth (the measure of accumulated worth rather than annual earnings) also trickled up rather than down. In 1979, the top 1 percent of Americans possessed 22 percent of the nation's total wealth. By the early 1990s, their share rose to 40 percent. Looked at another way, the top 1 percent of American households (834,000) held more wealth ($5.7 trillion) than did the bottom 90 percent ($4.8 trillion) comprised of eighty-four million households. This skewed profile resembled the distribution of wealth in the 1920s, before the introduction of progressive taxes. By the early 1990s, the gap among rich, middle class, and poor was bigger than at any time since 1945.

Economists attributed these growing disparities to several factors. The rising value of stocks and reduced tax rates benefited the wealthy most, boosting their net worth. At the same time, the incomes of skilled workers fell with the rise of automation, the decline of union power, the increasing number of service jobs, the growing use of part-time workers, and the foreign outsourcing of many higher-paid manufacturing jobs. A widening education pay gap also skewed incomes. For example, in 1980, a college graduate earned about 49 percent more than a high school graduate. By the early 1990s, the gap had grown to 83 percent.

Labor and Democratic leaders attacked Reagan–Bush-era economic policies as harmful to average Americans. In 1981, AFL-CIO chief Lane Kirkland characterized Reaganomics as "economic Darwinism, the survival of the richest." House Speaker Tip O'Neill charged that Reagan had created government "of the rich, by the rich, and for the rich." A Democratic campaign slogan in 1984 proclaimed, "It isn't fair. It's Republican."

Whether accurate or not, these criticisms gained little traction before 1992. Most Americans agreed that Democratic politicians cared more about helping the poor, working, and middle classes. But the same majority also saw the Democratic Party as ineffective. Many middle- and upper-class Americans, and especially white southerners, caricatured Democrats as little more than tax collectors for the welfare state. Many moderate- and low-income voters sensed that although Republican politicians might be allies of big business, they at least delivered some economic growth. Limited gains under Reagan and Bush appeared better than the losses under Carter.

During the 1980s, acquiring and flaunting great wealth became a source of public celebration. Money became the measure of one's value to society. Some of the decade's most popular television shows, such as *Dallas* and *Dynasty*, chronicled the flamboyant business and personal lives of rich extended families. Robin Leach, host of the reality TV show *Lifestyles of the Rich and Famous,* signed off with his trademark sound bite, "May you have caviar wishes and champagne dreams." Outspoken conservatives and "supply siders," such as New York Congressman Jack Kemp, economist Arthur Laffer, and writers Jude Wanniski and George Gilder, described financiers and deal-makers as secular saints who enriched society and deserved vast rewards. In his best-selling books, *Wealth and Poverty* (1981) and *The Spirit of Enterprise* (1986), and in frequent opinion columns in the *Wall Street Journal*, Gilder described capitalism as akin to religion. "Faith in man, faith in the future, faith in the return of giving, faith in the mutual benefits of trade, faith in the providence of God are all essential to successful capitalism," he proclaimed. Accumulating wealth represented the highest morality. Only losers blamed the system for their problems. The poor suffered because they "refused to work hard." President Reagan quoted Gilder frequently and in 1986 conferred upon him the White House Award for Entrepreneurial Excellence.

The real heroes of the age were flamboyant Wall Street operators such as Carl Icahn, T. Boone Pickens, Ivan Boesky, and Michael Milken and real estate speculator Donald Trump—men who earned billions of dollars buying and merging companies and constructing new office towers, apartment complexes, and resorts. Not since the days of the so-called robber barons in the nineteenth century had business leaders publicly voiced sentiments such as Boesky's ode to greed or Trump's boast that "I like beating my enemies to the ground."

Deal-makers and the financial institutions and money managers who backed them became celebrities during the 1980s. The deregulation of financial markets generated a great deal of media attention as people of even modest means followed discussions about new "financial instruments" such

Real estate magnate Donald Trump prepares to take a ride in his helicopter, 1980s. AP/Wide World Photos.

as 0-coupon bonds, options, stock index futures, mortgage-backed securities, and junk bonds. Employment in brokerages and investment firms doubled during the 1980s, while the number of shares traded on the nation's stock exchanges each year skyrocketed from twelve billion to more than forty billion. Wall Street, like Hollywood, became a glamour industry.

The "merger mania" of the 1980s reflected more than a natural evolution of capitalism. Changes in the 1981 tax law and the Justice Department's decisions in 1982 and in 1984 to relax enforcement of antitrust laws promoted a fever on Wall Street that burned for most of the decade. In 1980, about 1,500 companies had merged in deals valued at $32 billion. In 1987, 4,400 mergers valued at over $200 billion took place. Corporate raiders sometimes raised money by issuing so-called junk bonds, risky debt-bearing high-interest rates. Despite the costs, movers and shakers such as Boesky argued that these deals rewarded stockholders, eliminated incompetent management, and increased competitiveness.

Many of the nation's largest corporations, including R. J. Reynolds, Nabisco, Walt Disney, Gulf, Federated Department Stores, and R. H. Macy, were the objects of leveraged buyouts, some willingly and some under protest. Costly mergers did not necessarily or even often produce a more competitive company. The debt burden produced by mergers often left businesses unable to raise new funds for investment in plants and updated technology. Downstream profits went mostly to paying off bondholders. But the merger process generated immense fees for those arranging the takeovers, issuing junk bonds, or acting as consultants to the deals. For example, in 1987 Michael Milken earned about $550 million in fees. At age forty, he became a billionaire.

The merger mania slowed before the end of the decade. Following Boesky's conviction late in 1986, a series of investigations revealed widespread insider trading among many of the most successful financiers and institutions. In 1990, Milken received a ten-year sentence for financial fraud as well as a $600 million fine. Many others pled guilty to a variety of illegal practices. Drexel, Burnham, Lambert, Inc., Milken's trading firm and the giant of the junk bond industry, admitted to breaking the law and went bankrupt.

New tax and retirement policies had partly fueled the 1980s boom on Wall Street. Many small investors, wary of picking stocks, felt more secure putting money into mutual funds run by experts. Much of the money they invested came from individual retirement accounts (IRAs) and 401K retirement plans, which took their name from a provision in the tax code. During the 1980s, new rules permitted Americans to put up to $2,000 annually into an IRA and even more (depending on income) into 401K tax-deferred retirement accounts. At first, most of these funds went into traditional bank accounts. But as the public watched the rising value of stock indexes, people decided to get into the game. By the later 1980s, at least half of these retirement dollars went into stocks. Of course, to take advantage of these tax savings, you had to have surplus income beyond that needed for day-to-day living. This fact meant that higher-income Americans, not those of middle or lower income, benefited most from these tax-deferred retirement plans.

When the stock market bubble burst on October 19, 1987, known thereafter as "Black Thursday," the Dow Jones stock average fell over five hundred points. Curious and alarmed crowds of journalists, tourists, and investors milled around the New York Stock Exchange building that afternoon. Amidst the tumult, a man shouted, "The end is near! It's all over for the yuppies! Down with MBAs! It's all over! The Reagan Revolution is over!" A group of brokers attempted to restore calm by yelling back, "Whoever dies with the most toys wins!"

Over the next two years, the stock market regained its value. Fueled by a new bubble in computer and other technology companies, stock indexes rose much higher during the 1990s. But partly as a result of the crash of 1987, the junk bond market shrank dramatically, the number of large mergers decreased, and many heavily indebted companies defaulted on payments.

THE OTHER AMERICANS

As he did so often, Ronald Reagan got off one of the era's most memorable quips about poverty. For twenty years, he remarked, "We fought a war on poverty, but poverty won." As proof, he cited the nearly identical rate of poverty—about 13 percent—in 1963 and 1980. But this comparison obscured key facts. Before the Great Society reforms of Medicare, Medicaid, food stamps, and Social Security expansion, the elderly and disabled comprised the bulk of the poor. By 1980, these groups were much better off. The "new poor" consisted mostly of women and children.

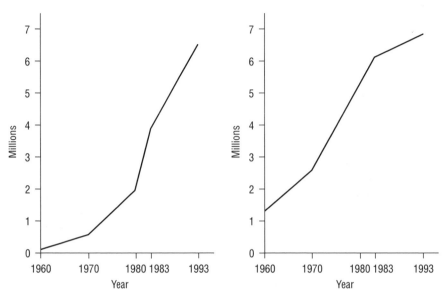

(left) Number of children living with single, never-married parent. (right) Number of children living with single, divorced parent. Results from the Census Bureau's annual report on marital status and living arrangements.

The prevailing attitude among conservatives during the Reagan-Bush era held that past efforts by liberals to reduce inequality and help the poor, although well intentioned, had been too costly and counterproductive. In 1984, social critic Charles Murray, whose research was generously supported by conservative groups such as the Manhattan Institute, the Scaife and Olin foundations, and the Liberty Fund, wrote the influential book *Losing Ground*. Murray argued that when the government "tried to provide more for the poor," it ended up "producing more poor instead." In its effort to remove barriers to progress through increased aid, affirmative action, and other remedies, government "inadvertently built a trap." White House Counselor Edwin Meese declared in 1984 that the "broken families, dependent mothers, and fatherless children that were spawned by a decade of aimless spending are the real victims of a well-meaning but misguided system of government aid and regulations."

Conservative economists such as Milton Friedman pointed out the fault he saw in making equality a primary goal. By doing so, "you end up with a society neither rich nor free." But a society that put freedom first ended up with both greater freedom and increased equality. Reagan's budget director, David Stockman, insisted that equality was a bogus principle for government to concern itself with. Government's only responsibility to the people was providing a modest safety net for those truly incapable of providing for themselves. "To go beyond that and seek to level incomes is morally wrong and practically destructive," he argued.

As the gap between richer and poorer Americans widened to the largest it had been since 1945, poverty increasingly became the lot of women and

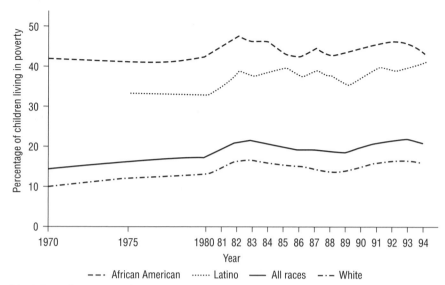

The ethnic dimension of poverty in America.

children. The "feminization" of poverty grew more severe during the 1980s, partly because of the rising rate of children born to single mothers. The rate of children living with a never-married mother soared by 70 percent between 1983 and 1993. In the early 1980s, 3.7 million children under age eighteen lived with a single parent who had never married. A decade later, 6.3 million children, or 27 percent of all children, lived with a never-married parent. An additional five to seven million children lived with single, divorced parents. In fact, after 1980, nearly half of all new marriages ended in divorce.

By the early 1990s, 25 percent of births in the United States were to unwed mothers; the rate for African-American and Hispanic women was about 50 and 33 percent, respectively. Compared with married women, unwed mothers were less likely to receive prenatal care, finish high school, or hold a paying job. The Reagan administration made the situation worse by slashing funds for the Women, Infants, and Children (WIC) program and other programs that provided prenatal and postnatal care to poor women and their children.

Although some of these funds were restored during the Bush administration, by 1992 about 22 percent of all American children under age eighteen lived in poverty. Among Hispanics and African-Americans, the numbers rose to 29 and 47 percent, respectively. One-third of thirty-four million Americans who lived below the poverty line resided in female-headed households. The overall poverty rate during the Reagan-Bush era hovered around 13 percent, about the average for the 1970s. The racial and ethnic profile of the poor remained highly skewed. In 1990, the poverty rate for whites was 10.7 percent; for Hispanics 28.1 percent; and for blacks 31.9 percent.

One of the most troubling economic trends of this period was the sharp increase in the number of people who worked full-time but could not lift them-

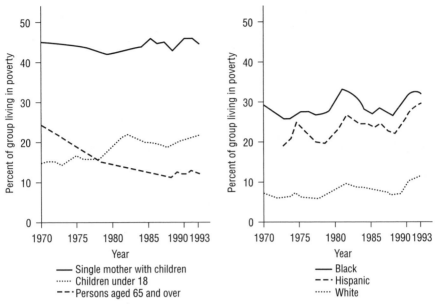

Poverty: the age and race factors.

selves and their families out of poverty. The number of Americans working full-time but earning less than a poverty-level income of about $13,000 per year for a family of four in 1991 rose by 50 percent from 1979 to 1992, from 12 percent to 18 percent. The trend toward lower wages was particularly sharp for young workers and those without college degrees.

The movement of so many manufacturing and service jobs out of cities and into new industrial and technology parks in the nation's suburbs—if not overseas—had an especially harsh impact on urban-based minority workers. Whereas more-educated and more-mobile African-Americans, for example, fared economically somewhat better during the 1980s, less-educated and lower-skilled African-Americans suffered a real decline in income and living standards.

This division held true for many women workers as well. At the start of the 1980s, women earned, on average, about 58 percent as much as men. Their average earnings rose to 68 percent by 1989. But this improvement reflected the entry of a large number of younger, better-educated professional women into the labor market. As a group, they earned about 80 percent of men's wages, much more than their less-educated and less-skilled sisters.

The growing phenomenon of homelessness and the worsening plight of a seemingly unreachable "underclass" alarmed both conservatives and liberals during the 1980s. The homeless included a variety of people, from women fleeing abusive spouses to the chronically mentally ill displaced by the closing of state mental institutions in the 1970s. Many lived on urban streets or in subway stations, begging for money and food. The plight of the homeless and urban underclass shocked public sensibilities, but it did not affect policy.

White House "spinners" deflected Democratic charges of Republican callousness by highlighting Reagan's uplifting rhetoric and life story. Aides stressed Reagan's humble background, his record of hard work and achievement, and his union activism as past leader of the Screen Actors Guild. To counter the Democrats' portrayal of him as an insensitive economic royalist, Reagan's handlers arranged for him to be photographed attending charity fundraisers, hosting Special Olympics for the handicapped, and speaking at events promoting education.

Proclaiming a doctrine of conservative populism, Reagan called the Republican Party the natural home of disillusioned working-class Democrats. As he put it an a speech in 1988, when the "left took over the Democratic Party, we [conservatives] took over the Republican Party. We made the Republican Party into the party of the working people, the family, the neighborhood, the defense of freedom, and yes, the American flag and the Pledge of Allegiance to one nation under God." The old Democratic Party "still exists," he explained, "except today it's called the Republican Party."

GOVERNMENT DEREGULATION AND THE PRIVATE SECTOR

Government regulation of business, the environment, and banking had been among the most important innovations of the New Deal. Conservative economists and some business leaders criticized government interference with market forces, even though regulators argued that they had improved markets by keeping them honest. Now, as the public expressed its own doubts about the competence of government, the Reagan administration initiated a major assault on federal regulatory powers. The Office of Management and Budget, the Commerce Department, a presidential commission chaired by businessman Peter Grace, and a task force headed by Vice President George H. W. Bush proposed eliminating hundreds of rules, including those dealing with hazardous waste disposal, air pollution, nuclear safety, workplace exposure to chemicals, and automobile fuel efficiency and safety.

During the late 1970s, the Carter administration began eliminating regulations that inhibited competition in the transportation and communication sectors. These eliminations lowered prices in the airline, railroad, trucking, and telecommunications industries. As a result of a federal lawsuit in 1981–1982, the nearly century-long telephone monopoly enjoyed by AT&T and its Bell System ended as AT&T spun off several local providers, and new companies entered the business. The newly competitive phone business led to improved service, lower rates, and technological innovation.

Reagan carried this policy much further because the president and his advisers saw virtually all government regulation as anticompetitive. In February 1981, he issued an executive order requiring federal agencies to perform cost-benefit studies of proposed new regulations to find the least costly alternatives. New appointees to federal agencies abolished many rules, rang-

President Reagan poses with his acerbic secretary of the interior, James Watt, 1981. David Hume Kennedy/Getty Images.

ing from those mandating stronger car bumpers to those placing environmental restraints on offshore oil drilling. This blasé attitude was typified by Reagan's choice to head the Federal Communications Commission, Mark S. Fowler. Dismissing calls to regulate broadcasting more carefully, Fowler described television as "just another appliance, a toaster with pictures." Ed Gray, whom Reagan chose to supervise the deregulated home loan industry, eventually came to regret the policy. The "administration was so ideologically blinded," Gray lamented, "that it couldn't understand the difference between" lowering airfares and removing vital oversight from parts of the banking system.

The budgets for federal regulatory agencies fell an average of 12 percent, and funding for the Environmental Protection Agency (EPA), the Occupational Safety and Health Administration (OSHA), and the Securities and Exchange Commission (SEC) was slashed, ostensibly to save tax dollars. Because of resulting staff shortages, these agencies were often unable to enforce regulations even if they wanted to. In a number of cases, Reagan appointed agency heads, such as Anne Gorsuch Burford of the EPA and James Watt of the Department of the Interior, who were openly hostile to the very regulations they purportedly enforced and who devoted their energies to weakening environmental protections.

Partly because he relished public attention, Interior Secretary James Watt became the point man for the deregulation crusade. Before joining the Reagan administration, Watt had founded the Mountain States Legal Foundation, a conservative antienvironmental, prodevelopment advocacy group partly funded by Joseph Coors. Describing the nation as divided between "liberals and Americans," Watt justified accelerated commercial development of federal lands by invoking the Bible. Scripture, he argued, "calls on us to occupy the land until Jesus returns." He interpreted this to mean that wilderness should be exploited, and he boasted that under his leadership "we will mine more, drill more, cut more timber." Reagan appointed Watt's protégé, Anne Gorsuch Burford, as head of the EPA. Her mismanagement (compounded by that of her top aide, Rita Lavelle) of funds earmarked for cleaning up chemical spills eventually led to Congress citing her for contempt. This development, and other legal troubles, forced her resignation. Two dozen top EPA appointees were either removed from office or resigned under fire. Lavelle went to jail.

Watt's aggressive antienvironmental actions included efforts to open up sensitive areas in Alaska, along the coasts, and in wilderness zones for energy development. He ordered that no more lands be acquired for federal parks and that no more animals or plants be placed on the endangered species list. Although a popular speaker and fundraiser for conservative causes, Watt became such a lightning rod for criticism that he could not implement most of his radical plans. He ultimately ran afoul of the president and first lady for his personal remarks rather than his public policies. In July 1982, he angered Nancy Reagan by barring the Beach Boys, a musical group she admired, from singing at a festival on the Washington Mall. In place of the Beach Boys, he invited Las Vegas lounge singer Wayne Newton. The last straw came in September 1983 when Watt sarcastically told a breakfast meeting of the U.S. Chamber of Commerce that he had appointed an advisory panel that included "every kind of mix you can have." It consisted of "three Democrats, two Republicans . . . a black . . . a woman, two Jews, and a cripple." With the Senate poised to condemn him, Watt resigned from the cabinet. William Clark, an equally conservative but less abrasive friend of Reagan, took over the Interior post.

Relaxed regulations, along with Reagan's indifferent attitude toward conflicts of interest among government officials, led to controversial policies or outright scandals in several government agencies during the 1980s. Close Reagan aides, including Michael Deaver and Lyn Nofziger, were convicted of ethics violations and influence peddling after they left White House service in the mid-1980s. Edwin Meese, first-term presidential counsel and second-term attorney general, barely escaped indictment by a special prosecutor for his personal involvement with the Wedtech corporation, a thoroughly corrupt Defense Department contractor. U.S. Attorney Rudolph Giuliani summed up the view of many in the Justice Department by calling the attorney general "a sleaze."

Besides problems at Interior and the EPA, major scandals costing taxpayers billions of dollars occurred in federal housing programs and Defense Department military procurements. Under Reagan, annual funds for the Department of Housing and Urban Development fell from $33 billion to $14 billion. HUD Secretary Samuel Pierce and his deputies steered billions of dollars in the remaining budget to cronies who used the money to build luxury apartments and golf courses, not low-income housing. After leaving the Interior Department, James Watt earned a half-million dollars merely by placing a few phone calls to friends in HUD on behalf of a construction company that hired him as a consultant. When asked by congressional investigators to justify this windfall, Watt retorted that just because the "system was flawed," that was no reason he should not profit from it. In 1990, Congress concluded that throughout the Reagan years HUD was "enveloped by influence peddling, favoritism, abuse, greed, fraud, embezzlement, and theft."

Midway through the two Reagan terms, congressional committees had exposed fifty cases of misconduct, mismanagement, or fraud by presidential appointees. In 1988, several dozen Defense Department officials and military contractors were convicted of rigging bids and faking quality control tests. By the early 1990s, at least two hundred Reagan appointees had been investigated and indicted for criminal acts related to their job performance.

But the worst instance of ideologically driven deregulation resulted in the collapse of the savings and loan (S&L) industry, a debacle sometimes called the "biggest bank job ever." The S&L debacle of the early 1990s resulted directly from mindless deregulation. Since the 1970s, savings and loan institutions, or "thrifts," had lost depositors because unregulated money-market funds paid higher rates of interest. To make commercial banks and S&Ls more competitive and to attract new deposits, Congress in 1980, at the end of the Carter administration, passed legislation that raised the federal insurance level to $100,000 on individual accounts and lifted the cap on interest rates. Two years later, Reagan convinced Congress to further deregulate S&Ls. Previously S&Ls made only low-risk loans, usually for the purchase of single-family homes. Under the new rules, they could invest depositors' funds in office parks, shopping malls, antique cars, bull sperm banks, or virtually anything else. The argument ran that bolder (i.e., riskier) loans would generate higher returns that attracted new depositors and increased the funds available for future home mortgages. If bad loans caused an S&L to collapse, depositors' accounts were protected by a government insurance pool. S&L owners had little personal liability.

S&L deregulation in the 1980s sparked a commercial construction boom for strip malls (whose number increased from twenty-two thousand to thirty-six thousand) and office buildings as the S&Ls lent money to hopefully high-yielding but risky ventures. Unfortunately, some S&L executives, such as the notorious Charles Keating, formerly an antipornography crusader in Ohio and now head of Lincoln Savings and Loan in California, colluded with builders to drive up the cost of commercial projects, producing bigger fees for all the principals. Keating's strategies for raising money included selling large amounts of uninsured "junk bonds" to unsuspecting bank customers. "The weak, meek, and ignorant are always good targets," he told his sales staff. Unscrupulous S&L executives also made dubious loans to business partners or paid themselves exorbitant salaries.

As early as the mid-1980s, many S&Ls were teetering on the brink of collapse. But rather than reining in the out-of-control lending policies, the Reagan administration cooperated with influential Democratic and Republican members of Congress who had industry ties to block stricter regulations. Then, in 1986, the major income tax reform bill reduced the tax benefit that wealthy investors received from putting money into commercial properties built with S&L loans.[1] Some investors simply defaulted on mortgages that no longer brought them tax breaks. Others stopped putting new money into what had become dubious commercial real estate. Soon the S&L industry found itself buried under a mountain of bad debt and vacant properties. Timely intervention by federal regulators might have contained the debacle by closing down badly run institutions. But S&L executives such as Charles Keating and the president's son Neil (head of a Colorado S&L) with close ties to both the White House and influential members of Congress, including Senator John McCain, lobbied successfully to keep business going as usual even as losses mounted.

A series of stopgap measures delayed the collapse of the S&L industry until after Reagan retired. Shortly after Bush took office in 1989, hundreds of S&Ls failed. To prevent a broader and costlier collapse, Congress created the Resolution Trust Corporation to take over a huge inventory of vacant buildings and obligations from the failed S&Ls. At a cost to taxpayers of several hundred billion dollars, this was the biggest bank heist in the nation's history. Yet, neither during nor after his presidency did Reagan ever bother to acknowledge the HUD, EPA, S&L, or military procurement scandals. (As for Iran-contra, he explained that he intended no wrong.) For the "Teflon president," it was as if they never happened. Perhaps because they involved complicated schemes, huge sums of money beyond the capacity of most people to understand, and presidential appointees rather than Reagan himself, the public remained largely indifferent to the Reagan scandals. In contrast, President Bill Clinton's personal and sexual transgressions, even though they involved neither much money nor public policy, fueled media-driven cries of outrage, his impeachment, and his near-removal from office.

CIVIL RIGHTS AND CONSERVATIVE JUSTICE

"Conservatives have waited over thirty years for this day," commented Richard Viguerie, a leading New Right fundraiser, when President Reagan nom-

---

1. Until 1986, most losses on commercial real estate investments could be deducted from other profits earned by a taxpayer. But the 1986 tax reform eliminated this provision, meaning that operating losses from, say, an office complex could not be used to reduce other income taxes owed by the investor. Thus, there was no year-to-year tax benefit to investing in or holding onto a money-losing venture in hope that its value would increase in the long run and when sold at a hoped-for profit would be taxed at a lower rate as a capital gain.

inated Judge Robert H. Bork in July 1987 to a vacant seat on the Supreme Court. Viguerie's remarks revealed anger that had accumulated since the Court's 1954 desegregation decision and many subsequent rulings by the Warren Court that expanded civil rights and liberties.

Like most conservatives, Reagan and Bush had criticized numerous Supreme Court decisions since the 1950s. Both presidents, along with other Republican leaders, complained that morally lax rulings by activist liberal judges had coddled criminals, promoted premarital sex and abortion, banished religion from public schools, and violated private property.

Reagan was especially critical of efforts by the federal courts and Congress to promote civil rights for minorities and equal rights for women. As governor of California, he had urged the legislature to repeal laws that barred property owners from discriminating in rentals on the basis of race. Reagan and George H. W. Bush had both opposed landmark legislation such as the 1964 Civil Rights Act, claiming it infringed on property rights. Reagan described the Voting Rights Act of 1965 as "humiliating" to southerners— apparently not counting the region's millions of disenfranchised blacks as noteworthy. Reagan was not "racist" in the narrow meaning of the term. When asked about his racial views he often recalled how while in high school he and his family had befriended black athletes shunned by teammates. Reagan's perception of race focused almost entirely on his personal feelings, not on the realities of life faced by minority groups. He could be remarkably obtuse on the subject. For example, when dining with the African-American GOP senator from Massachusetts, Edward Brooke, Reagan joked that in Africa "when they have a man for lunch, they really have a man for lunch."

Reagan, Bush, and many other Republicans believed in "conservative egalitarianism," the notion that government should oppose *both* racial discrimination and legal efforts to advance the rights of any group—even if members of the group, such as African-Americans or women, had suffered past injustice in areas such as education, housing, and employment. They also condemned affirmative action as, in effect, "reverse discrimination" against whites and men. The 1980 Republican platform stated that true "equal opportunity should not be jeopardized by bureaucratic regulation and decisions which rely on quotas, ratios, and numerical requirements to exclude some individuals in favor of others, thereby rendering such regulations and decisions inherently discriminatory."

Reagan excelled at using the language of liberty and freedom to justify doing nothing to challenge the racial and economic inequality inherent in the status quo. In practice, the administration sided with those who cited the principle of conservative egalitarianism to oppose "special privileges" conferred by government in areas beyond race. For example, recognizing labor unions as the agent of workers, requiring employers to pay minimum wages, and providing the progressive income tax, welfare programs, and food stamps were all labeled special privileges that unfairly discriminated in favor of or against certain Americans. In pursuit of equality, they violated liberty.

Reagan's own discomfort with addressing racial problems and implicit support for the Nixon-era "southern strategy" of expanding the GOP appeal among white southerners and blue-collar northern Democrats showed in several ways. He endorsed a constitutional amendment to outlaw school busing, opposed a federal holiday honoring Martin Luther King Jr., attempted to restore tax benefits to private segregated schools (disallowed by the IRS under Carter), and called for gutting the 1965 Voting Rights Act when it came up for renewal in 1982. Only strong opposition by congressional Democrats and several Supreme Court rulings (including an eight-to-one decision in 1983 against restoring tax breaks to private segregated academies) blocked these initiatives.

Reagan had better luck implementing his antiaffirmative action views through his executive appointments to the Justice Department and other federal agencies. The president's choice for attorney general, William French Smith, and head of the Justice Department Civil Rights Division, William Bradford Reynolds, reflected Reagan's opposition to affirmative action and similar programs. They vehemently opposed any special protection for groups or remedies based on rectifying past mistreatment, including voluntary school busing programs based on race. Presidents Reagan and Bush also changed the direction of the federal Equal Employment Opportunity Commission and Commission on Civil Rights by reducing their budgets and by appointing conservative members who opposed most efforts to challenge racial or gender discrimination or its legacies. In what seemed a contradiction, the Reagan administration supported creation of several black-majority voting districts in the South. By concentrating African-American voters in a few areas, it ensured the election of a handful of blacks to Congress. But, more importantly, it ensured that a much larger number of white Republicans would be elected from districts that now had fewer minority and Democratic voters.

GOP leaders faulted federal courts for a series of decisions since the 1960s that expanded protections for criminal defendants, including informing defendants of the right to remain silent and to have an attorney and other limits on evidence that police could use at trial. Public fear over rising crime rates in the 1980s prompted both Republican and Democratic legislators at the state and national levels to mandate longer, mandatory prison sentences for many crimes, especially those related to the possession or sale of drugs. As discussed in the following chapter, Reagan and Bush did not create this harsh anticrime wave, but they rode it skillfully for partisan purposes.

One particular crime in the 1980s captured the public's fear of random violence. On December 22, 1984, a mild-mannered electrical engineer named Bernard Goetz shot four young African-American men on a New York City subway train. Goetz claimed the teenagers (who carried sharpened screw drivers and had previous brushes with the law) were about to rob him, although they insisted they merely asked for five dollars. Some observers felt he reacted so violently, shooting one of the group in the back and another multiple times after he had fallen wounded, because he had been mugged twice before. Even though one of the four wounded teens, Darrell Cabey, was paralyzed in the shooting, much of the public embraced Goetz as an "avenging angel."

The incident resembled the plot of the first two *Death Wish* films (1974 and 1981) starring Charles Bronson, and tabloids quickly dubbed Goetz the "subway vigilante." In 1987, a jury acquitted Goetz of attempted murder, but convicted him of the lesser charge of criminal possession of an unlicensed weapon. He served six months in jail. In 1994, Cabey won a $45 million civil award against Goetz, who promptly filed for bankruptcy.[2]

Aside from a booming prison industry, the most lasting impact that the Reagan and Bush administrations had on legal affairs lay in their judicial appointments. Reagan appointed nearly four hundred federal judges—a majority of all those sitting in 1988—as well as a chief justice of the Supreme Court and three associate justices. Bush appointed two justices to the Supreme Court as well as many other federal judges.

Presidents since the nation's founding had routinely nominated judges who shared their general outlook. However, under Reagan and to an extent under Bush, this became a fine art. As presidential Counselor Ed Meese put it, appointing the "right judges" would institutionalize the "Reagan Revolution so it can't be set aside, no matter what happens in future elections." In moving the vetting process from the Justice Department to the White House, Reagan established the special Judicial Selection Committee (JSC) to recruit and screen candidates. Shunning advice from traditional legal groups such as the American Bar Association, the JSC relied primarily upon conservative organizations such as the Federalist Society for assistance in identifying prospective judges. Potential nominees were screened in lengthy sessions during which they were probed for their views on crime, affirmative action, abortion, and other sensitive issues.

When Republicans controlled the Senate from 1981 to 1986, it easily confirmed Reagan's first three Supreme Court appointments: Sandra Day O'Connor, the first woman justice, the staunchly conservative Antonin Scalia, and William Rehnquist, promoted to chief justice. Most Democratic senators respected these nominees' abilities and voted to confirm them even if they disagreed with their judicial ideology.

The situation changed after the Democrats regained control of the Senate in 1987. That year Reagan nominated Robert Bork to fill a Supreme Court vacancy. Bork was an unusually outspoken, many thought abrasive, conservative. As solicitor general (the number three position in the Justice Department) in 1973, he had carried out Nixon's firing of Watergate prosecutor

---

2. Although Goetz insisted from the beginning he only wanted to "go back to being an anonymous stranger in New York," he ran for mayor of that city in 2001 on a platform of "militant vegetarianism." He blamed the 1984 attack and his reaction on the influence of "red meat." His change in diet had not mellowed him much, however, as he told incredulous listeners in his lonely campaign for office that AIDS had proven a "tremendous help in getting rid of the crappiest elements of society."

Archibald Cox after Attorney General Elliot Richardson and his deputy quit rather than do so. Many ordinary Americans as well as congressional Democrats never forgave Bork for acting as Nixon's hatchet man. Bork infuriated even moderate Republicans by insisting that the Constitution offered few protections for personal privacy, free speech, women, and minorities. His arrogant demeanor at his confirmation hearing, as well as his trumpeting what many people saw as extremist views, led a majority of senators, including some Republicans, to vote against his appointment to the Court. After this defeat, Reagan nominated Anthony Kennedy, a respected conservative judge, whom the Senate easily confirmed. The Bork episode revealed that in the future both liberals and conservatives would treat court appointments as essentially high-stakes political poker that would determine the direction of national policy.

As the number of conservative justices increased after 1984, the Supreme Court whittled away at "liberal" decisions dating from the Warren era of the 1950s and 1960s. Court rulings loosened requirements that police alert suspects of their constitutional rights. Other decisions made it easier to deny bail to criminal suspects, affirmed most state death penalty laws, and allowed prosecutors to present certain illegally seized evidence to juries.

In 1983, the Justice Department urged the Supreme Court to limit the guarantees contained in Title IX of the 1972 Education Act. This landmark act barred sex discrimination by educational institutions receiving federal funds. Title IX had opened a wide variety of athletic and academic programs to women. But the Court agreed with the Reagan administration's narrow interpretation. In the 1984 *Grove City College* case, a majority of justices found that Title IX had a limited application and that the institutions could skirt its provisions by using nonfederal money to finance discriminatory programs. When Congress attempted to restore federal protection against sex discrimination by passing the 1988 Civil Rights Restoration Act, Reagan vetoed the bill—only to have Congress, in a rare display, override his veto.

During 1989, the conservative majority in the Supreme Court handed down several other decisions that eroded employees' ability to sue private employers for acts of racial, age, sex, or disability discrimination. The Democratic majority in Congress responded by passing the Civil Rights Act of 1990, which provided new legal remedies for those who suffered workplace mistreatment. Bush vetoed the bill, arguing that it would result in frivolous lawsuits and put pressure on business to set racial hiring quotas. A year later, however, following the bruising fight to confirm Clarence Thomas for the Supreme Court, Bush signed a modified version of the same bill in an apparent effort to repair his shaky standing with women and minorities.

The focus on the family cited so frequently by Presidents Reagan and Bush often seemed a focus on the unborn. Reagan endorsed an antiabortion constitutional amendment, ordered that no public money go to domestic or international family planning organizations that tolerated (or even discussed) abortion as a means of birth control, and convinced Congress to fund legislation that created "chastity clinics" where teenagers were encouraged to avoid sex. At White House urging, Congress continued to ban Medicaid-funded abortions as well as some forms of birth control and counseling. This attention to the preborn often seemed to end at birth. The Reagan administration cuts funds for infant nutritional programs, opposed the expansion of federally funded day care, and ignored calls to establish a national family leave policy to permit new parents to get off from work.

Bush, who—in what seemed like another age—had run for Congress as a "pro-choice" Republican in 1966, embraced the pro-life, antiabortion position as soon as Reagan asked him to join the ticket in 1980. Despite his unflagging loyalty to their position, many religious and social conservatives doubted Bush's commitment to overturning the 1973 *Roe v. Wade* decision, which established a woman's constitutional right to choose an abortion. Bush tried to reassure skeptics in 1986 by endorsing a "human life" amendment to the Constitution designed to overthrow *Roe*.

When Bush became president in 1989, he retained Reagan's tight restrictions on funding family planning groups who did not oppose abortion. Then Louis Sullivan, his nominee to head the Department of Health and Human Services, revealed to startled Republican senators that he was "pro-choice." Bush demanded that Sullivan publicly recant as the price for continued White House backing for his nomination. The Sullivan episode increased the uneasiness that the religious and social right felt toward the new president.

Bush responded by taking a still higher-profile stand against abortion rights. When the Supreme Court reviewed a state law that imposed strict limits on abortion providers, he instructed the Justice Department to file a brief supporting the restrictions and urged the Court to go further and overturn *Roe*. In 1989, a five-to-four majority of Supreme Court justices ruled in *Webster v. Reproductive Health Services of Missouri* that states could strictly regulate—but *not* ban outright—abortions. (They reaffirmed this ruling in *Planned Parenthood v. Casey* in 1992.) The outcome disappointed the "right-to-life" movement but gave some solace to the "pro-choice" camp, who had feared an outright ban. Bush applauded the Court's decision to "protect the unborn" but renewed his call for Congress to pass a constitutional amendment outlawing abortions.

Because Democrats controlled both the House and Senate, this proposal went nowhere. In fact, Democrats felt emboldened by the *Webster* decision and passed several bills designed to loosen federal restrictions on funding abortions. Between 1989 and 1992, Congress passed and Bush vetoed ten abortion-related bills, including one that called for funding the procedure for poor women if their pregnancy resulted from rape or incest.

Liberal concerns and conservative hopes for the future direction of the Supreme Court intensified when associate justices William Brennan and Thurgood Marshall retired from the Supreme Court. The departure of these two stalwart liberals gave Bush an opportunity to tip the ideological balance of the Court. To replace Brennan in 1990, the president nominated, at the urging of his chief of staff, John Sununu, the virtually unknown David Souter of New Hampshire. Unlike Robert Bork, who had a long record of touting ex-

Law professor Anita Hill testifies against her former boss, Clarence Thomas, 1991. Jennifer K. Law/Getty Images.

treme conservative positions, Souter had served for only a few months as a lower court federal judge and had not expressed himself publicly on controversial issues such as abortion, the right to privacy, and the death penalty. He maintained silence on these matters during the Senate confirmation process and easily won confirmation. Conservative Republicans assumed that Sununu's stamp of approval meant Souter could be counted on to vote "right." Democrats hoped that his silence before the Senate meant he would keep an open mind. To nearly everyone's surprise, Souter emerged as a voice of moderation on abortion and most other issues that came before the justices. Conservatives complained that Bush had undermined their effort to construct a solid ideological majority on the Court.

To make up for the Souter debacle, Bush resolved to fill the Supreme Court vacancy left by the retirement of Thurgood Marshall—the Court's first African-American justice—with a reliable and high-profile conservative. The president announced that the "most qualified American" to replace Marshall was Clarence Thomas, a forty-three-year-old African-American federal appeals court judge. Thomas, a staunch conservative, had criticized as deeply flawed many past Supreme Court rulings on abortion, school prayer, privacy rights, and the death penalty. As a Reagan appointee to the Equal Employment Opportunity Commission, Thomas had dismissed most complaints of unfair treatment brought by women and minorities. Despite this record, Thomas won tacit support from many civil rights organizations and black

Supreme Court nominee Clarence Thomas defends himself against accusations of sexual harassment, 1991. CNP/Getty Images.

leaders who favored appointment of another African-American to replace Marshall. Thomas appeared headed for speedy confirmation until a journalist revealed that Thomas had been accused of sexual harassment by one of his former colleagues, law professor Anita Hill.

The all-male Senate Judiciary Committee reluctantly interviewed Hill (but ignored other women prepared to testify about Thomas's offensive behavior) in a tense, televised hearing. Her detailed allegations of harassment, Thomas's vehement denial and description of the hearing as a "high-tech lynching," and the committee's condescending treatment of Hill proved a sorry spectacle. In the end, many Democrats joined Republicans in voting to confirm Thomas. As Bush hoped, Thomas emerged as perhaps the most conservative justice on the Court. The episode aroused strong misgivings, especially among feminists, over Bush's judgment in making the nomination. Unexpectedly, it brought into the mainstream the larger issue of sexual harassment in the workplace.

THE PRISON/INDUSTRIAL COMPLEX

Even while the United States lost large numbers of traditional manufacturing jobs in the 1980s, it rapidly increased employment in one service industry that was almost impossible to "outsource": prisons. At least in this area, conservatives favored expansion of the government's reach. In 1980, state prisons held about 300,000 inmates and federal prisons about 25,000 more. Another 200,000 Americans served shorter terms in local jails. By 1990, the state and federal prison population had swelled to nearly 800,000, while local jails housed 400,000 inmates. By the mid-1990s, these numbers increased by another 50 percent. This growth curve would thrill any CEO.

The expansion of the prison population followed twenty years of increased public resentment over rising crime rates during the 1960s and 1970s. In that period, the number of all reported crimes quadrupled, and the rate of violent crimes grew even faster. Fear of violent crime became especially severe in cities and merged with issues of race. African-Americans, for example, comprised about 12 percent of the population in this period but in victim surveys represented 30 percent of the perpetrators of assault and 62 percent of robberies.

Several factors contributed to this increase, including a surge in the number of teenage boys and young men most likely to engage in criminal behavior, the loss of blue-collar urban jobs, and the growing number of single-parent families. Conservatives often blamed the problem on a "permissive" attitude among liberal Democrats, educators, and judges who worried more about the rights of criminals than the violence perpetrated against honest citizens. In the mid-1960s, 48 percent of Americans described courts at all levels as "too lenient" toward defendants. By 1980, that number soared to 83 percent. As crime became a political issue, Reagan and Bush pledged to appoint federal judges who favored a "strict" interpretation of the Constitution and imposed tougher sentencing. State legislators and members of Congress responded by imposing harsher penalties on lawbreakers. Whether or not more jail time reformed criminals or lowered crime rates, politicians knew that keeping offenders locked up longer made people feel safer, just as executing murderers provided a sense of closure even if it had no impact on future crime.

State legislatures, which retained jurisdiction over most crime, mandated longer prison terms, limited parole, treated more juvenile offenders as adults, and imposed "three strikes and you're out" laws. In California, for example, a voter-passed initiative stipulated that a third conviction for even a minor, nonviolent felony could result in a sentence of twenty-five years to life. As a result, hundreds of men and women received life sentences for stealing items such as golf clubs, videocassettes, and, in one case, a pizza.

As described in the next chapter, during the 1980s the war on crime merged with the war on drugs. Middle-class Americans feared not only drug use by their children, but also the violence associated with the sale of "crack" cocaine in the 1980s. Although rates of overall drug use did not actually rise after 1980, several high-profile deaths among celebrities and violence among

As public attitudes toward crime hardened, many states revived chain gangs as a form of punishment and humiliation. AP/Wide World Photos.

dealers created a climate of fear. National and local politicians escalated the war on drugs by devoting more funds to law enforcement and prison cells. Congress and state legislatures imposed new mandatory minimum prison sentences for drug and other offenses in the 1980s and 1990s, often without holding hearings on the impact—both financial and human—of this policy.

As a consequence, federal, state, and local prison populations nearly tripled between 1980 and the early 1990s. At the federal level, drug offenders accounted for 60 percent of this increase and for 33 percent of new state prisoners. More than half of the new inmates were African-American and Latino. The number of women in state and federal custody surged fourfold, from about 12,000 to about 50,000, during the 1980s and doubled again to 100,000 by 1999. One-third of these women were imprisoned for drug offenses.

By the mid-1990s, the cost of building and running local jails and state and federal prisons exceeded $30 billion annually. States, which paid most prison costs, have since the mid-1990s spent more annually on prisons than on higher education. By 1995, for example, the fifty states spent $2.6 billion on building prisons and $2.5 billion on building colleges. In California, between the mid-1980s and the mid-1990s, overall prison spending grew by 200 percent, compared with a 15 percent increase for higher education funding.

Advocates of strict sentencing insisted that the high cost, often reaching $25,000 or more per prisoner per year, served the public well. Prolonged incarceration, they claimed, accounted for the steady drop in the crime rate beginning in the 1990s. In other words, keeping criminals out of circulation definitely inhibited their ability to commit crimes, whatever its larger impact. But evidence confirming this success proved hard to find. New York, for example, experienced a significantly greater *drop* in violent crime rates than did California, even though New York had the second-slowest-growing prison system in the country, whereas California had one of the fastest and imposed harsher penalties for similar crimes. Similarly, whether or not a state imposed the death penalty for capital crimes or longer terms for drug offenses had little apparent impact on the rate at which murders or drug crimes occurred. So many factors other than length of incarceration influenced crime rates (for example, birth rates, economic conditions, family stability, the certainty as distinct from the duration of punishment, etc.) that criminologists were far more cautious than politicians in explaining cause and effect.

No one, however, could dispute that America's incarceration policies have disproportionately impacted minorities, especially African-Americans and Latinos. By the early 1990s, for example, African-Americans comprised around 12 percent of the overall population but 50 percent of the prison population. One in three of all black males between the ages of twenty and twenty-nine was under some form of criminal justice control. Looked at another way, at current levels of incarceration, black males born in 1990 have about a one-in-four chance of going to prison in their lifetimes, whereas Hispanic males have a one-in-six chance, and white males have a one-in-twenty-three chance.

Harsher drug laws accounted for some of these disparities. Either because of less effective legal representation or prior offenses, blacks and Latinos received longer sentences than whites convicted of similar offenses. State and federal laws also punished those possessing or selling "crack" cocaine far more harshly than those arrested for possessing or selling powder cocaine. Under federal guidelines, one gram of crack is treated like one hundred grams of powder cocaine. Because African-Americans used and sold crack more commonly than did middle- and upper-class whites, courts routinely sentenced them more harshly.

Incarceration carried other social stigmas. Most states barred voting by convicted felons, while in custody or on probation or parole. Several states disenfranchised felons for life or required elaborate legal procedures to regain voting rights. As a result, about 13 percent of the black adult male population has lost the right to vote. In a few states, 33 percent of African-Americans have been permanently disenfranchised. This issue surfaced nationally in the disputed 2000 presidential election when thousands of eligible voters in Florida were barred from casting ballots because their names appeared, often incorrectly, on lists of disenfranchised ex-felons.

The rapid expansion of the prison population after 1980 created a web of public and private groups eager to collect some of the billions of dollars spent on incarceration. These groups ranged from prison guard unions to construction firms to private correctional companies to businesses that supply meals, uniforms, and other institutional staples. Organizations such as the American Correctional Association (a national trade organization), the

American Legislative Exchange Council (a conservative public policy lobbying group funded in part by the private prison industry), and labor unions representing prison guards in California, Texas, and New York routinely lobbied state legislatures in support of stricter law enforcement and sentencing.

To control the high costs of incarceration, state and federal officials often reduced funding for education, counseling, and drug treatment programs while also turning to the private sector. Since the 1980s, conservatives have pushed for eliminating the government's monopoly by partially privatizing the prison system. Among the largest of the private companies that rose to the occasion is the Corrections Corporation of America (CCA), which by the 1990s ran the sixth-largest prison system in the United States, after Texas, California, the federal government, New York, and Florida. CCA's dozens of "privatized" prisons, based loosely on the model of publicly funded, privately managed "charter schools," held nearly sixty thousand inmates. Several smaller private firms supervised about eighty thousand state and federal prisoners. Despite spending huge sums on prisons, lawmakers paid little attention to rehabilitating prisoners or helping them find a role in society when their sentences ended.

New Americans

Although Presidents Reagan and Bush and many of their supporters stressed what they called "continuities" and "traditions," the United States became a more socially and culturally diverse society during the 1980s. A surge in immigration accelerated the creation of a polychrome and multicultural society.

In his speech accepting the presidential nomination at the 1980 GOP convention, Reagan paid homage to the nation's self-image as a place of refuge and an "island of freedom" in a dangerous world. He asked delegates to join him in thanking "divine providence" for opening America to past victims of oppression and disaster. Nine years later, in his "farewell" to the American people, Reagan repeated this theme. He read from a letter sent to him by a sailor serving on the aircraft carrier *Midway* in the South China Sea. When the crew saw a refugee-laden boat about to capsize in heavy swells, they risked their own lives to send out a rescue launch. As one of the brave sailors stepped on board the refugee boat, a frail Indochinese man "stood up and called out . . . Hello, American sailor, Hello, freedom man." To Reagan, this symbolized America's promise to the world.

Although a wonderful example of the president's inspirational storytelling, the anecdote did not reflect his administration's record toward immigrants and refugees. For example, in 1981 he responded to the chaos in Haiti by ordering the Coast Guard to tow back to sea any boats laden with desperate Haitians approaching the American coast. For these unfortunate souls, American sailors were hardly "freedom men."

At the end of the Carter administration, Congress had enacted the Refugee Act of 1980, designed to protect those fleeing to the United States because of a "well-founded fear of persecution" on religious, political, or racial grounds.

The act called for treating all refugees equally. But under Reagan and then Bush, Washington implemented the act's provisions quite selectively. Nearly anyone fleeing leftist Cuba or Nicaragua automatically received refugee status. Those fleeing violence and poverty in El Salvador, Guatemala, or Haiti, whose regimes Washington counted as allies, were generally turned away as inadmissible "economic refugees."

Some Americans considered this differential treatment of refugees a violation both of law and morality. In the mid-1980s, some church leaders and lay activists defied the Reagan administration by assisting Central American refugees on their own. The so-called Sanctuary Movement functioned like the "underground railroad" in pre–Civil War America, helping transport and relocate individuals and families. These activists organized a network of churches and other institutions to shelter refugees who would otherwise be deported. Boston and Cambridge, Massachusetts, declared themselves "sanctuary cities," and in Tucson, Arizona, local ministers and concerned citizens crossed the desert border with Mexico to provide water and food to some undocumented migrants and to lead to safety Central Americans refused legal entry into the United States. The government labeled sanctuary leaders "alien smugglers" and convicted several of violating immigration law. However, to avoid making them martyrs, the Justice Department declined to send them to prison. After 1986, some of the tension eased when the Reagan administration agreed to allow many Central Americans already in the United States to remain until the violence in El Salvador and Nicaragua subsided.

Aside from the conflict over refugee policy, immigrants continued to be a major part of the American experience. In fact, about as many foreign-born (twenty-five million) entered the country in the fifty-five years since 1945 as came during the fabled years of unrestricted immigration from 1880 to the early 1920s. Most of the post–World War II surge followed the 1965 immigration reform act that abolished the restrictive ethnic and racial code dating from the 1920s. During the 1980s, more than seven million immigrants arrived, and nine million more arrived in the 1990s. The percentage of foreign born among the total U.S. population increased from 6.2 percent (14 million out of 226 million) in 1980 to nearly 8 percent (20 million out of 248 million) in 1990. In this period, immigrants accounted for a third of the nation's total population increase.

Since 1980, around 45 percent of immigrants came from Asia and the Middle East, and about as many came from Latin America and the Caribbean. Europe provided only about 10 percent of immigrants, and Africa provided far fewer. The surge of migrants from Mexico and South America raised the Latino portion of the U.S. population to 13 percent during the 1990s, surpassing the percentage of African-Americans. Between 1980 and the early 1990s, the Asian-American population doubled, with the arrival of 3.5 million Filipinos, Chinese, Koreans, Indians and Vietnamese, Cambodians, and Laotians. These newcomers settled everywhere but concentrated in the cities of California, New York, Florida, Texas, New Jersey, and Illinois. Even though

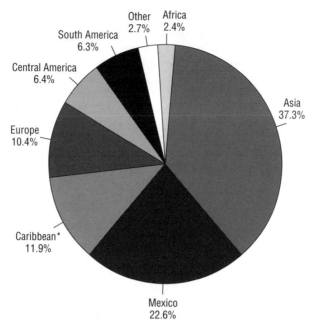

Asia and Latin America come to the United States. Immigrants to the United States 1981–1990, by origin. Source: Center for Immigration Studies, 1990 Immigration and Naturalization Service Yearbook.

*Antigua-Barbuda, the Bahamas, Barbado, Cuba, Dominica, Dominican Republic, Grenada, Haiti, Jamaica, St. Kitts and Nevis, St. Lucia, St. Vincent and Grenadines, and Trinidad and Tobago.

New York City's Chinese population increased from 33,000 to 400,000 between 1960 and 2000, Los Angeles replaced New York as the major port of entry for Asian and Latino immigrants. In 1992, a fourth of the nine million inhabitants of the Los Angeles area were recent arrivals. By then, Hispanics comprised 25 percent of California's population and Asians 10 percent.

The San Fernando Valley of greater Los Angeles epitomized the new pattern of migration and ethnicity. Just before the 1965 immigration reform, its population was nearly 90 percent white and overwhelmingly middle class. Thirty years later, the 1.3 million valley residents were one-third foreign born and about one-half Latino. Although some problems associated with the "inner city" existed in this suburban extension of Los Angeles, the valley's mixed economy actually outperformed the rest of the city in job creation.

Besides the large Latino and Asian migration to the states named earlier, many immigrants found their way to places such as Minnesota, North Carolina, Georgia, and Arkansas. For example, about thirty thousand Hmong, a Laotian tribal group who had sided with the United States during the Vietnam War and fled after 1975, resettled around Minneapolis with the assistance of state, church, and voluntary aid groups. Sometimes whole village populations from Mexico and Central America moved to small cities in the American South, where they worked in textile, furniture, and food-processing plants. This influx of workers allowed the South to sustain its economic growth.

New immigrants worked in all areas of the economy, from performing unskilled agricultural labor to running small shops to staffing hospitals to designing computer software. They filled American cities with the sounds of new languages and diversified religious life as millions of Muslims, Buddhists, Hindus, and Sikhs joined the traditional mix of Protestants, Catholics, and Jews.

The increase in immigration aroused mixed feelings among the general public, even though the new arrivals often filled jobs shunned by other Americans and helped to revitalize the cores of many cities. In Florida, for example, many African-Americans resented what they saw as favored treatment given to those coming from Cuba. The large number of undocumented Mexicans living in the United States drew special concern. Some whites feared the erosion of English as the national language with the proliferation of new cultures and tongues. Voters in California, Arizona, and Florida passed laws declaring English the official state language. Some states denied driver's licenses to non-English speakers and moved to limit social services to the undocumented.

After years of debate about how to control immigration, Congress passed the 1986 Simpson-Rodino Act. This bipartisan legislation offered legal status to several million undocumented aliens already living in the United States but fined employers who hired new undocumented workers. Despite hopes that the act would ensure orderly immigration procedures, it had little impact on undocumented immigrants or on those employers who hired them. In 1990, Congress authorized nearly 700,000 regular entry slots per year, with an additional 100,000 visas for refugees. In addition to legal entrants, about 300,000 undocumented immigrants arrived each year. Some of them stayed for short periods of time, but others stayed indefinitely. By the early 1990s, they totaled at least five million. Because of its proximity, Mexico was the country of origin for at least half the undocumented immigrants. During the 1990s, around one million people immigrated legally or otherwise to this country each year, historically a very high number. The human flow from abroad abated only with the economic downturn at the end of the decade and the imposition of stricter controls following the terrorist attacks of September 11, 2001.

America's economy, legal system, and social structure evolved in often-contradictory ways during the 1980s. The top fifth of Americans enjoyed real economic growth, whereas most others remained in place or even slid back. Wall Street financiers elevated "greed" to traditional value status, whereas traditional families seemed ready to be placed on the endangered species list. To reverse the legacy of "liberal activist" judges, Presidents Reagan and Bush appointed large numbers of "conservative activists" to the federal bench. To keep America safe, state legislatures and Congress passed laws and sentencing guidelines that locked up record numbers of their fellow citizens. Historically high numbers of immigrants poured into the United States, while federal and local authorities pondered ways of limiting the flow. As we shall see, American culture also pulled in contrasting directions as ordinary people and government policymakers grappled with the challenges posed by drugs, sex, changing gender roles, new technologies, foreign competition, and an education system nearly everyone loved to hate.

Sources and Further Readings

Numerous authors have evaluated the intentions and impact of "Reaganomics" on the national economy and individual Americans. Among the best studies are John W. Sloan, *The Reagan Effect: Economics and Personal Leadership* (1999); Kevin Phillips, *The Politics of Rich and Poor: Wealth and the American Electorate in the Reagan Aftermath* (1990); Kevin Phillips, *Wealth and Democracy: A Political History of the American Rich* (2002); David Stockman, *The Triumph of Politics: How the Reagan Revolution Failed* (1986); W. Brownlee and Hugh Graham Davis, eds., *The Reagan Presidency: Pragmatic Conservatism and Its Legacies* (2003); John Ehrman, *The Eighties: America in the Age of Reagan* (2005).

For a discussion of the debate over income inequality, corporate excesses, and the "culture of greed," see Barbara Ehrenreich, *The Worst Years of Our Lives: Irreverent Notes from a Decade of Greed* (1990); Benjamin Friedman, *Day of Reckoning: The Consequences of American Economic Policy under Reagan and After* (1986); William Greider, *The Education of David Stockman and Other Americans* (1986); Robert Lekachman, *Greed Is Not Enough: Reaganomics* (1982); Michael Lewis, *Liar's Poker* (1989); William A. Niskanen, *Reaganomics: An Insider's Account of the Politics and the People* (1988); Donald T. Regan, *For the Record: From Wall Street to Washington* (1988); Connie Bruck, *Predator's Ball: The Junk Bond Raiders and the Man Who Staked Them* (1988); Allan Murray and Jeffrey Birnbaum, *Showdown at Gucci Gulch: Lawmakers, Lobbyists, and the Unlikely Triumph of Tax Reform* (1988); John Taylor, *The Circus of Ambition: The Culture of Wealth and Power in the Eighties* (1989); Nicholas Mills, ed., *Culture in an Age of Greed* (1990); James Traub, *Too Good to Be True: The Outlandish Story of Wedtech* (1990); Michael Katz, *The Undeserving Poor: From the War on Poverty to the War on Welfare* (1990).

Changing patterns of international trade and American indebtedness are discussed in Clyde V. Prestowitz Jr., *Trading Places: How We Allowed Japan to Take the Lead* (1988); Martin and Susan Tolchin, *Buying into America: How Foreign Money Is Changing the Face of Our Nation* (1988).

The savings and loan crisis is analyzed by Martin Mayer, *The Greatest Ever Bank Job: The Collapse of the Savings and Loan Industry* (1990); Stephen Pizzo, Mary Fricker, and Paul Muolo, *Inside Job: The Looting of America's Savings and Loans* (1989).

Conservative justice is examined by Herman Schwartz, *Packing the Courts: The Conservative Campaign to Rewrite the Constitution* (1988); Jane Mayer and Jill Abramson, *Strange Justice: The Selling of Clarence Thomas* (1994).

Changes in immigration patterns and refugee policies from the 1970s through the 1990s are analyzed in Gil Loescher and John Scanlan, *Calculated Kindness: Refugees and America's Half Open Door, 1945 to the Present* (1986); David Reimers, *Still the Golden Door: The 3d World Comes to America* (1992); Otis Graham, *Unguarded Gates: A History of America's Immigration Crisis* (2004).

6

WEIRD TO WIRED

Complexities of American Culture

If an unfriendly foreign power had attempted to impose on America the mediocre educational performance that exists today, we might well have viewed it as an act of war.

SECRETARY OF EDUCATION TERREL BELL, 1983

Even as some politicians and their theological allies celebrated the nation's conservative political drift, new technologies and media, such as the personal computer, cable television, the Walkman, and national newspapers, altered how Americans entertained and informed themselves. A shrinking number of households conformed to the traditions embodied by "traditional family values." More people than ever used illegal drugs, while gender roles continued to evolve, often in "untraditional" ways. Bedrock institutions such as public education came under growing attack, while new diseases and social anxieties challenged faith in modern medicine and science. As the last decade of the century began, some Americans feared that their nation had lost its competitive edge and might soon be eclipsed by its protégé and rival, Japan. Many of these trends seemed unconnected to formal politics and defied obvious conservative or liberal solutions.

YUPPIES

The go-go world of Wall Street in the 1980s had room at the top for only a handful of Trumps, Milkens, and Boeskys. Farther down the food chain, demographers and journalists identified a related but more common sociological type—the yuppie. As a group, "yuppies"—an extended acronym for "young upwardly mobile urban professionals"—exulted in their lifestyle during the 1980s. Journalists used the term lavishly in 1983 and 1984, partly to describe Senator Gary Hart's unexpected following among young Americans as he campaigned for the Democratic presidential nomination. *Newsweek* dubbed 1984 "The Year of the Yuppie" and applauded the group's eagerness to "go for it" as a sign of the "yuppie virtues of imagination, daring, and entrepreneurship." Unlike socially concerned protesters or hippies of the 1960s, these young adults had little interest in overthrowing what their predecessors had called the "rotten system." They came of age eager to consume. As *Newsweek* put it, yuppies existed "on a new plane of consciousness, a state of Transcendental Acquisition." As we shall see, they acquired even their own disease, a mysterious ailment called "chronic fatigue syndrome" or the "yuppie flu."

Despite the hoopla, yuppies were easier to parody than to pigeonhole. Between two million and three million of the thirty million or so baby boomers born during the 1950s and early 1960s were true yuppies—urban professionals or managers earning over $40,000. As candidate Hart learned, they could not be relied upon as a liberal Democratic voting bloc. Even though they embraced permissive views on abortion, sex, and the use of recreational drugs, many supported Reagan's economic policies. Yuppies aspired to become investment bankers, not social workers. For example, in 1985, one-third of Yale University graduates applied for jobs as financial analysts with the high-flying First Boston Corporation.

Yuppies enjoyed creature comforts, spending, and overspending on "leisure products" such as Porsches and BMWs, designer sneakers, state-of-the-art electronic equipment, and gourmet foods. They embraced the fitness craze, patronizing health clubs, jogging, selecting garments made from natural cloth, and eating high-fiber diets. Yuppies placed a premium on looking good. Novelist Tom Wolfe parodied the subculture—as well as the distance that separated yuppies from the urban underworld they usually glimpsed only through the windshields of their Porsches—in his biting satire, *The Bonfire of the Vanities* (1987).

Yuppies were voracious consumers of business advice books whose origins stretched back to Benjamin Franklin's *Poor Richard's Almanac* and Horatio Alger's uplifting novels of the late nineteenth century. Dale Carnegie's *How to Win Friends and Influence People* (1936) and Norman Vincent Peale's *Power of Positive Thinking* (1952) continued the tradition. Like these earlier inspirational texts, those published in the 1980s offered a relentlessly upbeat collection of aphorisms, many with a vaguely Christian or spiritual theme. A smile, a shoeshine, and a positive attitude, they implied, could meet and beat Japanese and other competitors.[1] Also, like their predecessors, many sold remarkably well.

For example, *The One Minute Manager* (1981) by Kenneth Blanchard and Spencer Johnson, *In Search of Excellence* (1982) by Thomas J. Peters and Robert H. Waterman, and *The Seven Habits of Highly Effective People* (1990) by Stephen R. Covey quickly sold five million or more copies each. Spinoffs and audiobooks that could be listened to on car tape decks while driving or on

---

1. In the 1980s, books with titles such as *The Art of Japanese Management* portrayed that nation's techniques as a model for American executives and workers to emulate. The praise turned to anger under the pressure of trade competition by the early 1990s. Predictions that Japan would soon dominate the world fell flat when that nation experienced a prolonged decline after 1993.

mobile players drove sales still higher. Most of what they advised made good sense, even if it covered familiar ground: prioritize decisions; make lists; have a goal but remain flexible; don't be afraid to ask questions; respect co-workers; encourage productivity by saying nice things to subordinates. By 1989, when Wess Roberts published *Leadership Secrets of Attila the Hun*, it was unclear to readers and reviewers whether or not the author meant it to be taken seriously or was having fun with the genre.

Several of these authors became extraordinarily rich pitching advice. But some were already rich and sought respectability by sharing their insights. Chrysler executive Lee Iacocca described how to revive a moribund company in his 1986 autobiography and 1989 memoir *Talking Straight*. Wall Street raider and future felon Ivan Boesky provided tips on how to make billions in *Merger Mania* (1985). Donald Trump dished out advice to young entrepreneurs in *The Art of the Deal* (1987), which became a best-seller in part because Trump bought so many copies himself. The ever-expanding variety of "how to" and "advice" books on business, sex, marriage, investments, and health became such a dominant part of the publishing market that after 1984 *The New York Times Book Review*'s weekly list of best-sellers ranked them in a category of their own.

Some social commentators implied that many yuppies were merely reformed radicals making up for lost time. To make a point, they highlighted the careers of several former Black Panthers and Students for a Democratic Society (SDS) activists. For example, Eldridge Cleaver returned to America from exile to become a born-again Christian, Republican activist, and clothing designer. Fellow Panther Bobby Seale, famous for shouting, "Burn, Baby, Burn," reinvented himself as a gourmet chef whose promotional video bore the evocative title *Barbecuing with Bobby*. (He urged backyard grillers *not* to burn the baby-back ribs.) Student radical David Horowitz flipped sides, becoming a conservative pundit who visited college campuses to expose leftist professors. Rennie Davis, a defendant in the celebrated Chicago conspiracy trial of 1968, reemerged as a stock broker. Radical actress Jane Fonda, denounced as "Hanoi Jane" for her trips to the enemy capital during the Vietnam War, made a fortune producing exercise videos. Some other 1960s radicals, such as Mark Rudd and Abbie Hoffman, emerged from hiding to resume quiet lives or to work for peaceful social change. Former Weather Underground fugitive Bernadine Dohrn, for example, joined the law faculty at Northwestern University, where she ran a program assisting the children of imprisoned mothers. But whether they sought publicity or not, these were exceptions who had little in common with most yuppies.

The Wall Street crash of October 19,1987, dimmed the mystique surrounding young entrepreneurs. By 1988, "yuppie" had devolved into something of a slur. *Newsweek*, which had celebrated its discovery of yuppies four years before, now described the group as in "disgrace" and suggested that the 1980s had already ended, two years early. The *Wall Street Journal* reported that "conspicuous consumption is passe." *New York* magazine, a purveyor to fine tastes, ran a cover story celebrating the return of altruism. "Had it with pride,

Yuppies, initially admired, soon became objects of ridicule. DOONESBURY © 1985 G. B. Trudeau. Reprinted with permission of UNIVERSAL PRESS SYNDICATE. All rights reserved.

covetousness, lust, anger, gluttony, envy and sloth?" the magazine asked. The time had come to "start doing good." Not many yuppies took oaths of poverty or donated their wealth, property, or BMWs to charity; but it seemed that the outright celebration of greed during the Reagan era had lost some of its appeal.

SOCIETY AND CULTURE IN THE 1980s

In the social and cultural sphere, as in the judicial system, the 1980s brought a resurgence of conservative values. Presidents Reagan and Bush and many of their supporters stressed family values, clean living, public observance of religion, attention to the basics in education, and cultural conformity. At the same time, however, the nation experienced a renewed drug crisis, a decline in the reputation of public education, a series of scandals among television evangelists, an AIDS (acquired immune deficiency syndrome) epidemic, and a large influx of immigrants, which made the United States even more culturally diverse.

During the 1980s, as the scourge of AIDS and increased drug use aroused public concern, a health and fitness craze swept the nation. Beyond yuppies, middle-class Americans in general paid increasing heed to warnings that their sedentary lives, along with their high-fat diet, and use of alcohol, tobacco, sugar, and caffeine placed them at risk for many diseases. Exercise at health clubs became popular as did jogging while plugged into a Sony Walkman. (In a revealing contrast, inner-city, minority youth flaunted norms by playing music in public on large, loud "boom boxes," sometimes derided as "ghetto blasters." More affluent teens and young adults listened to their music on equally expensive but miniaturized personal listening devices whose headphones insulated them from the world.) Fashion designers marketed expensive lines of workout clothes and high-technology athletic shoes that were the rage across class and racial lines. Shopping at "natural food stores" and comparing brands of bottled water became a social activity. Breweries and soft drink manufacturers could barely turn out enough "light beer" and diet soda to slake the nation's thirst. When the popular press warned about

Is it fair to force your baby to smoke cigarettes?

By the 1980s, antismoking messages were everywhere. Frank Barratt/Getty Images.

the "deadly white powder," one had to scan the article carefully to see if it referred to salt, sugar, saccharin, or cocaine.

In the 1970s, the California branch of the American Cancer Society (ACS) began an annual "smokeout" day to encourage people to quit smoking cigarettes for twenty-four hours. By 1980, the California campaign had grown into the nationally publicized ACS "Great American Smokeout." Each November celebrities joined ordinary citizens at public rallies, where they pledged to not smoke for at least one day and hopefully longer. By the end of the decade, state and local governments, again led by California, raised "sin taxes" on tobacco products to finance antismoking campaigns. Many localities implemented workplace and restaurant clean air ordinances that limited smoking to designated areas, often outside buildings.

In spite of their general disdain for government regulations, both the Reagan and Bush administrations actively promoted antitobacco programs. Building on the anecdotal evidence of the 1940s that linked smoking to many diseases, the many scientific studies of the 1950s that confirmed the risk, and the 1964 report issued by the U.S. surgeon general that declared smoking a cause of lung cancer, Reagan's surgeon general, C. Everett Koop, escalated the federal antismoking campaign. Koop, who called himself "the nation's doctor," directed public health agencies to warn the public that tobacco use put them at risk for cancer and many other diseases and that nicotine was as addictive as heroin or cocaine. Koop committed his considerable prestige to a campaign to create what he called a "smoke-free society" by the year 2000. In 1985, warning labels that had been on cigarette packs for nearly two decades and on print ads since the early 1970s became more explicit. Koop's successor in the Bush administration, Surgeon General Antonia Novello, pursued the same goal. Schools played an especially important role in communicating the danger of tobacco use as children were encouraged to lecture smoking parents on the risk they faced. Efforts by government and voluntary agencies between the 1960s and early 1990s helped reduce by half the proportion of Americans who smoked cigarettes, one of the great but sometimes overlooked public health success stories of the era.

Probably because of the nation's unhappy memories of prohibition, public officials generally downplayed the fact that alcohol use by underage drinkers, along with overconsumption by adults, remained one of the most common and harmful forms of substance abuse. Law enforcement agencies, insurance companies, and highway safety groups had long complained that judges and legislators minimized the problem of drunk drivers out of concern that they themselves might become victims of stricter enforcement.

The situation changed dramatically after 1980, when Candy Lightner organized Mothers Against Drunk Driving (MADD) following the death of her twelve-year-old daughter at the hands of a repeat drunk driver. The charismatic Lightner, the subject of a sympathetic movie and extensive television coverage, organized regional and national MADD chapters that worked closely with educators, the insurance industry, automobile companies, transportation safety groups, and law enforcement agencies to lobby state and federal lawmakers to stiffen penalties for drunk driving. As a result, new federal and state regulations reduced the amount of alcohol permitted in drivers' blood and increased sharply the penalties for those caught driving under the influence (DUI). Americans convicted of DUI became one of the fastest-growing categories of those in prison.

THE AMERICAN DISEASE

In the earlier discussion of crime and prisons, we noted that during the Reagan and Bush administrations, the war on crime merged with the war on drugs. Both presidents joined the ranks of nearly all their predecessors since Woodrow Wilson in crusading against narcotics. Neither declarations of war nor proclamations of victory had much impact on what has sometimes been called "the American disease." During the 1980s and early 1990s, an estimated forty million Americans, nearly one in six, consumed an illegal substance at least once each year. A 1987 survey revealed that half of all citizens under age forty-five had smoked marijuana at least once.

The federal war on drugs began in 1914 when the Harrison Act outlawed personal opiates and restricted medical use of opiates. The law defined all drug users as criminals and kept them in that category for the rest of the century. Congress effectively criminalized marijuana possession in 1937, as most states had already. Under Presidents Truman, Eisenhower, and Nixon, federal laws extended the range of banned substances and increased penalties for their possession, sale, or use. Nixon replaced the Narcotics Bureau with the more powerful Drug Enforcement Administration (DEA). Reagan and Bush bolstered the DEA's power and budget, while Congress extended federal jurisdiction over many common drug crimes that had previously been state offenses. Just as the Japanese had been accused of purveying drugs during World War II, politicians often linked drug smuggling to the Soviet Union, China, and Cuba during the Cold War.

Federal antidrug efforts in the 1980s continued to focus on eradicating foreign supplies, stopping imports, and arresting dealers and users. Narcotics convictions sent thousands of small-time users and pushers to prison but barely impacted the larger trade. In fact, despite the immense costs of the drug war during the 1980s and early 1990s, the price of cocaine and most other street drugs fell sharply. Patterns of drug use, most medical authorities agreed, waxed and waned in a rhythm all their own, barely influenced by government crackdowns. Although people from all backgrounds used various drugs, the patterns of use varied among economic, ethnic, and racial groups.

In the early 1980s, public concern over drug use ranked well below economic and foreign policy concerns. In 1985, barely 1 percent of Americans surveyed listed illicit drugs as a major national problem. But four years later, more than 50 percent of those surveyed described drug use as the gravest threat to national security.

To a large extent, the change stemmed from the appearance of "crack," an inexpensive cocaine derivative that became widely available by mid-decade. Print and electronic media carried frightening stories: robberies inspired by addicts' need for money to buy crack; pregnant crack users and parents who ignored or abused their children; gun-toting preteen dealers in turf wars that mowed down innocent bystanders. Especially harrowing accounts circulated of newborns writhing in agony from crack withdrawal.[2]

The 1986 death of Len Bias, a promising basketball player at the University of Maryland who died from cocaine poisoning shortly after signing a contract with the fabled Boston Celtics, highlighted the problem. The circumstances

---

2. In fact, these babies suffered from a combination of prenatal exposure to a variety of drugs, as well as alcohol, poor nutrition, and little health care. Crack was just one of several problems. The pediatrician who first brought public attention to so-called crack babies tried to explain the broader problem in a follow-up study—but politicians and the media ignored him.

of his death led many people to question why such a promising athlete had turned to drugs. Only a few cynics asked how Bias had managed to become a college senior eligible to play despite failing most of his courses.

Another factor that increased public attention was the receding Cold War threat after 1985. Thereafter, the focus placed on the drug issue by President and Mrs. Reagan contributed to a national obsession. To an extent, the drug war replaced the Cold War as a national security issue. The administration and journalists friendly to the White House spoke of threats from "narcoterrorists," often linked to left-wing regimes in Nicaragua and Cuba, who replaced the Soviet Red Army as "enemy number one." In 1986, Reagan's National Security Council issued a directive calling drug smuggling a major threat to American security .

After consulting with political advisers rather than mental health professionals, the president and first lady launched their antidrug campaign under the slogan "Just Say No." In a widely covered story, Mrs. Reagan visited nurseries that treated so-called crack babies. What she observed, the first lady told reporters "would make the strongest hearts break." Ronald and Nancy Reagan (whose own children later wrote about their drug use in the 1960s and 1970s) condemned drug use as immoral and criminal and insisted that the best prevention and cure came from promoting religious values, imposing harsher school discipline, and strictly enforcing antidrug laws. In 1986, the president issued an order mandating that federal workplaces be "drug free" and called for routine urine testing for workers in "sensitive positions." Congress followed up in 1988 by passing the Drug Free Workplace Act, which mandated that universities accepting federal grants and contractors taking federal dollars maintain a "drug-free workplace." In the private sector, this typically involved requiring new employees to submit to urine testing, a process derided by its critics as "jar wars."

By 1990, federal and state expenditures for enforcing drug laws ran to over $10 billion annually, with most of the money spent on law enforcement and incarceration. About 750,000 Americans were charged each year with violating drug laws (most often related to marijuana), and those convicted of possession and sales became the fastest-growing part of the state and federal prison population.

Most experts believed that drug use among white Americans and the middle class peaked in the late 1970s or early 1980s and then leveled off. Local police tended to make more "busts" when pressed to do so by public officials or when they were given more resources based on their arrests. Drug seizures, whether up or down, did not directly correlate to use patterns and had little impact on availability or price because suppliers could produce enough drugs to meet virtually any market demand.

When cocaine and its derivatives such as crack became popular, the greatest concentration of users was among poor, inner-city, minority youth. For some of these young people, staying high relieved the miseries of daily life. For others, selling drugs provided one of the few avenues of economic and social mobility available to them.

In a typical year in this period, illegal drugs killed about four thousand to five thousand Americans. Another eight thousand or so died in turf wars and drug-related violence. Although tragic, these grim numbers should be viewed in context. In fact, the toll was *less* than half the number of Americans who died each year from adverse reactions to over-the-counter medicines and prescription drugs. It represented a tiny fraction of the several hundred thousand Americans estimated to die prematurely each year from illnesses linked to tobacco and alcohol use.

Like most Americans, the president and first lady appeared more concerned with reducing drug-related violence than with answering the questions of why youth and others used drugs or how to rehabilitate them. Both the Reagan and Bush administration policies continued to define drug use as a criminal problem, not a public health problem, with policy focused on intercepting supplies, arresting dealers, and jailing users. For example, Reagan put Vice President Bush in charge of a task force to reduce smuggling into Florida. With the deployment of military units to the region, seizures increased, then declined. Reagan and Bush claimed success. In fact, smugglers simply operated in less-policed areas until the campaign subsided.

Upon becoming president in 1989, George H. W. Bush declared a bold new offensive in the drug war, dispatching military units freed from Cold War duties in Europe to stop drug smugglers along the border with Mexico and on the high seas. One of the president's main justifications for invading Panama and seizing strongman Manuel Noriega was to punish him for cooperating with Colombian drug cartels. In a dramatic televised presentation from the Oval Office, Bush displayed a vial of crack cocaine that DEA agents had purchased in Lafayette Park, just a block from where he spoke. (He did not reveal that to provide the prop for the TV speech, undercover agents had cajoled a naïve and reluctant pusher to meet them at the park, which he did not know was across the street from the White House.)

The president upgraded his drug war by appointing William Bennett, Reagan's outspoken secretary of education (see later), as the director of the Office of National Drug Control Policy. In selecting Bennett as his so-called drug czar, Bush hoped to please social conservatives who admired the sharp-tongued philosophy Ph.D. and considered him a possible presidential candidate. But the administration's overall approach remained the same: appropriating more money for police and jail cells, assigning more police and armed forces to interdict smuggling, and making a token effort at diverting young offenders.

Bennett, a chain-smoking "nicotine addict" and compulsive gambler, proved especially ill suited for the job. During his frequent appearances on television, he condemned the media for romanticizing drug use and dissipated his energy by exchanging insults with anyone who questioned his views. The drug czar called for arresting and jailing more small-time users and ridiculed critics who would place more emphasis on education and rehabilitation. He called swift, sure punishment the only deterrent. Despite a promise to show quick results, Bennett achieved virtually nothing during his two years on the job. Recognizing that excitement over the Gulf War and domestic economic problems had displaced the interest of the president and public in his campaign, Bennett resigned in 1991 and devoted his energy to writing a best-selling book on "virtue."

EDUCATION

In the past century, each generation of Americans discovered a "crisis" in public education. For example, following the *Sputnik* scare of 1957, when the Soviets launched the first artificial satellite, Americans worried that the nation's schools lagged behind those of its Cold War rival. Just before the Soviet achievement, an educator had published a best-selling critique of American schools entitled *Why Johnny Can't Read*. The nation's largest-circulation magazine, *Reader's Digest*, combined that critique with a bleak warning in a 1957 article entitled "Why Johnny Can't Read . . . and Ivan Can." *Sputnik* spurred Congress to pass the National Defense Education Act, which provided substantial federal funds to local school districts. During the 1980s, Americans feared that their high schools turned out functional illiterates unable to compete with Japanese and South Korean students, the new "threat" as the Soviet threat began to fade.

The Reagan administration had little sympathy with those who called for more federal aid to basic education. As a candidate, Reagan criticized Carter's creation of the cabinet-level Department of Education and hinted he would abolish it. Although Reagan did not follow through on his threat, he selected Terrel Bell to serve as secretary of education, assuming that the conservative Mormon educator from Utah favored slashing federal school funds. In fact, Bell had a deep commitment to public schools and quickly fell out with the president's more conservative advisers.

Angered by pressure from the White House to weaken enforcement of antidiscrimination laws and to join the chorus that called for reducing federal education spending, Bell struck back. In an adroit maneuver, he convened a blue-ribbon panel to assess the condition of American schools. The resulting report issued in 1983, *A Nation at Risk: The Imperative for National Reform*, declared that "if an unfriendly foreign power had attempted to impose on America the mediocre educational performance that exists today, we might well have viewed it as an act of war."

Many Americans sympathized with the tone of the report, but few agreed on a remedy. Conservatives blamed school problems on the influence of teachers' unions, wasteful spending, and a lack of attention to the "basic three Rs." Liberals countered that public schools were chronically underfunded even as they were pressed to provide a growing list of services ranging from hot meals to sex education to computer skills.

Schools in the United States faced a situation unique among industrialized countries. Unlike in Japan, South Korea, or even the Soviet Union, in the United States over 90 percent of all public school funding came from local, not federal, taxes. Elected state officials and local school boards, not federal agencies, set educational policies and standards. The federal government played only a limited funding and advisory role. Typically, schools in affluent areas with a strong tax base tended to be well financed and successful, whereas those in poor areas struggled to make ends meet.

To further complicate matters, the urban middle class abandoned public schools in growing numbers. Continuing the trend of the 1970s, many middle-class parents, both white and black, enrolled their children in private and parochial schools with selective admission policies. With their more affluent and motivated students gone, urban public schools struggled to educate a larger proportion of poor, minority, and non-English-speaking children. The flight of middle-class students further reduced school districts' ability to raise needed revenues. Parents paying tuition for private education had little incentive to vote for higher taxes. The gradual aging of the American population also contributed to the school crisis because the elderly—with no young children of their own to educate—tended to oppose additional expenditures on schools. These problems accelerated the decline of faith in public education, making it still harder to fund schools adequately.

Reagan's advisers realized that in the wake of Bell's scathing report on education, a sizable portion of the public blamed the president for these problems. White House staff orchestrated a series of "photo ops" in which Reagan visited public schools over a several-week period. At each location, he posed with a popular teacher or honor student and said a few cheery words about the importance of education. After a month of these appearances, polls showed renewed public confidence in Reagan's education policy, even though he continued to oppose increased federal funding.

By then Secretary of Education Bell's fate had been sealed. Shortly after winning reelection in 1984, Reagan fired him. The president selected William Bennett as Bell's replacement. An outspoken critic of teachers' unions and innovative curricula, Bennett declared that public schools should impose stricter discipline, not request more money.

While running for the presidency in 1988, George H. W. Bush set a different tone. Recognizing that Bennett's abrasive style had alienated many potential supporters, Bush spoke of his own desire to be known as the "education president." Once elected, Bush appointed the soft-spoken Lamar Alexander to head the Department of Education and endorsed the New American Schools Development Corporation, a public-private partnership that called for reforms to "unleash America's creative genius" by forming the "best schools in the world." The group promised that within a decade American students would become the best in the world in science and mathematics. Bush also cooperated with a group of state governors, including Bill Clinton of Arkansas, in promoting ideas for school improvement.

Nevertheless, in practice, federal policy changed little under Bush. Few new dollars were budgeted, and education took a backseat to most other issues. Conservatives, meanwhile, explored several new educational ideas that later gained traction, such as using standardized tests to rate schools and teachers, creating so-called charter schools (publicly funded but privately run schools), and providing vouchers from tax receipts that students could use to attend private and parochial schools.

RELIGION IN PUBLIC LIFE

Continuing a process that began in the late 1970s, evangelical Christianity became more closely identified with the Republican Party. With between 20 and 40 percent of Americans describing themselves as "born again," Reagan, Bush, and their advisers recognized the immense impact that a large number of disaffected Christians could have if they were energized behind national and local candidates. Republican officials capitalized on the ability of television ministers, or televangelists, to mobilize an audience of millions on behalf of the Republican cause. As one GOP official put it, the Reagan administration intended to embrace conservative Christians so tightly "they could not move their arms."

Reagan, who was raised in a religious household but who while president seldom attended church, spoke with verve and certainty on religious matters. He described the Bible as containing answers to "all the world's complex and horrendous problems." Reagan endorsed "creation science" as an alternative to the theory of evolution and urged amending the Constitution to permit official school prayer.[3] White House staffers consulted regularly with evangelical groups, conveying their concerns to the president.

Opinion surveys revealed that younger and socially liberal voters believed that the once-divorced Reagan, who had many gay friends in Hollywood, was "winking" at them when he criticized homosexuality, divorce, premarital sex, abortion, and recreational drug use. Yet, self-described Christian conservatives took his statements at face value. As a group, they voted for Reagan over his opponents by almost a four-to-one margin. The religious right never felt as comfortable with George H. W. Bush as it had with Reagan, but Bush received the same ratio of votes from Christian conservatives in 1988. Equally important, religiously motivated voters formed a growing proportion of participants in Republican primaries that selected candidates.

During the 1980s, the religious right focused its ire against abortion, restrictions on school prayer and religious displays, gay rights, and politicians who were on the "wrong side" of these issues. Despite their assertions that the Bible was the unerring word of God, most high-profile televangelists glossed over biblical injunctions to help the poor or to avoid accumulating worldly goods. By 1985, these electronic ministries, including Jerry Falwell's Moral Majority, Pat Robertson's 700 Club, Jim Bakker's PTL ("Praise the Lord") Club, and Jimmy Swaggart's televised ministry, raised over $1 billion annually.

---

3. On this issue, the president spoke for most Americans. Polling data showed that a large majority of his fellow citizens doubted that Darwin's theory of random mutations and natural selection could account for the appearance of human life, even if it might explain the evolution of other species.

Televangelists Jim and Tammy Faye Bakker celebrated wealth and faith in the early 1980s. Will and Deni Mcintyre/Getty Images.

Many televangelists were honest and sincere, less inclined to flamboyant exaggeration and flagrant fundraising than were Swaggart and the Bakkers. The Reverend Billy Graham, for example, had used television to preach the gospel since the 1950s. Although he was a politically conservative Christian who befriended Republican presidents from Eisenhower through George W. Bush, Graham did not demonize Democrats or those who did not follow his faith, and he showed no hint of financial or personal impropriety. For their part, not all viewers accepted the political dogma put forth by the more strident media preachers.

Several prominent televangelists found themselves engulfed by scandal in the late 1980s. Money and sex, two reliable temptations, proved their undoing. For several years, White House pressure had dissuaded the IRS and Justice Department from pursuing tips about improper business and personal behavior among TV preachers. In 1988, the *Charlotte Observer* ran an exposé of an investment scam run by Jim Bakker that bilked investors out of $158 million they had put into his religious theme park, Heritage USA. The Justice Department then indicted Bakker on numerous counts of fraud and conspiracy, for which a federal jury convicted him. Meanwhile, a rival preacher revealed that Bakker had pressured a church member, Jessica Hahn, to have sex with him and had used donated funds to pay her several hundred thousand dollars in hush money.

Bakker blamed much of his trouble on rival Jimmy Swaggart who, he charged, lusted after the PTL theme park. Hahn parlayed her notoriety into a nude photo shoot and interview with *Penthouse* magazine. As she explained to those who read the magazine ostensibly for its interview, Bakker manipulated her into having sex with him by saying "when you help the shepherd, you help the sheep."

Swaggart, Bakker's nemesis, got caught up in a web of scandal when one of his other rivals presented evidence that Swaggart frequented prostitutes. At first Swaggart denied such dalliances. But after one woman came forward with detailed recollections of his "really kinky" proclivities, Swaggart made a tearful televised confession.

Pentecostal faith healer and university founder Oral Roberts became an object of derision when he locked himself in a prayer tower, claiming that God would "take" him in thirty days unless his flock mailed him $8 million. When initial contributions fell short, a prominent gambler anted up enough money to save Roberts.

Airing of this dirty laundry did not doom either the evangelical movement or the electronic church. In 1988, Pat Robertson declared himself a candidate for the Republican presidential nomination, provided he received spiritual support and cash contributions from three million followers. He received the money but lost the nomination to George H. W. Bush. The minister's campaign had not been helped by his public prayer to divert a hurricane from Virginia to New York. Robertson remained active in politics, establishing the Christian Coalition, a group who lobbied to ban abortion, restore school prayer, and oppose equal rights for homosexuals. Walking a fine line between religion and politics, the Christian Coalition prepared detailed "voter guides" it distributed to its two million members and many more churchgoers that effectively endorsed candidates. Robertson and his group took credit in the early 1990s for promoting the activities of politicians such as Newt Gingrich and for helping the GOP to gain majority control of the House of Representatives in 1994.

Evangelical Christianity and media remained tightly entwined during the 1990s, especially with the expansion of cable television and "talk radio." Robertson's Christian entertainment empire expanded with the creation or takeover of the Family Channel, International Family Entertainment, MTM Productions, and the Ice Capades. New evangelical organizations such as the Promise Keepers attracted large numbers of male supporters. Although Jerry Falwell's Moral Majority disbanded in 1989, successor groups such as James Dobson's Colorado Springs-based Focus on the Family ensured the continued influence of the religious right on American cultural and political life. As Billy Graham's health failed in the 1990s, his son Franklin, who had strayed from religion as a youth, picked up God's cudgels and became a close friend of another fortunate son who found solace in faith, President Bush's son and a future Texas governor and president, George W. Bush.

CHANGING GENDER ROLES

In the 1987 film *Fatal Attraction*, actress Glenn Close portrayed a thirty-something career woman who has a weekend affair with a married colleague, played by Michael Douglas. Douglas's philandering comes back to haunt him when the distraught Close stalks him, threatens his wife and children, and slaughters the family's pet bunny. The film echoed themes voiced by conservative politicians and their religious allies: feminism and sexual independence harmed women's mental health and endangered the family. In this view, single, childless, career women were social misfits and potential moral outlaws who threatened society. Marriage, monogamy, and motherhood, like faith, prevented women from becoming homicidal maniacs and kept society stable.

When Republicans convened to nominate a president in 1980, two issues evoked real passion among delegates writing the party platform: repealing the fifty-five-mile-per-hour highway speed limit and implementing the New Right social agenda on women and reproductive rights. In a sense, conservative activists wanted to allow men to drive faster down the highway but to force women to drive more slowly down the highway of life. This approach reflected Republican efforts to woo not only religious conservatives but also white southern men and northern blue-collar Catholics who had traditionally voted Democratic. The GOP platform called for a constitutional amendment to ban abortion and also opposed ratification by state legislatures of the still-pending Equal Rights Amendment to the Constitution. This agenda formed part of the "traditional family values" mantra recited by Republicans. But the agenda carried a clear message: women should stay at home, obey their husbands, and raise children.

During the 1980s and early 1990s, American society seemed to pull in contrary directions regarding gender issues. At one level, the nation appeared increasingly tolerant of nontraditional lifestyles. Out of choice or necessity, well over half of all single and married women, including those with young children, now worked outside the home in a variety of professions. Sexuality in general was depicted much more openly in the arts and entertainment, and homosexuality was widely acknowledged, if not fully accepted, as part of the human experience. At the same time, religious conservatives and other members of the New Right in and out of the Republican Party denounced gays, abortion, gender equality, pornography, and a host of other "sins" as the progeny of "secular humanism."

Reagan and the religious right celebrated what they called the "traditional family," consisting of a breadwinning husband and a wife who served as mother and homemaker. Many Americans found this image of family life appealing. Yet, the so-called traditional household continued to decline in the 1980s. In 1970, 40 percent of the nation's households still conformed to that ideal; by 1980 that proportion had dropped to 31 percent, and by 1990 to 26 percent. The decline reflected several trends. For example, as the population aged, many wives outlived their husband and lived singly after his death. The number of unmarried couples living together rose sharply during the decade, as did married couples who chose to defer or not have children. The steeply increasing rates of both divorce and out-of-wedlock births further reduced the number of "traditional households."

With women holding such a large share of the nation's paying jobs, feminists continued to press harder for affordable child care, ratification of the

Equal Rights Amendment, and an end to gender discrimination by employers. But despite the administration's verbal support for a "pro-family" agenda, Reagan and congressional Republicans opposed efforts to develop a national child-care policy, opposed creating a national work-leave policy for new parents, cut funds for infant nutritional programs, and blocked reconsideration of the Equal Rights Amendment when the deadline for state ratification expired in 1982.

Also in 1982, when the results of the midterm congressional election showed a widening of the gender gap that favored Democrats, Reagan undertook several "pro-woman" initiatives. He appointed Margaret Heckler as secretary of health and human services and Elizabeth Dole as secretary of transportation to his formerly all-male cabinet. They complemented his 1981 naming of the first woman justice to the U.S. Supreme Court, Sandra Day O'Connor. Although all three women were well qualified for their positions, none identified with or promoted a feminist agenda. The president sometimes trivialized their roles by referring to Heckler as "a good little girl" and laughing while his aides parodied Dole as "schoolmarmish." Reagan appointed several New Right activists to the less-visible Civil Rights Commission and the Equal Employment Opportunity Commission, where they routinely dismissed claims of gender discrimination.

During the Bush administration, the president tempered many of Reagan's harsher criticisms of social programs, women, and minorities. First Lady Barbara Bush, unlike Nancy Reagan, enjoyed very positive press coverage, especially of her campaign to promote childhood literacy. Bush himself spoke often of promoting a "thousand points of light," a sometimes-confusing allusion to citizens volunteering through private charities (rather than government programs) to solve social problems. He restored some funds to childhood nutrition programs and spoke more positively about the federal role in promoting education. But budget constraints and opposition within Republican ranks limited his initiatives.

Bush's gentlemanly demeanor often clashed with the harsher demeanor of his vice president, Dan Quayle. This clash was especially apparent in April 1992, when Los Angeles erupted in flames. Following the acquittal of several police officers tried for the videotaped beating of black motorist Rodney King, thousands of outraged, mostly African-American Angelinos went on a rampage. Both black and Latino rioters vented much of their anger at Asian-owned retail stores in their neighborhoods. During several days of rioting, fifty-two people died, and the city sustained nearly a half-billion dollars in property damage. Bush himself waited several days before commenting on the unfolding tragedy and nearly a week before visiting the damaged city. This lassitude contributed to the public's growing sense in the wake of the liberation of Kuwait that despite Bush's keen interest in foreign affairs he seemed largely indifferent to domestic problems.

Vice President Quayle did not hesitate to step into the breach. Anxious to step out of Bush's shrinking shadow (and overcome his gaffe of misspelling *potato* during a televised spelling bee) before the upcoming election, in May

YOU CAN'T LIVE ON HOPE.

The fight against AIDS included a public education campaign to alert people to the danger. Illustration by Sandra Shap/Bernstein & Andriulli, Inc.

Quayle delivered a strident speech in San Francisco. Ignoring nearly all the factors that underlay the violence (including decades of hostility between the police and the African-American community, racial tensions between blacks and more recent Hispanic and Asian immigrants, high levels of unemployment, etc.), Quayle blamed the riot on a "poverty of values." He went on to denounce the behavior of a television sitcom fictional character, Murphy Brown, played by actress Candice Bergen. Brown, a single thirty-something career woman, had become pregnant. Rather than have an abortion, she opts to give birth and raise the child alone. Instead of praising the character's decision to have the child, Quayle accused the show's writers of mocking the importance of fathers and of denigrating traditional family values. This terrible "lifestyle choice," as Quayle described it, somehow set the stage for the semidestruction in Los Angeles.

Most Americans, along with late-night TV hosts, ridiculed these remarks and questioned why Quayle debated a fictional character. Some White House staffers suggested dropping him from the ticket that autumn.

Although Bush distanced himself from the remarks, the incident further eroded public confidence in the quality of his leadership and the judgment of those around him.

Some commentators lamented and others cheered the notion that the 1980s marked the end of the sexual revolution that began during the 1960s. More than anything else, the outbreak of the AIDS epidemic in the early 1980s precipitated a health crisis that made Americans more cautious about sexual relations. The result of a virus probably originating in Africa, AIDS destroys the immune system and leaves victims vulnerable to opportunistic infections. The deadly human immunodeficiency virus (HIV) that causes AIDS is transmitted from one person to another through the exchange of body fluids, particularly blood and semen. In the early years of the epidemic, sexual transmission was especially prevalent among gay men. Intravenous drug users who shared needles were also at grave risk, as were their sex partners. Before tests were developed to check the nation's blood banks, many hemophiliacs contracted the virus through transfusions. By the end of 1993, some 200,000 Americans had died from the disease, and an estimated one million others carried the deadly HIV infection. AIDS struck much harder in other countries, especially in Africa, Brazil, and parts of Asia.

Because most of those first diagnosed with AIDS were gay men or drug abusers, many Americans, including President Reagan, were uncomfortable even discussing the disease. During his first term, Reagan opposed spending much federal money on AIDS research or preventive education. The president remained silent on the subject while televangelists spoke of God sending a "gay plague" to punish sinners. Perhaps the cruelest remarks came from Reagan aide Patrick Buchanan: "The poor homosexuals. They have declared war on nature and now nature is exacting an awful retribution." Scientists urged public officials to endorse a "safe sex" program promoting the use of condoms in order to reduce transmission of the virus. Providing clean needles to intravenous drug users might also inhibit infection. But many religious authorities and cultural conservatives condemned these ideas, arguing that promoting safe sex encouraged promiscuity and that giving junkies clean needles endorsed heroin addiction.

In October 1985, Rock Hudson, a popular film star and a personal friend of the Reagans, died of AIDS. His death humanized the disease, both for the president and for much of the public. The president appointed a commission who recommended much higher levels of funding for government and private research, education programs, and treatment. The virus had been identified by 1984, and now a search for ways to prevent or cure the disease began in earnest. Although Reagan urged compassion for people with AIDS, he seldom spoke on the subject except to assure potential blood donors that they could not become ill by donating blood. The president refused to endorse Surgeon General Koop's call for launching a publicity campaign to encourage the use of condoms.

During the Bush administration, federal policies toward AIDS and its victims became somewhat kinder and gentler, to use one of the president's phrases. In 1989, Congress created the National Commission on AIDS, and Bush authorized greater federal spending on medical research and prevention programs. First Lady Barbara Bush posed for photographers while holding a baby born with AIDS. But Bush's own discomfort with the subject and his wariness of offending his conservative base and further antagonizing rivals such as Patrick Buchanan resulted in his maintaining a low profile on the subject.

BLACK HELICOPTERS, MILK CARTONS, AND MYSTERIOUS AILMENTS

Americans in every era have lived with their own social fears and demons, from witchcraft in seventeenth-century Salem to the domestic Red Scare in the 1940s and 1950s. But each generation finds a distinct way of expressing its anxieties, whatever the underlying cause. In the 1980s, the AIDS epidemic challenged a core belief held by Americans in the decades after World War II: that science, medicine, and psychiatry could prevent or cure most common disorders and ensure a good life. The advent of antibiotics such as penicillin in the 1940s, the Salk vaccine's triumph over polio in the 1950s, the growing use of radiation and chemotherapies against cancer in the 1960s, the development of antipsychotic and mood-stabilizing drugs in the 1970s, and the proliferation of electronic consumer marvels from the personal computer to the microwave oven reassured the postwar generation that life had become safer and more comfortable.

During the 1980s, however, new afflictions beset American society. Besides the AIDS crisis, virulent strains of antibiotic-resistant bacteria evolved. The wars on drugs and crime reflected fears of disorder and the vulnerability of children. Radio and television talk show hosts such as Phil Donahue (starting in the mid-1970s) and Oprah Winfrey (nationally syndicated since 1986) provided a national podium for real and pseudo-scientists to alert the public to frightening new problems and dubious solutions. Often speaking a language derived from twelve-step recovery programs such as Alcoholics Anonymous (which had a good track record in helping people stay off booze), these new, usually self-appointed experts described entirely new categories of what critics called "the culture of victimization." Chocoholics, sex addicts, and nicotine fiends (a term dating from the early twentieth century) joined compulsive eaters, dieters, and gamblers as part of an ever-expanding "culture of addiction." Popular entertainment merged with and promoted these anxieties.

Media pundits warned of rampant child kidnapping, convincing food distributors to place photographs of missing children on milk cartons. Until 1980, local police generally handled child disappearance cases, and reliable data were hard to find. Congress expanded federal oversight by passing the 1980 Parental Kidnapping Act and the 1982 Missing Children Act. In 1984, Reagan signed a law creating the National Center for Missing and Exploited Children (NCMEC).

A real (but rare) stranger kidnapping in the 1980s contributed to hysteria about satanic abuse and other cults. AP/Wide World Photos.

The new agency's initial findings shocked the nation: nearly 750,000 children went missing each year. Terrified parents worried that losing sight of a toddler in the supermarket or playground for even a moment might result in his or her being snatched by roving bands of kidnappers lurking in the fresh food aisle or behind park shrubs. In fact, about two-thirds of the missing children—500,000—were teenage runaways who fled home on their own and usually returned. Nearly all the rest were children taken by a parent or relative during divorce-related custody fights. True "stranger kidnappings," which often result in death, thankfully remained a rare crime, with about one hundred occurring annually. This more detailed data, so much less compelling than the headline-grabbing number of 750,000, received far less media scrutiny.

Supermarket tabloids, word-of-mouth rumors, and even respectable periodicals informed the public about suspicious new diseases that caused chronic fatigue and afflicted veterans of the Gulf War. People were urged to recover their "repressed memories" and to discover whether they had "multiple personalities" caused by satanic ritual abuse or alien abduction. Conspiracy theorists on late-night radio warned that government officials colluded with an all-powerful United Nations to dispatch squadrons of "black helicopters" as part of a nefarious plan to strip Americans of their freedom.

Incidents of what today might be called "reincarnation," "channeling recovered memory," "chronic fatigue," "multiple personality," "satanic abuse", and "alien contact" can be found in folk tales and other accounts stretching back centuries. More recent popular books, such as *The Search for Bridey Murphy* (1956), *The Three Faces of Eve* (1957), *Rosemary's Baby* (1967), and *Sybil* (1973), as well as films such as *Close Encounters of the Third Kind* (1977), had enthralled millions of readers and viewers. Case studies of multiple personality, such as those of Eve and Sybil, stressed the rarity and uniqueness of the condition. To put it bluntly, they proclaimed, "I may be crazy, but I'm special." In the 1980s, the increasingly common portrayals of multiple personality disorders, recovered memory, and various kinds of abuse stressed inclusivity. "We are all crazy as victims of abuse," they declared, "and you are, too, if you'd only admit it."

The frequent overlap of media entertainment and news reporting created a snowball effect during the 1980s and early 1990s that transformed individual testimonials of illness, abuse, or abduction into ritualized tales of organized family, community, and government conspiracies. Self-published authors and self-credentialed experts who called themselves "traumatists", "ufologists", "experiencers", "survivalists", and "recovered memory specialists" exposed what they saw as the misdeeds of unsympathetic doctors, abusive parents, and evil government agencies. They put their own scientific gloss on the subject by often placing medical-sounding labels on the conditions they probed. Even if no cure existed, both society and "victims" found a certain comfort in receiving a medical diagnosis of a mysterious condition.

The appearance of chronic fatigue syndrome (CFS), the "malaise of the eighties" or the "yuppie flu," as *Newsweek* labeled it in 1986, set a pattern. In 1984, a physician near Lake Tahoe reported on several patients who complained of headaches, soreness, fatigue, rashes, and difficulty concentrating. Most of these (and later) victims were well-educated women in their twenties and thirties whose symptoms defied standard diagnosis. After media outlets as diverse as *Rolling Stone* magazine and *The New York Times* reported on this first cluster, tens of thousands of patients around the country came forward to report similar problems. Although some doctors initially linked the malaise to Epstein-Barr virus, a cause of mononucleosis, this link proved inaccurate.

In 1988, the federal Centers for Disease Control (CDC) in Atlanta recognized CFS as a medical syndrome, meaning that it described a cluster of symptoms even if its cause remained unclear. Few CFS sufferers actually met the eight-point criteria outlined by the CDC. By then, most doctors concluded that the aches, pains, and exhaustion experienced by CFS victims were probably physical manifestations of an underlying psychological or perhaps autoimmune disorder—not an infectious disease. Ultimately the CDC recommended treating patients with antidepressants.

Since Louis Pasteur's discoveries in the late nineteenth century, the common understanding of disease attributed it to infectious agents. Overstressed young adults and mothers, the typical CFS patients, found comfort in applying a medical label to their exhaustion. Many journalists, authors, and ordinary people misunderstood the CDC position, believing the agency's designation of CFS as a syndrome meant it must be either a communicable disease or a mental disorder. This left the general public confused and CFS sufferers angry at what they saw as a callous medical establishment that either ignored their plight or labeled them as crazy.

A related collision between orthodox science and "populist" or "junk" science came into sharp relief a few years later in the wake of the 1991 Gulf War. No sooner had coalition forces liberated Kuwait from Iraqi occupation than the mass media reported that at least 10 percent of the 700,000 American troops deployed in the region after August 1990 suffered from "Gulf War Syndrome" (GWS). Symptoms of this mysterious disorder, including joint pain, fatigue, memory loss, and mood swings, resembled symptoms of CFS. (British and other coalition troops who fought alongside Americans reported a much lower rate of complications.) On the basis of initial and later studies, most military doctors and independent researchers concluded that the veterans suffered from symptoms typical of posttraumatic combat stress. In previous conflicts, soldiers were discouraged from complaining about—or even discussing—physical or emotional difficulties in readjusting to civilian life. But the military's post-Vietnam culture encouraged speaking out. When the medical establishment described their symptoms as emotionally based, veterans angrily rejected the implication that they were "nut cases." They allied with advocacy groups, including some organized by CFS sufferers, who blamed GWS on exposure to risky inoculations, exotic viruses, or chemical toxins released by burning oil wells and weapons.

Far from being indifferent or hostile to their plight, both the Bush and Clinton administrations empathized with Gulf War veterans. Both presidents lamented the often-shabby treatment meted out to Vietnam-era soldiers who were exposed to carcinogens such as Agent Orange or who suffered from undiagnosed emotional trauma. The Defense Department and Veterans Administration began monitoring reports of GWS in 1991 and after 1994 authorized disability payments to ill veterans even though no link had been found between GWS and deployment in that conflict. Nevertheless, an unlikely coalition of liberal and conservative politicians, advocacy groups, and journalists accused government doctors and bureaucrats of disparaging sick veterans and orchestrating a coverup.

Mistrust of scientific and government authority proved a common thread among several other syndromes that surfaced during the 1980s. Accounts of people who reported being abducted by aliens or sexually abused by satanic cults proliferated in the media. These victims—some of whom developed "multiple personality disorder" (MPD)—confronted a wall of silence—or worse—when they sought help from the police and mental health professionals. They found relief only by turning to unconventional therapists who helped them recover—and prevail over—suppressed memories of real traumas.

During the 1980s and early 1990s, best-selling books, tabloid stories, and celebrity confessionals (e.g., Roseanne Barr and Rosie O'Donnell) highlighted the painful legacies of incest and child abuse. Injuries suffered in childhood, they reported, often had lifelong consequences. It was hard to dispute this assertion or to deny that American society had often turned a blind eye toward the plight of abused children. But these accounts went much further, claiming that one-third or more of all children had been sexually abused and that highly organized satanic cults sometimes based in day-care centers raped and mutilated large groups of children. Victims reportedly repressed memories of these traumas, causing some to develop multiple personality disorder.

The most influential treatment of the subject, *The Courage to Heal* (1988) by Ellen Bass and Laura Davis, sold a million copies within a few years of its appearance and inspired many copycat self-help texts. The authors provided a seventy eight-point checklist of symptoms that revealed a history of sexual abuse. Pretty much everything, it seemed, might be evidence of molestation. Judith Herman, author of the best-selling *Trauma and Recovery* (1992), asserted that female rape and incest victims, like combat veterans, suppressed memories of assaults and suffered a wide array of physical and psychological problems. Because traditional psychotherapy ignored their plight, patients were encouraged to find help through unorthodox treatments, such as hypnosis, role-playing group therapy, and drug-induced states. Recovery also required confronting family members who had inflicted or tolerated these crimes. A culture that had previously underestimated the incidence of abuse now saw it everywhere.

Victims of especially severe abuse were said to suffer from multiple personality disorder, later renamed "dissociative identity disorder." (Mainstream psychiatrists and psychologists considered this an extremely rare condition.) In these cases, memories of especially awful trauma were offloaded onto separate deviant personalities—known as "alters"—while the child continued to develop. Treatment, usually under hypnosis, required putting a patient in touch with the "alter" to bring out the truth about past abuse. MPD became a frequent plot element in low-budget films about serial killers. It provided a gloss of science to macabre story lines and allowed producers to pay just one actor to play the part of several villains. By 1990, hypnotists, reflexologists, and aroma therapists had diagnosed twenty thousand cases of the disorder and estimated that two million or more Americans might suffer from MPD. Even more frightening, MPD therapists reported that half their patients recounted acts of cannibalism, child sacrifice, and mass rape by satanic cults that sounded like something out of a medieval nightmare.

Several high-profile child abuse cases seemed to verify that something like satanic ritual abuse (SRA) might be occurring in plain sight. In 1983, for example, police swooped down on the McMartin preschool in Manhattan Beach, California, after children alleged that staff members had raped, brutalized, and threatened to kill them. In 1984, prosecutors charged seven staff members with molesting over three hundred children. Two years later, a new prosecutor dropped charges against five of the care providers but brought the two remaining defendants to trial. In what became California's longest, most complex, highly publicized, and emotionally draining trial (until the O. J. Simpson case in the 1990s), jurors listened to more than three years of testimony between 1986 and 1990. After nine weeks of deliberations, the jury acquitted one defendant of all charges and could not decide on the guilt or innocence of the second. A shorter retrial of the sole remaining defendant also ended in a hung jury, after which all charges were dropped. Meanwhile, in the late 1980s and early 1990s several other day-care operators in New Jersey, Massachusetts, North Carolina, and elsewhere were charged with similar offenses.

The 1988 manifesto on recovered memory, *The Courage to Heal*, affirmed that children's reports of satanic abuse were credible. Several other best-selling books reported that children were commonly victims of unspeakable violence at the hands of wandering bands of satanists. To be sure, disturbed *individuals* sometimes acted out satanic and occult fantasies, in private or public. But this had nothing in common with the supposed network of powerful devil worshippers who lived normal lives and whose jobs, families, and standing in their community were merely a cover for demonic attacks on innocents.

Not surprisingly, reports of assaults on children by trusted caregivers horrified the public. Child abuse, like child kidnapping, is a painful reality. But it seldom if ever occurred in the way the proponents of satanic abuse alleged or the media graphically reported. The typical sexual predator was not a stranger but rather most often a relative or family friend—in other words, Uncle Bill fondling his niece in the basement during the Thanksgiving meal, not Miss Laura or Mr. Tom engaged in lurid sado-masochistic rituals during nap time at the Merry Moppets day-care center.

Most of the day-care center cases became media circuses, or pop-culture "show trials." The cases typically began when parents sensed that their child was unhappy over something that happened at day care. In several instances, a parent became irate upon hearing that his or her child had been disciplined by a care provider, perhaps with a sharp word or mild swat. Once the event was reported to the police, the authorities themselves or "recovered memory specialists" (usually *not* trained mental health professionals but rather self-credentialed experts) who were brought in for the investigation asked leading questions of the child and then other children. Being eager to please the adults (who promised rewards ranging from McDonald Happy Meals to trips to Disneyland) and picking up on their interrogators' fascination and anxiety, many children recounted increasingly graphic tales of evil clowns and demons who performed grotesque sexual rituals and slaughtered babies and animals in secret rooms or aboard spaceships. Children who denied seeing or participating in these events were often classified as "in denial." Despite the absence of corroborating physical evidence, in many cases police arrested, courts tried, and juries convicted dozens of day-care providers and others accused of assisting them. Whereas the McMartin defendants were eventually released, others accused of similar crimes received life terms in prison.

Before this feeding frenzy abated in the mid-1990s, and most of the convictions were overturned, it seemed beside the point that police discovered no dead children, boiled bunnies, or secret torture chambers. Nor could pediatricians identify any physical signs of sexual violation of the children. Most striking was that not a single parent or investigator *ever* witnessed the elaborate satanic rituals inflicted on hundreds of young victims despite the constant picking up and dropping off of children at the suspect facilities. Still, true believers among the parents, therapists, police, and prosecutors insisted that the absence of evidence only confirmed the power and cunning of those engaged in the conspiracy.

One step beyond multiple personality disorder and satanism lay alien abduction. Abductees, like most victims of chronic fatigue, repressed memory, multiple personality disorder, and satanic abuse, were disproportionately women. However, in this instance they were typically poorer, less educated, and more rural than their counterparts, more likely Wal-Mart clerks than corporate managers. Modern reports of forced contact with aliens began in the late 1940s during the "flying saucer" craze associated with the early Cold War and fears of the Soviet Union. The "buzz" on UFOs held that the U.S. government not only knew about alien visitations but also actually stored the bodies of dead aliens and spaceship parts at secret locations such as "Area 51" or Roswell, New Mexico. By the 1970s, the number of people reporting abduction had grown large enough for them to hold annual conventions.

Building on the popular low-budget "creature features" of the 1950s and 1960s, several of Hollywood's top-grossing films of the 1970s and 1980s dealt with alien contact. These films included Steven Spielberg's immensely popular *Close Encounters of the Third Kind* (1977) and *E.T.* (1982), as well as director Ron Howard's *Cocoon* (1985). Interestingly, in these cinema treatments, it is humans who seek contact with shy aliens and find the encounters inspiring, not terrifying. The aliens in *Cocoon* actually solve the problem of what to do with elderly Americans whose quality of life has deteriorated: beam them aboard the mother ship and fly to a retirement community in another galaxy.

But most tabloid and memoir accounts of alien contact painted a far grimmer portrait of the abduction experience. Two best-sellers, *Missing Time* (1981) by Bud Hopkins and *Communion* (1987) by Whitley Streiber, detail terrifying close encounters. In the late 1980s, Hopkins created the Intruders Foundation as a support group for traumatized abductees.

Accounts of alien abduction followed a similar pattern. After experiencing strange memory lapses and emotional anguish, the as-yet-unaware abductees sought help from a sympathetic unconventional therapist, often a hypnotist. Under hypnosis, they recalled being taken at night from home or a car on a deserted road and transported aboard a spacecraft. Aliens probed the restrained humans to steal their DNA, eggs, or sperm as part of a diabolical plan to create mutant life-forms. Impregnated women were returned home but reabducted so aliens could harvest their half-human babies.

These lurid, often-tearful accounts made for riveting tabloid journalism. Even cynics recognized that self-described abductees suffered from something. Psychologists pointed to "night terrors," a condition in which a sleeper partially awakens from a nightmare but cannot move or shake the thought. Prodded by hypnotists who suggest that aliens may have caused the trauma, the distraught subject latches on to that explanation. Among poor, rural, and uneducated women abductees the clear fascination with high-tech phenomena such as spaceships and advanced life-forms seemed especially poignant. Women who recounted forced impregnation followed by the loss of a baby clearly experienced ongoing pain but probably not as a consequence of intergalactic sexual assault. Among skeptics, such stories evoked a headline supposedly printed in the supermarket tabloid *National Enquirer:* "MARTIAN RAPES NUN—ESCAPES IN UFO."

From the Weird to the Wired: Information Technology and Culture

Technological change accelerated in the 1980s, affecting popular culture and entertainment in novel ways. The personal computer and cable television, for example, transformed the way ordinary people produced, received, and exchanged information. Until 1980, a Xerox photocopier or an IBM Selectric typewriter was probably the most sophisticated office machine used by the average American office worker. Television sets were ubiquitous, but whether you lived in Los Angeles or Atlanta, they carried no more than four (ABC, CBS, NBC, and PBS) network signals and perhaps those of two additional local broadcasters.

Modern computers emerged from World War II–era research in the United States, Great Britain, and Nazi Germany. As they evolved, these giant "mainframes" required specially trained programmers to operate them. For decades, most of the critical "hardware" and "software" developed for computers came from costly, often tax-funded, large-scale research projects at government, university (e.g., MIT, Cal Tech, Stanford), and corporate (e.g., Bell, IBM, Xerox, Texas Instruments) research laboratories. During the 1960s, at least two-thirds of all the computer-related research funding in the United States came from DARPA, the Pentagon's Defense Advanced Research Projects Agency. Lone, sometimes eccentric entrepreneurs and bold "venture capitalists" played a role much later on, primarily in marketing computers. Even as vacuum tubes gave way to transistors, then to microchips in the 1960s and 1970s, most computers were used by government agencies and a few large businesses, usually to store and retrieve data and to execute various military applications. In 1970, the Intel Corporation developed the microprocessor, a device that shrank the size and increased the speed of a computer's central processing unit. In 1981, IBM began marketing small desk-top "personal computers" (PCs) for home and office use, almost casually initiating a computing revolution. (Apple unveiled its PC in 1977 but lacked the market reach of IBM. It launched the innovative Macintosh in 1985.)

Two young entrepreneurs, Bill Gates and Paul Allen, who founded a startup company named "Microsoft" in 1975, recognized the emerging market for "user friendly" software to operate the new personal computers. Gates and Allen acquired the rights to a little-used existing computer program, altered it slightly, and licensed it to IBM at $10 per unit as MS/DOS (disk operating system). In 1983, Microsoft launched its Word and Windows programs, run by a "mouse," while another company, Lotus, marketed its popular 1-2-3 spreadsheet for business applications. By the early 1990s, nearly a fourth of all households owned a personal computer and used it mostly to word process, manage finances, and play games. By then, Microsoft had expanded from three to almost six thousand employees, and annual revenue exceeded $1 billion. Bill Gates became the richest person in the world.

IBM fared less well. For obscure business reasons, it neglected to acquire exclusive rights to the memory chips or programs that ran the PC. Thus, any manufacturer could put Intel chips and Microsoft software into a PC "clone" that worked as well as an IBM computer and usually cost less. This situation opened a vast market to Dell, Compaq, and numerous other domestic and foreign computer makers who eventually took the lead in manufacturing. By 1983, personal computers had become so pervasive that *Time* magazine honored the PC as "the machine," in place of the man "of the year."

Although use of e-mail and the Internet did not become commonplace until the 1990s, their origins also lay in DARPA-funded research in the 1960s and 1970s. In 1969, DARPA sponsored a primitive network of linked computers, designed partly as an emergency communication system in case of war. The first "Advanced Research Projects Agency Network (ARPANET)" message flashed that year between giant computers at UCLA and Stanford. In the early 1980s, civilian agencies such as the National Science Foundation (NSF) promoted the use of what was now called the "Internet" as a way for groups of allied researchers to easily post and exchange information. In 1993, NSF released the Internet for general use, and programmers quickly developed software that allowed personal computers to log in to the system. Soon millions of Americans were communicating through e-mail and beginning to browse the emerging "World Wide Web." The diminishing cost of computers, the greater ease in using them, and their growing capabilities fueled the 1990s explosive growth in dot-com companies and e-commerce.

Americans watched more and more television during the 1980s. On average, at least one set was turned on for about seven hours daily in each household, up from about six hours per day in 1970. Depending on age and gender, individual viewing ranged from three to four hours per day. At the same time, the growing segmentation of television and other media markets meant that Americans of different age groups, genders, regions, and so forth viewed fewer shows in common. With most new TVs operated by hand-held remote control, viewers, often dubbed "couch potatoes," rapidly "channel surfed" among shows, hoping to avoid commercials.

The remote control, along with color receivers and larger receivers, was one of the handful of innovations in television since its inception after World War II. The TV universe changed dramatically during the 1980s. Network (ABC, CBS, NBC, PBS, and, after 1988, Fox) broadcasting began the decade with a near monopoly of 90 percent of viewers. By the early 1990s, the advent of cable expanded the channel range from five or six options to several hundred, and the networks lost almost half their audience.

Cable neatly complemented the deregulatory movement of the early 1980s. Under Reagan, the Federal Communications Commission dropped many of its long-standing restrictions on cross-ownership among radio, television, newspaper, and magazine companies and allowed a single company to acquire several radio and television stations. Although the FCC continued to have authority over broadcast radio and television, the 1984 Cable Television Act largely freed cable from any government regulation. Media mergers became common in the belief, misguided in most cases, that a company owning, say, a movie studio, a broadcast or cable station, and other forms of entertainment would enjoy business "synergy" that would maximize profits. Thus, ABC merged with Capital Cities and then Disney. CBS merged with Westinghouse, and General Electric purchased NBC. Fox had links to newspapers, cable stations, and other media.

Cable channels of all sorts, many on a twenty-four-seven schedule, proliferated. Some, for example, specialized in news (CNN), religion (CBN), sports (ESPN), popular music (MTV), country music (CMT), children's shows (Disney), public affairs (C-Span), erotica (Playboy), recent films (HBO), or consumer products (Home Shopping Network). As providers added ever more cable channels, they further divided the market by catering to specialized tastes in everything from cooking to stock car racing. In a struggle to stay afloat, the broadcast networks began operating their own specialized cable channels, further segmenting traditional audiences. By 1990, 90 percent of American homes had access to cable, and about 60 percent actually subscribed.

Like the hand-held remote and cable, the videocassette recorder (VCR) further altered viewing patterns. VCRs had been invented in the 1960s but came into common use in the 1980s when mass production made them affordable, and the Supreme Court ruled that home recording of television shows did not violate copyright law. By the end of the decade, three-fourths of all households owned a VCR. Once viewers mastered the sometimes frustrating controls—which some viewers never did, leaving the LED indicator on the front panel to flash endlessly—viewers could rent feature films from ubiquitous video stores or record TV shows and watch them (fast forwarding through commercials) at their leisure.

Other forms of mass entertainment also became more segmented during the 1980s. Radio stations adopted increasingly specialized formats. Now, in addition to "top forty," "easy listening," and "classic rock" stations, broadcasters aimed their signal at specifically African-American or Latino audiences or at those who preferred all-talk, all-sports, or all-news radio. Shock jocks and strident conservative talk show hosts became staples of radio, signifying, depending on one's perspective, the decay or advance of civilization. The appearance of the compact disc in 1982 posed additional challenges to radio broadcasters, as its quality and mobility led many music lovers to replace home and portable radios with CD players.

Since the 1930s, mass-market magazines such as *Reader's Digest* and later *Time, Life,* and *Newsweek* had been staple sources of news and entertainment for millions of Americans. Television had gradually eroded their subscriber base, leading to *Life's* demise in 1972. By the 1980s, general interest news and literary magazines lost large numbers of readers. As the old periodicals faltered and sometimes stopped publishing, readers turned toward specialty magazines, such as those focusing exclusively on topics such as the Civil War, celebrity lifestyles, pets, retirement, fitness, travel, cooking, regional color, and investments.

These new technologies gradually called into question the role of traditional news sources. By the early 1980s, less than a fourth of Americans still considered newspapers the "most believable" news source. Half the public described television reporting as more believable. Newspaper circulation peaked at about sixty two million copies per day in the 1980s, held steady for a few years, and declined steeply after 1990. To survive, many newspapers merged. The remaining readership tended to be older, richer, and better educated than the general public.

Unlike most other countries, the United States lacked a "national" newspaper before the 1980s. Even the largest dailies, such as *The New York Times* or *Los Angeles Times*, had circulations of only about one million and were read primarily by local subscribers. In contrast, Japan's three large national dailies each had about twelve million readers. The appearance of *USA Today* in 1978 altered the face of American journalism. Edited centrally but printed and distributed locally, *USA Today*, which critics derided as "McNews," soon reached a daily audience of over two million. Lacking local color or a strong editorial voice, its short, general interest stories and emphasis on weather, finance, and sports, offended no one. By the end of the 1980s, other papers, such as the *Wall Street Journal* and *The New York Times*, used new technology to publish regional editions.

The content of the first national newspaper, like that of many cable television channels, demonstrated the strengths and weaknesses of the digital and computer revolution. The media possessed a greater ability to communicate more rapidly to more people than ever before, but it did little to raise the level of public discourse and resulted in more and more Americans sharing less and less of a common culture. This divide mirrored the economic, religious, and political divisions that had become hallmarks of American society during the 1980s.

The tendency of opinion leaders, politicians, and ordinary people to externalize national problems suggested that a residual insecurity underlay the Reagan-Bush era's veneer of prosperity and pride. Although it never reached the fevered rhetorical pitch or military standoff of the Cold War, by the late 1980s and early 1990s many Americans accused Japan of launching an economic offensive against the United States. As the annual trade deficit with Japan passed the $50 billion mark in 1985 and kept on growing, the dean of American political journalism, Theodore White, wrote in *The New York Times* that Japan's political and corporate leaders used exports of Toyotas and VCRs like "guided missiles" in their offensive to dismantle American industry and to show "who finally won the war fifty years before." Other journalists, members of Congress, and spokesmen for veterans groups dredged up similar military metaphors. Japan's export "offensive" targeted America's manufacturing base, along with good jobs, and was nothing less than "a new Pearl Harbor."

The Japanese "threat" even contributed to a brief infatuation with "junk science." In 1989, for example, two scientists working at the University of Utah, B. Stanley Pons and Martin Fleischmann, announced they had discovered a way to produce energy from "cold fusion" at room temperature with off-the-shelf equipment. If true, this would not only revolutionize physics, but also solve the world's energy problems. Overnight, as one astute observer noted, the Japanese "became to cold fusion what the Soviets had been to the defense community . . . the evil empire" that justified big spending.

Pons and Fleischmann hired as their shill lobbyist Ira Magaziner, who in April 1989 urged a congressional committee to ignore the usual peer review process and give the Utah visionaries special monetary grants to perfect their discovery. Japan, Magaziner noted, had appropriated earlier American technologies such as color TV, the computer chip, and the VCR. Now, he warned, strategists in Tokyo were "working on a plan" to monopolize the big enchilada—cold fusion. Instead of "dawdling" while pencil pushers at the National Science Foundation wasted time "proving" the science behind the exciting discovery, Congress must, Magaziner implored in Reaganesque rhetoric, "for the sake of my children and all of America's next generation" fund a cold fusion institute. Fortunately, Congress dawdled a bit longer and allowed Utah officials to pony up most of the seed money for the project. This proved a prudent decision because a few months and tens of millions of dollars later, more reputable scientists debunked the cold fusion claim as a hoax. Pons and Fleischmann dropped from sight. Magaziner, however, prospered. President Bill Clinton tapped him in 1993 to draft a national health-care plan. The convoluted plan not only failed to pass, but also proved so unpopular that it helped Republicans win control of the House of Representatives in 1994.

Meanwhile, during the 1980s and early 1990s, union leaders and millions of displaced workers complained to little avail as steel, ceramic, textile, and electronics manufacturing plants closed. Even had they wished to act in defense of domestic markets, neither Reagan nor Bush had much leverage. In fact, Japan's government, central bank and private investors recycled a big part of their dollar trade surplus by purchasing about a third of the U.S. federal debt generated from 1981 to 1992. In effect, the Japanese lent back to the U.S. Treasury much of their trade profits to finance the American arms buildup and tax cuts of the Reagan-Bush era.

By the late 1980s, the bilateral relationship grew more testy as the Japanese began using some of their vast dollar surplus to buy up American real estate and corporate assets. These included shopping malls, Hawaiian resorts and golf courses, entertainment companies such as CBS Records, Columbia Pictures, and Universal Studios, and trophy properties such as New York's Rockefeller Center. Even through British and Dutch investors owned far more American assets than did these Asian latecomers, popular resentment focused on Japan, whose economy seemed to be crushing its one-time patron.

Newsweek described Sony's purchase of Columbia Pictures as "Japan invades Hollywood." Andy Rooney, the acerbic commentator on CBS's *60 Minutes*, squinted his eyes and spoke derisively in inflected English about how Japan would follow its purchase of "Lockafella Center" by buying "the Gland Canyon and Mount Lushmore." A Pontiac dealer in New York placed an ad warning Americans who bought Toyotas and Hondas that next Christmas the "Hirohito (formerly Rockefeller) Center" would replace its giant holiday tree with a bonsai in a pot.

Popular novelist Michael Crichton weighed in with a lurid political-economic thriller in 1992 (followed by a much toned-down movie) entitled *Rising Sun*. The wooden plot featured a murder of a Los Angeles callgirl by Japanese industrialists and their American lackies who planned to buy up U.S. technology companies at bargain rates. In their relentless drive for world domination, Crichton warned, the Japanese bought and sold American politicians and companies and made whores out of white women. So many Japan-bashing books appeared in the early 1990s that some bookstores created a section all their own.[4]

---

4. Crichton and his fellow "bashers" such as Clyde Prestowitz (*Trading Places*, 1988) and Pat Choate (*Agents of Influence*, 1990) were poor forecasters. After 1993, the Japanese economy went into a decade-long slump that forced the sale of many recently purchased U.S. assets, including Rockefeller Center, at huge losses. By then, however, China's surging economy picked up the slack and became an even larger exporter to the United States. Like Japan in the 1980s, since 2001 China has lent back to the U.S. government much of its huge trade surplus to finance the record budget deficits run up by the defense spending and tax cuts under President George W. Bush. Much of the racially tinged resentment formerly directed at Japan now went toward China.

In January 1992, in an effort to calm Japanese investors who worried about the ever-growing U.S. government deficit, and also to show American voters that he could persuade the Japanese to limit their exports, President Bush traveled to Tokyo. Almost fifty years before, as a young Navy pilot, Bush had fought the Japanese. Now he led a delegation of industrialists across the Pacific to get the Japanese to import more American products and export fewer of their own. But, aside from agreeing to open a branch of Toys R Us, the Japanese made few commitments.

Unfortunately, at the state banquet honoring the president, a fatigued George H. W. Bush succumbed to an acute stomach flu. Suddenly he slumped over Japanese Prime Minister Miyazawa Kiichi, vomited into his host's lap, and fainted. Live television caught the awful scene of the shocked prime minister cradling Bush's head on the floor while the president regained consciousness. Shortly afterward Miyazawa publicly remarked that American workers were "illiterate," "lacked a work ethic," produced shoddy goods, and had no one but themselves to blame for their economic troubles. South Carolina's Democratic Senator Ernest Hollings struck back by telling a group of factory workers that they should "draw a mushroom cloud and put underneath it: Made in America by lazy and illiterate Americans and tested on Japan." The humiliating visit and its angry aftermath further eroded Bush's stature and seemed a metaphor for the unraveling of America's Cold War dominance.

Bashing the Japanese, however, would not restore national productivity and pride. Although most Americans remained wary of big government, by 1992, faced with a steep recession and mounting job losses, they had also lost patience with conservative leaders who responded to all problems by calling for more tax cuts. In that year's presidential election, voters selected Bill Clinton, seizing the national steering wheel and correcting course back toward the center—at least for a while—from a right turn.

SOURCES AND FURTHER READINGS

The best overview of the impact of drugs and antidrug policies in twentieth-century America is that of David Musto, *The American Disease: Origin of Narcotic Control* (1999); other useful studies that focus on the drug war and crime are Dan Baum, *Smoke and Mirrors: The War on Drugs and the Politics of Failure* (1996), Erick Schlosser, *Reefer Madness: Sex, Drugs, and Cheap Labor in the American Black Market* (2003); Dale D. Chitwood and others, *American Pipe Dream: Crack, Cocaine, and the Inner City* (1995).

The debate over the quality of American education is the subject of books by Terrel H. Bell, *The Thirteenth Man: A Reagan Cabinet Memoir* (1988), and Diane Ravitch and Maris A. Vinovskis, eds., *Learning from the Past: What History Teaches Us about U.S. School Reform* (1995).

Televangelism and the "culture wars" are discussed in Jeffrey K. Hadden and Anson Shupe, *Televangelism: Power and Politics on God's Frontier* (1988); Quentin Schultze, *Televangelism and American Culture: The Business of Popular Religion* (2003); Billy Graham, *Just as I am: The Autobiography of Billy Graham* (1997); John Morone, *Hellfire*

Nation: The Politics of Sin in American History (2003); James D. Hunter, *Culture Wars: The Struggle to Define America* (1988); Martin E. Marty and R. Scott Appleby, *The Glory and the Power: The Fundamentalist Challenge to the Modern World* (1992).

Political and cultural conflict over the changing role of women in American life is examined in Susan Faludi, *Backlash: The Undeclared War against American Women* (1991), and Tanya Melich, *The Republican War against Women* (1996).

The impact of AIDS on American life and politics during the 1980s is the subject of Randy Shilts, *And the Band Played On: Politics, People and the AIDS Epidemic* (1987).

Chronic fatigue, mass child abuse, and other syndromes of the 1980s are examined by Elaine Showalter, *Hystories: Hysterical Epidemics and Modern Culture* (1997); Dorothy Rabinowitz, *No Crueler Tyrannies: Accusations, False Witness, and Other Terrors of Our Times* (2003). See also Francis Wheen, *Idiot Proof: Deluded Celebrities, Irrational Power Brokers, Media Morons, and the Erosion of Common Sense* (2004), and Jodi Dean, *Aliens in America: Conspiracy Cultures from Outerspace to Cyberspace* (1998); Philip Klass, *UFO Abductions: A Dangerous Game* (1989); Susan Clancy, *Abducted: How People Come to Believe They Were Kidnapped by Aliens* (2005).

The rapidly growing literature on the impact of computers on American life includes Janet Abbate, *Inventing the Internet* (1999); Neil Randall, *The Soul of the Internet: Net Gods, Netizens and the Wiring of the World* (1997); John Naughton, *A Brief History of the Future: From Radio Days to Internet Years in a Lifetime* (2000).

The changing content and format of news coverage are discussed by Steven M. Barkin, *American Television News: The Media Marketplace and the Public Interest* (2003); Leonard Downey Jr. and Robert J. Kaiser, *The News about the News: American Journalism in Peril* (2002); Eric Alterman, *Sound and Fury: The Triumph of the Punditocracy* (2002); on U.S. relations with Japan, see Michael Schaller, *Altered States: The United States and Japan since the Occupation* (1997).

INDEX

Bold page numbers indicate photographs